T0286891

The New American Anti-Semitism

The New American Anti-Semitism

The Left, the Right, and the Jews

By Benjamin Ginsberg

INDEPENDENT
INSTITUTE

Independent Institute
100 Swan Way, Oakland, CA 94621-1428
Telephone: 510-632-1366
Fax: 510-568-6040
Email: info@independent.org
Website: www.independent.org

Cover Design: Denise Tsui
Cover Image: Dm/Adobe Stock #578413255
Cover Image: budastock/123rf.com #99477572
Cover Image: loft39studio/123rf.com #207161092

Library of Congress Cataloging-in-Publication Data:

Names: Ginsberg, Benjamin, author.
Title: The new American anti-Semitism : the left, the right, and the Jews / by Benjamin Ginsberg.
Description: Oakland : Independent Institute, [2023] | Includes index.
Identifiers: LCCN 2023030480 (print) | LCCN 2023030481 (ebook) | ISBN 9781598133868 (cloth) | ISBN 9781598133875 (paperback) | ISBN 9781598133882 (ebook)
Subjects: LCSH: Antisemitism--United States. | Jews--United States--Social conditions. | Right and left (Political science) | United States--Ethnic relations.
Classification: LCC DS146.U6 G56 2023 (print) | LCC DS146.U6 (ebook) | DDC 305.892/4073--dc23/eng/20230731
LC record available at https://lccn.loc.gov/2023030480
LC ebook record available at https://lccn.loc.gov/2023030481

Contents

Preface

ON THE MORNING of October 7, 2023, the Palestinian Hamas militia began firing rockets into Israel from positions in Gaza. Under the cover of the rocket barrage, a large force of Hamas fighters, likely armed by Iran, stormed across Gaza's border into Israel, where they brutalized and murdered hundreds of Israeli civilians, including entire families, in their homes. The fighters then killed several hundred young people attending a music festival being held nearby. Some two hundred Israelis as well as a number of American citizens were taken as hostages and moved to Gaza.

Hamas and its Iranian backers hoped that the plight of the captives would leave the Israelis with little choice but to attack Gaza, where, in house-to-house fighting, heavy casualties might be inflicted upon the Israeli Defense Forces (IDF). As a bonus, Israel would surely be castigated by pro-Palestinian elements of the "international community" as well as the liberal Western media for the civilian casualties and humanitarian crisis that an Israeli attack on Gaza likely would produce. As an added bonus, Arab states like Saudi Arabia would be compelled to break off nascent ties with Israel.

Israel called up its military reserves and began a massive bombing campaign against Hamas targets in Gaza, saying it would launch a ground invasion to destroy Hamas and, if possible, free the prisoners. The IDF warned the residents of Gaza City to flee south, where they would be less likely to be caught up in the coming battle. Israel's critics declared that this warning represented an attempt at the ethnic cleansing of Gaza rather than a humanitarian gesture.

Most Americans, including President Biden, seemed appalled by Hamas's savagery. Voices, however, quickly were raised in support of Hamas's actions.

Among the first of them were those of three members of Congress, Ilhan Omar (D-Minn.), Cori Bush (D-Mo.), and Rashida Tlaib (D-Mich.), who blamed Israel for the attack on its own citizens and called for an end to US military aid to Israel as a solution to the problem. The views of Congress's left-liberal "squad" were soon echoed by more than a few left-liberal intellectuals and celebrities in America and Europe, by student groups on several college campuses, and, of course, by Muslim demonstrators throughout Western Europe.

The expressions of sympathy for Hamas and antipathy for Israel help illustrate and underscore some of the key points raised in this book. First, anti-Zionism has become pervasive on the liberal Left in both America and Europe. In Western Europe, after the Hamas attack, 2,000 prominent intellectuals and celebrities signed a manifesto denouncing Israel for what they called the "unprecedented cruelty being inflicted on Gaza." In America, while Republican politicians supported Israel unanimously, the Democrats were divided, with some, like the members of the congressional squad, denouncing Israel and pointing to Israeli policies as the root cause of the problem. Jews, of course, have been loyal Democrats since the New Deal but might wish to rethink that affiliation.

Second, recent events illustrate the close relationship between anti-Zionism and anti-Semitism. Those two ideas might be distinguishable philosophically, but in practice they are not so different. The conflict between Israel and Hamas sparked an enormous upsurge in anti-Semitic incidents in the United States, with attackers making no distinction between Zionists and Jews. In Europe, Jews were urged to avoid any outward display of their religious affiliation lest they be targeted. As we shall see, in polite American society, vehement criticism of Israel is often little more than a veiled form of anti-Semitism. The Hamas charter actually offers some intellectual clarity on this point. The charter seems to call for the destruction of all the Jews, not just the Zionists. The self-proclaimed Jewish anti-Zionists represented by groups like Jewish Voice for Peace and IfNotNow who held noisy demonstrations supporting Hamas and demanding that Israel end its "genocide" in Gaza might profit from reading and actually thinking about what their friends have to say.

Third, the Hamas attack and the Israeli response revealed the extent to which anti-Semitism and anti-Zionism have become entrenched in the political ecosystems of many major college campuses. They include such elite schools as Harvard, Columbia, and the University of Pennsylvania.

Pro-Palestinian student groups, especially Students for Justice in Palestine (SJP), have been active on American campuses for some time now. SJP has built coalitions with left-liberal American students and politically progressive faculty who oppose Israel because they see the Jewish state as a "colonialist" oppressor and agent of American imperialism. Pro-Palestinian students have also entered alliances with other liberal student groups who are not focused on the Palestinian or geopolitical issues but advocate for a variety of other causes—Black Lives Matter activists, environmental activists, LGBTQ+ activists, and so forth, in what often is called an "intersectional" coalition. In such a coalition, groups that view themselves as opposing one form of oppression will combine with campus groups that claim to oppose other forms of oppression, each supporting the goals of the others.

Generally, the disruptive and aggressive tactics of these alliances, as when they shout down speakers with whom they disagree or harass Jewish students, are ignored by university administrators who, for reasons to be discussed later, generally seek to avoid confrontations with the hard campus Left. Administrators will cite their love of the First Amendment when asked to disown hate speech by leftist groups while showing less concern with the Constitution when it comes to protecting ideas expressed by conservatives.

Predictably, in the aftermath of the Hamas attack on Israel, pro-Palestinian groups and their campus allies charged that Hamas's atrocities should be understood in the broader context of Israeli oppression of the Palestinian people. For example, Swarthmore College's SJP chapter released a statement on October 10, justifying Hamas's violence by saying, "Since early Saturday morning, Palestinians in Gaza and the West Bank have valiantly confronted the imperial apparatus that has constricted their livelihoods for the past seventy-five years." The statement also said that "decolonization is far from a metaphor confined to the classroom" and that "There exists only a colonizer and colonized, an oppressed and an oppressor. To resist is to survive, and it is our right."

In 2023, major donors seemed surprised to learn that their beloved alma maters had become hotbeds of anti-Semitic agitation. They should have been paying more attention before writing the checks.

As an author, I am usually pleased when events prove my points. In this case, however, I'm sorry to have been right.

Introduction

MANY AMERICAN JEWS believe that their most dangerous foes today are on the political Right. Indeed, the fact that a few thousand white nationalists supported Donald Trump was a major reason that close to three-fourths of Jews surveyed voted for Joseph Biden in 2020, despite Trump's efforts to gain Jewish voters and, of course, his personal, family interest in combating anti-Semitism. To his credit, Trump was one of the most pro-Israel presidents since Harry Truman. Yet white nationalists or supremacists, sometimes virulently anti-Semitic, often stole the headlines. Individuals linked to far-right groups have carried out a majority of the violent domestic terror attacks in the United States in recent years, including the 2018 shooting at Pittsburgh's "Tree of Life" synagogue, killing eleven worshippers and wounding six others. During the storming of the Capitol on January 6, 2021, white nationalist imagery was also noticeable. This included a "Camp Auschwitz" sweatshirt worn by one rioter and a shirt declaring "6MWE" (6 million weren't enough) worn by another.

To focus exclusively on the Far Right, however, misses the lethal and growing anti-Semitism threat from the political Left. Jews should by nature be aware of the existence of anti-Semitism anywhere. The question is, Do they downplay or ignore such threats? Black Lives Matter (BLM) protestors in the summer of 2020, for example, used anti-Semitic rhetoric and even engaged in looting and vandalism directed at Jewish-owned property. In May 2021, several vicious attacks on Jews by pro-Palestinian thugs in the wake of Israel's bombing of Hamas bases in Gaza were met with indifference by some on the Left, most notably the members of the progressive congressional "squad," who refused to condemn anti-Semitism except by piously intoning that all lives matter. This comment was a conscious imitation of those on the political Right who use the phrase "all lives matter" to counter Black Lives Matter. Nevertheless, most Jews support liberal causes and tend to dismiss anti-Semitism on the political Left as relatively insignificant. Some Jewish organizations deny that left-wing anti-Semitism even exists. After BLM protestors defaced and vandalized synagogues in a heavily Jewish neighborhood of Los Angeles in May 2020, the Anti-Defamation League (ADL) declared that "claims of targeted anti-Semitic violence [on the part of BLM demonstrators] have been exaggerated or misrepresented."[1] The venerable ADL has, in recent years, positioned itself as a politically progressive organization and endeavors to look the other way when its friends make rude comments about Jews. In Yiddish, one might say that the leaders of the ADL *machen sich nit wissendik* (prefer to look the other way). In fairness, we should not single out the ADL for criticism. In a reflexive spasm of virtue signaling, many synagogues also festooned their front lawns with BLM posters and banners. In May 2021, Senator Bernie Sanders suggested that pro-Palestinian hate crimes directed against Jews were linked to "right-wing extremists."[2]

Yet even if the anti-Semitism of the Far Right is at times violent and leads the news, the anti-Semitism of the political Left is the greater threat to the place of Jews in the United States today. Why is this so? The political and social standing of Jews in the diaspora, except in Israel, has been dependent always on non-Jews. In the last several decades, the influence of American Jews has been mostly dependent on their alliance with the gentile liberal bourgeoisie and the Democratic Party. This is an alliance forged in the anti-Nazi coalition of the 1930s and renewed during the great progressive political struggles of the 1950s, '60s, and '70s.

Without question, this alliance has been instrumental in Jews achieving unprecedented prominence and influence in the United States. Consequently, the large and growing number of progressives who continually engage in an anti-Semitic discourse camouflaged by anti-Zionism or anti-Israel rhetoric represents a greater threat to America's Jews than the spasmodic violence of the Far Right. The latter should be easily curbed by the police if they are not "defunded." The former is insidious, a lasting threat to US Jews, which resembles the periodic rise and fall of Jews throughout history: in Spain, in Germany, or in the book of Esther in the Bible.

The origins of my scholarly interest in anti-Semitism are more than academic or religious. Both my parents were victims of Nazism, and had they not overcome improbable odds to survive the Holocaust, my scholarly career, let alone I, would not exist. For my mother, one night toward the end of 1941 in Ukraine, Germans and their Ukrainian auxiliaries entered her *stot* (village) and began rounding up Jews, beating and shooting many of them on the spot, and collecting the others for what was euphemistically known as resettlement. Some Jews ran, while others hid; a few resisted. My mother hid in an empty barrel, and, through sheer blind luck, no one lifted the lid. She survived but may have been the only survivor of that night's murderous *Aktion*. She even had to watch her own mother taken away, never to see her again. My mother then went into hiding for months until she was able to reach safety behind Russian lines.

Raised in Vienna, Austria, my father fled to Poland after the *Anschluss*; then the Germans arrested him after the fall of Poland. Escaping from a German labor camp in 1940, he fled east and managed to reach the Soviet Army. Conscripted on the spot, he trained to serve in an artillery regiment, where he took advantage of the math he'd learned in his Viennese *Gymnasium*. When the Soviets deployed large numbers of Katyushas—the famous Soviet rocket artillery—in 1942 and 1943, my father, using his math skills, guided deadly rocket salvos at the Germans.

Ironically, these Soviet rockets developed by Jewish engineers were extremely effective against German infantry. In response to the late Holocaust scholar Raul Hilberg's inaccurate comment on the insignificance of armed Jewish resistance, one might say that salvos of hundreds of deadly rockets developed by Jews and fired by a Jew were an exceedingly robust form of armed Jewish resistance. Even Hannah Arendt, who professed embarrassment at the Jews' alleged complicity in their own destruction, would have had no reason to feel ashamed of my father. The Germans, fearing the Katyushas, would have had to agree too, if they had known who was shooting at them.

As victims of Nazism, both my parents were grateful to the Russians for saving their lives. Nevertheless, after a taste of life in the Soviet Union, the brutality and idiocy of Communism and the anti-Semitism of the government repelled them, and my parents set out for America. My parents' experiences influenced deeply my conviction that neither the political Right nor the political Left has a monopoly on arrogance, stupidity, or hatred of Jews. Unlike many American Jews, I have always kept my eyes on the Left too.

In the book of Exodus (32:9), God tells Moses that the Jews are a "stiff-necked people." It would appear today that the necks of some Jews have become so stiff from looking over their right shoulders that they are unable to turn enough for a quick peek to the left. America has been good for the Jews (and vice versa), but if Jewish history offers any lessons, among the foremost is that nothing good lasts forever. Most American Jews view the United States as *their* country, but Jews in the diaspora have never been able to take the future for granted anywhere or at any time. I hope this book is a wake-up call for the complacent. During the long course of Jewish history, friends have become enemies and friendly lands have turned hostile. Often enough, as darkness gathered, the Jews were slow to see peril. Hannah Arendt also castigated Germany's Jews for their political innocence and denial of the Nazi threat as it gathered around them.

A wealthy and successful American Jew recently asked me, "Where could Jews go if they had to leave the United States?" The question may seem fantastic, but then again, Jewish history offers ample reason for fatalism. One of my goals is to acquaint American Jews with their history and to help them take a clear-eyed view of contemporary prospects, threats, and possibilities by considering that history. My advice from a lifetime of study, experience, and family trauma is to keep an eye on, and a sense of proportion regarding, the entire political spectrum for anti-Semitism.

I want to thank Christopher Briggs and Stephen Thomson for all their advice and their confidence in the book. And I want to thank the wonderful production team headed, as we started the process, by George Tibbitts and now by Anne Lippincott.

I

Anti-Semitism Today: Three Questions to Ask Anti-Semites

IN WHAT WAYS can criticism of Israel and Zionism be anti-Semitic? Obviously, the Jewish state, like all other sovereign governments, is culpable at certain times and places for its actions and is thus open to criticism. I can, however, offer three questions that suggest veiled or not-so-veiled anti-Semitism in criticism of Israel. First, does the putatively anti-Zionist group or individual make use of well-established anti-Semitic imagery and tropes or comment on Jews specifically when censuring Israel? In a well-known case discussed later in this chapter, Alison Weir, an anti-Zionist journalist writing in *CounterPunch*, resurrected and reaffirmed the infamous medieval "blood libel" against the Jews in an article accusing Israeli troops of harvesting the organs and blood of Palestinian children. Or take the Oxford poet Tom Paulin, who thought that one Jew was the same as another and declared that "Jews from Brooklyn" settled the West Bank. Paulin also thought that Jewish settlers were "Nazis" and should be "shot dead."[1]

The second question involves an iniquitous comparison. Is the evidence proffered of no malice toward Jews proportionate to vehemence toward Israel? The UN Human Rights Council in 2017 declared Israel to be the world's worst human rights violator. That's a far-fetched assertion in a world that includes such brutal regimes as those in North Korea, Syria, Iran, Myanmar, and Saudi Arabia, yet it is expected from an organization that includes many Arab states. Certain progressives in the United States and Europe share this view. And while they should know better, they also show little interest in the brutal conduct of other notorious governments toward their citizens. These individuals or groups, however, have a unique reason to demonize Israel.

Vehemently denouncing the actions of Israel serves to knock Jews off the moral pedestal they claimed after the Holocaust, a moral pedestal that was renewed with strong Jewish support for the American civil rights movement and opposition to America's colonial wars in Asia and the Middle East. Exemplifying this principle is the statement of a prominent French journalist who, responding to a photo of a Palestinian boy killed (allegedly) by Israeli troops, wrote, "This death erases, replaces, the picture of the boy in the Warsaw ghetto."[2] Hence denunciations of Israel that seem to be over the top are useful to diminish the moral stature of the Jews in general.

The third question is, What evidence do anti-Zionists offer to deny being anti-Semites? Is it proportional? Take, for example, Linda Sarsour, a prominent Palestinian American political activist. Sarsour is vehement in her denunciations of Israel and supports boycott, divestment, and sanctions (BDS) directed against the Jewish state. To bolster her claim that she is not an anti-Semite, Sarsour recently launched a campaign to raise money to repair vandalized graves in a Jewish cemetery in St. Louis. A nice gesture, but a campaign on behalf of a handful of already deceased and entombed Jews is hardly proportional to a campaign against the 6 million Jews still living in the state of Israel.

Most of my politically progressive anti-Zionist, anti-Israel acquaintances and colleagues would give an incriminating answer to at least one of these questions; many would supply two, if not three, incriminating answers. Finally, in listening for answers to these questions, we should also consider what politically progressive Jews are saying and doing that gives ammunition to anti-Semites. This includes several prominent Jewish intellectuals and such groups as Jewish Voice for Peace (JVP), who are vociferous anti-Zionists, calling for BDS and other measures directed against Israel. In a *Washington Post* op-ed, Rebecca Vilkomerson, former executive director of JVP, cheered the findings of a Pew Poll saying that liberal Democrats now showed more support for the Palestinians than for Israel.[3] In 2020, JVP sponsored a campaign called "Deadly Exchange," which promoted the idea that American police brutality toward black persons had come about because Israel had trained American police forces to employ racist and brutal tactics.[4]

Jewish self-hatred is hardly a new phenomenon. Recall the turn-of-the-century anti-Semitic Austrian philosopher Otto Weininger, whom Adolf

Hitler praised as "the one decent Jew"—praise indeed from the author of *Mein Kampf* and the Final Solution. It would, of course, be too easy to explain away *all* Jewish anti-Zionism as just another example of this traditional self-loathing. But this conclusion is unavoidable when a Jewish anti-Zionist begins a talk or written presentation with a veiled "I am not one of those kikes" disclaimer by declaring "I am a Jew, but I am not a supporter of Israel." I will return to the topic of Jewish anti-Zionism later, but, for now, let me report a strange conversation I had last year with a Muslim student in one of my seminars at Johns Hopkins.

After the seminar, during which several liberal Jewish students castigated Israel and called for its elimination in favor of a new state in which Palestinians and Jews would live together peacefully, this individual, an immigrant from a Middle Eastern nation, approached me to express his bewilderment with some of his Jewish classmates' views. In his country, as everywhere in the Middle East, he said, teaching hatred of Jews was commonplace. "Are these liberal students too naïve to realize it, or is it that they don't care that without their state and army, many, if not all, the Jews of Israel would be massacred?" I told him it was an excellent question.

Campus Coalitions of (Mostly) Leftist Hate

Aside from the irony of a Muslim student commenting on Jewish naïveté, a larger phenomenon was occurring. Overt expressions of hostility toward Jews, sometimes couched as anti-Zionism, sometimes crudely not, have become more common on American college campuses than anywhere else outside Europe, the Middle East, and North Africa, and they indicate, according to the growing number of verbal and physical attacks on Jews, where anti-Semitism is headed in America at large, including in the Democratic Party and on the floor of the House of Representatives. One Jewish organization, AMCHA, a Hebrew word meaning "grassroots" or "ordinary people," publishes a periodic inventory of events at America's colleges that negatively affect Jewish students and faculty. In 2016, for example, AMCHA cataloged 519 such events. By my count, of these events, 104, or 20 percent, could be expressions of right-wing antipathy toward Jews. These consisted of such things as swastikas painted on the walls of Jewish fraternities, an email sent to Jewish students declaring

"Heil Hitler," or the anonymous note sent to a Jewish professor with the pithy comment "Gas Jew Die!"

A much larger number of events cataloged by AMCHA, however, represented expressions of anger directed at Israel and/or Jews by left-liberal activists drawn from campus coalitions that include militant Muslim and African American students as well as some feminists, LGBTQ+ activists, and radical campus critics of social ills they attribute to capitalism and Western imperialism, such as members of the revived Students for a Democratic Society (SDS). Each of these groups feels a different stake in antipathy to Israel, and even where no direct stake is clear, the diverse forces of the liberal Left form a logrolling coalition to support one another's agendas.

The doctrine of "intersectionality," which holds that all forms of oppression stem from common racial and economic sources, encourages such progressive logrolling. Since Jews are wealthy whites, and the Jews of Israel, their critics say, mistreat people of color, anti-Zionism and anti-Semitism arise naturally from intersectional thinking. Left liberals interpret intersectionality, moreover, to mean that they must all support one another's causes. Thus, while Students for Justice in Palestine (SJP), a mostly Muslim group, often takes the lead in organizing anti-Israel protests as well as making demands that colleges break all cultural and economic ties with Israel, the local chapters of SDS and the Black Student Union often join SJP. For their part, LGBTQ+ activists may chime in to accuse Israel of "pink-washing," that is, falsely representing itself as a safe haven for LGBTQ+ people. Activists for other liberal groups often accuse Israel of also "greenwashing" and "veganwashing." At Washington University in St. Louis in November 2016, SJP went a step further, accusing a Jewish LGBTQ+ group of ignoring Israeli violence against gay Palestinians. The Jewish LGBTQ+ group had angered SJP by claiming (correctly) that Israel was the only state in the Middle East in which known LGBTQ+ persons were safe from imprisonment, torture, and even execution. Similarly, in 2017 the organizers of Chicago's "Dyke March" and "Slut Walk" banned Jewish LGBTQ+ marchers from carrying Jewish LGBTQ+ pride flags (a Star of David embossed over a rainbow) on the grounds that the Jewish star was a symbol of Zionist oppression. Organizers further dismissed Jews as "Zios," an anti-Semitic slur popularized by neo-Nazi David Duke.

While these examples are actions nominally directed against the Jewish state, similar events often cross the line into obvious anti-Semitism. Examples include an October 2016 Students for Justice in Palestine event designed to disrupt Rosh Hashanah services or a September 2016 pro-Palestinian protest at the University of California, Berkeley, whose posters declared that "Jewish bullies" promoted support for Israel. In 2020, Jewish students at the University of Illinois charged that campus administrators ignored their complaints of scrawled swastikas across the campus, the smashing of windows in Jewish fraternity houses, and vandalized menorahs and mezuzahs. Jewish students also charged that members of Students for Justice in Palestine tried to use university diversity training for "anti-Israel indoctrination." On several campuses, Jewish students celebrating Israel's Independence Day or hosting pro-Israel speakers have been verbally or even physically assaulted.

It is exceedingly difficult, therefore, to attack Israel without mentioning Israel's Jewish supporters. A slippery slope, the situation on America's campuses has led to enough complaints that two members of Congress, Senator Bob Casey Jr. (D-PA) and Senator Tim Scott (R-SC), introduced legislation requiring the Department of Education to investigate campus anti-Semitic incidents more forcefully. In 2020, President Donald Trump issued an executive order requiring federal agencies to treat anti-Semitism as a civil rights violation and cutting off federal aid to colleges that tolerated anti-Semitic activities on campus. This order had some effect. At the University of Illinois, administrators acted against anti-Semitic activity when threatened with a Department of Education investigation.

It Can Happen Again

What is occurring on US college campuses and elsewhere is a recurring theme of Jewish history. American Jews are powerful, as at other times in their history. They are prominent in several key industries, universities, and professions, and play important roles in the political process and hold many major national offices. Though Jews constitute barely 2 percent of America's citizens, about one-fourth of the nation's wealthiest four hundred individuals are Jewish, along with a similar percentage of the partners in America's most powerful law firms. In 2020, two prominent contenders for the Democratic presidential nomination, Bernie Sanders and Michael Bloomberg, were Jews. The percentage of congressional seats held by Jews has declined some in recent years yet is still more than three times the percentage of Jews in the US population. One recent book declared, "From the Vatican to the Kremlin, from the White House to Capitol Hill, the world's movers and shakers view American Jewry as a force to be reckoned with."[4]

Jews, talented and ambitious, have risen to power in many times and places, from the medieval Muslim world and early modern Spain to Germany and the Soviet Union in the twentieth century. In most instances, though, Jewish power proved to be evanescent. No sooner had the Jews become "a force to be reckoned with" than they found themselves banished to the political margins and, in some more infamous cases, forced into exile or murdered. Though Jews may rise to commanding heights, their power usually rests on insecure foundations, such as on college campuses today.

The question is, Are the episodic rises and falls of Jewish history even relevant to America today? In short, yes. Jews can never afford to ignore them, for Jewish history shows that the power of the Jews in the diaspora, while often significant, is seldom stable. Jews, a small group, are not so firmly or fully integrated into surrounding societies, including America, as they often appear. Their power is like an immense tower with a weak and shallow foundation—impressive at first glance but unstable in a strong wind or earth tremor. Could a shift in the nation's prevailing political winds or tectonic social plates attenuate the place of America's Jews? Given Jewish history, the better question is *when* it will happen, not *if*. And this time it will come from the liberal Left, not the radical Right.

By choice, Jews have been outsiders; their history, ethnic solidarity, faith, religious practices, and communal institutions have guaranteed that they will appear different from everyone else. In other words, the Jews are marginal; they are never quite 100 percent French, English, or German, or, for that matter, American, even if they speak the local language perfectly, dress correctly, and cheer vigorously for the best sports teams. Despite the advantages that might accumulate from fuller assimilation in any given society, Jews keep separate. This is the source of their strength and weakness.

Their scant numbers coupled with social marginality guarantee that, outside the state of Israel, the Jews can seldom aspire to reach the highest pinnacles of national power on their own and achieve greater security. Where and when Jews achieve political prominence, it is usually in alliance with some indigenous elite—in America this has been an urban, liberal, upper-middle-class alliance within the Democratic Party since the 1930s. Before, in the seventeenth and eighteenth centuries, in similar fashion, Jews were allied with monarchs and noblemen who relied on Jewish administrators, advisers, financiers, and tax collectors to manage the affairs of state. Jews were especially useful partners precisely because they could not aspire to power independently and, thus, were no threat to their noble patrons. During the nineteenth century, western European Jews became politically important in alliance with the liberal bourgeoisie and played major roles in the formation of the bourgeois French and Italian states, as they did later in the construction of Germany's short-lived Weimar Republic. In the early twentieth century, an alliance of Jews and gentile Communists led the Bolshevik Party, and, by helping to create the Soviet state—three of the six members of Vladimir Lenin's first Politburo were of Jewish origin—Jews briefly rose to positions of enormous power in the USSR.

In all these cases, while Jews achieved considerable influence and status, they never fully integrated into or won full acceptance from society. In the cases of Germany and Russia, outside the small elite to which they belonged, Jews were the objects of considerable popular antipathy. Indeed, the rise of the Jews to positions of prominence worsened popular anti-Semitism and later stimulated ill will toward those gentile groups believed responsible for the Jewish rise to power. The Nazis, taking it a genocidal step further, looked to capitalize on both these sources of anger toward Jews when they called Weimar a *Judenrepublik*—that is, a regime of Jews and apostate Germans who abetted the Jews' rise to power. Patrick Buchanan evoked a similar idea in the United States when he referred to the US Congress as "Israeli-occupied territory"; so did Professors John Mearsheimer of the University of Chicago and Stephen Walt of Harvard in 2007, when they tried to expose the machinations of the pro-Israel lobby in the United States.[6] Certainly, in 2019, Muslim congresswoman Ilhan Omar meant to question the legitimacy of Jewish prominence in America when she tweeted that it was "all about the Benjamins," a reference to the $100 bills allegedly wielded by Jewish influence peddlers.

In contemporary America, Jewish integration has happened only in a narrow and privileged sliver of the liberal bourgeoisie, and Jews have little presence outside that stratum. Even where they have considerable influence, Jews are under attack today. Jews are typically found living in affluent residential areas, attending better colleges and universities, working as managers and professionals, and engaging in upscale forms of recreation. Few Jews are found in blue- or pink-collar worlds or in America's rural and small-town "heartland." The ascendance of the Jews and their prominence in liberal society has certainly not gone unnoticed among certain Americans outside the liberal bourgeoisie. Witness the anti-Semitic claims spouted by QAnon conspiracy theorists and the "You will not replace us" (YWNRU) slogan used by white supremacists to refer to the idea that the Jews are engaged in replacing the white race with nonwhites, whom they can better control. Still, the bigger problem for Jews today is not the extreme Right but certain Jewish "allies" among America's liberal bourgeoisie, like their counterparts in Western Europe, who have already engaged in "anti-Zionism" leading to anti-Semitism. Typically, the nominal target of their ire is the state of Israel, which they condemn as a racist and imperialist entity, illegally occupying stolen Arab land. This discourse has become deafening on college campuses where faculty and students celebrate "Israel Apartheid Week" and call for boycotts of Israel. In the political arena, it is difficult to hate Israel while not developing some anger toward Israel's Jewish defenders. Hence an anti-Zionist discourse inevitably, if gradually, takes on a more generally anti-Semitic tone. It has, for example, become an article of faith in some sections of the liberal Left that American Jews overemphasize the European Holocaust to deflect attention from a far worse crime, Israel's ongoing genocide against the Palestinians.

August Bebel, one of the founders of Germany's Social Democratic Party, viewed the susceptibility of German workers to the anti-Semitic propaganda that was commonplace in nineteenth-century Europe as a dangerous source of division within the socialist movement. Indeed, he saw agitation against the Jews as a snare designed to lure workers into alliances with reactionary forces in German society. Hence Bebel famously referred to anti-Semitism as the "socialism of fools."

Today anti-Semitism, often couched as anti-Zionism, is the "liberalism of fools." Expressions of antipathy to Jews on the part of some Left liberals produce divisions within the progressive political camp and align portions of the liberal community with strange and unsavory bedfellows, such as the Iranian government, the Saudi royal family, European fascists, and American "white nationalists," whose agendas are hardly liberal or progressive. The European Left loudly proclaims its anti-Zionism by denouncing Israel as a racist and apartheid state and calling for support for the anti-Israel BDS (boycott, divestment, and sanctions) movement. The BDS movement is active in the United States as well.

Most of Europe's socialist and even moderate press saw Israel, for example, as blameworthy during the 2014 Gaza War, supported anti-Israel demonstrations throughout Europe, and blamed Jewish self-defense organizations for fomenting violence when they sought to protect synagogues from mobs. With less fanfare, European leftists engage in "an anti-Jewish discourse" at dinner parties, during university seminars, and in the media.[7] In the United States, a CNN Poll taken during the war showed that support for Israel among Republicans stood at 73 percent, while only 44 percent of Democrats sympathized with Israel in the conflict.[8] In the United States, left-liberal anti-Zionists are joined by prominent African Americans who, like their white compatriots, sometimes conflate anti-Zionism and anti-Semitism. How else shall we interpret Professor Cornel West's description of Harvard's Jewish former president, Larry Summers, as the "Ariel Sharon of higher education"? During the 2014 Gaza War, West declared on national television that he saw a relationship between the ghetto of Gaza and the ghettos of America, but he left viewers to wonder who was responsible for both sets of ghettos.[9] In 2016, progressive presidential candidate Bernie Sanders—a Jew—named West to the Democratic Party's platform committee, where he advocated for a pro-BDS plank.

In 2020, Black Lives Matter, a movement developed to protest the killing of young black men by police officers in several American cities, also demonstrated the power of intersectionality by declaring that "Zionists" were somehow to blame for police violence against blacks in America.[10] Some progressive groups have demanded that local police departments stop sending officers to Israel for antiterrorism training, saying that they would learn lessons that would lead to the deaths of more black men.[11]

Many Left liberals who are fond of denouncing Israel and Zionism deny that they are anti-Semites and claim to be driven by nothing more than a moral commitment to ending what they see as the brutality and mendacity of the Israelis, who they say threaten the peace of the entire world.[12] It is certainly possible to possess separate and distinct attitudes toward the state of Israel and the Jewish people and, perhaps, even to like Jews while believing that Israel constitutes the chief threat to world peace today, however far-fetched. It is difficult to understand fully, however, why anyone without at least a bit of antipathy toward Jews would choose to focus his or her special moral outrage against the Jewish state. Israel, to be sure, is neither inhabited nor governed by saints. Its policies, like those of other countries, may call for severe criticism.[13]

Yet many on the political Left appear to single out Israeli policy while paying little or no attention to other regimes' behavior. The Israelis stand accused, for example, of the crime of pursuing an ongoing policy of stealing Arab land. Unfortunately, some in Israel do regard the continuing expropriation and settlement of Arab land as a divine mission.[14] However, the political Left asserts that *the very existence* of the state of Israel itself is an illegitimate theft of Arab land. Jacqueline Rose, a progressive British scholar and frequent leader of anti-Israel boycotts, echoes the Arab view that the creation of Israel in 1948 was a tragedy or catastrophe (*al nakba* in Arabic).[15] Without question, Arabs, Jews, and others have historical, religious, and legal land claims in the Middle East that merit attention, yet why single out Jewish claims to the land of Israel as particularly lacking in legitimacy? There is no square inch of earth on the planet whose rightful ownership is uncontestable. Most contemporary Arab states are artificial entities created by the British and other colonial powers and have little historical legitimacy. At least the United Nations created Israel, not the British Foreign Office.

It hardly needs saying, moreover, that the United States occupies millions of square miles of territory taken from the Native Americans as well as land grabbed by force from the Mexicans, whose Spanish forebears had taken it from Native Americans. The ancestors of the modern-day Europeans took their land too—look at the continued shifting of borders throughout European history. But because most of these land grabs occurred long ago, the rightful ownership of western European territory is mostly uncontested these days. In the case of America, European settlers battled the original landowners and later confined them to reservations, where they were unable to press their claims with much vigor.

The main difference between the Israelis and other contemporary land-owners is that Israel has existed as a state only for several decades and tried to accommodate its Arab enemies. Should Israel, therefore, deserve relegation to the status of a pariah for having been insufficiently warlike? One suspects that a certain number who declare that Israel and the Zionists are the world's chief villains might have begun with hostile attitudes toward Jews in the first place.

Again, in principle, it is possible to become anti-Zionist without first being an anti-Semite. But even those for whom anti-Zionism begins as something other than a politically correct form of anti-Semitism can find it difficult to remain vehemently opposed to Israel for long without developing a certain hostility toward Jews. Perversely, those who regularly clash with the Jews can come to see the Jews' enemies as their friends. This process explains the "green/brown" alliances that have sprung up in Europe between progressives and neo-Nazis, who find common ground only in their hatred of Jews.[16]

Such alliances have also arisen in the United States. A case in point is a recent article in the left-liberal newsletter *CounterPunch* claiming that Israel makes a practice of capturing Palestinians to harvest their organs for transplantation.[17] Is this merely an anti-Zionist screed? Well, not exactly: The article's author, Alison Weir, founder of the anti-Israel organization If Americans Knew and veteran of many battles against Israel and its supporters in America, intimates that this alleged Israeli practice comes directly from the ancient Jewish tradition of murdering gentiles to obtain their blood for ritual purposes. And to whom does a contemporary progressive turn for help in understanding and reinventing this hoary blood libel? Weir purports to rely, among other sources, on a blogger known as Israel Shamir, whose postings under the title "Bloodcurdling Libel" explain that a small group of medieval Jews did engage in the ritual murder of Christians.[18] Interestingly, this Israel Shamir is neither a biblical scholar nor a historian. The name *Shamir*, as it turns out, is one of the many pseudonyms employed by a shadowy European neo-Nazi based in Sweden.[19] Anti-Zionism, in this case, becomes difficult to distinguish from anti-Semitism and, as August Bebel might have predicted, leads a left-liberal activist to find common ground with a Nazi.

2

How Anti-Semitism Became a Progressive Ideology

WHAT ACCOUNTS FOR the vehement anti-Semitism currently found on the political Left? To be sure, leftist anti-Semitism is not new. The virulently anti-Semitic, anti-Zionist Soviet campaigns of the 1960s and '70s quickly come to mind.[1] And, of course, Karl Marx himself was pathologically critical of the role played by Jews in the rise of capitalism. Yet, history aside, contemporary left-wing anti-Semitism is rooted in modern political struggles.

As a starting point, most Jews are themselves politically liberal—many are left-liberal, believing in big government—and associate anti-Semitism with their traditional enemies on the political Right. But whether the source is left-wing or right-wing, Jews often ascribe anti-Semitism to irrationality, scapegoating, and what some call "enduring myths" about the Jewish people, and not to rational politics or self-interest. And certainly, like other ethnic and racial hatred, anti-Semitism involves a substantial element of mythology and irrationality. Otherwise, how can we explain certain far-fetched myths propagated by the Arab media and heard throughout the Muslim world? According to the Egyptian and Jordanian press, Israel was responsible for the COVID-19 pandemic; Israel distributes drug-laced chewing gum and candy designed to make women sexually corrupt and to kill children; Israel deliberately infects Palestinian children with the HIV virus; Israel poisons Palestinians with uranium and nerve gas; Jews use the blood of gentiles to make matzah for Passover; the 9/11 terrorist attacks were perpetrated by Jews, not Arabs; and so forth.[2] Some of these claims have gained traction in the West, with many Europeans and Americans prepared to believe the most outlandish tales about the Jews. Indeed, in August 2014, the *New York*

Times contributed to this demonology by publishing a front-page story asserting that Israel was the center of the global gray market in human organs for transplantation.[3] Israel's role in this gray market is disputed, but, in any case, could the editors of the *New York Times* have failed to perceive that the story contributed to the malicious trope already promoted by anti-Semites?

Where anti-Semitism becomes an important feature of political discourse, however, more is involved than simple irrational malice toward, and traditional myths about, the Jews.[4] A reservoir of anti-Jewish sentiment is a necessary but insufficient condition for the emergence of anti-Semitic politics. In politics, principles and rhetoric are tools and weapons that are seldom brandished unless they serve some set of political interests. In the case of the current anti-Semitic rhetoric of the Left liberals, three sets of progressive forces have found reason to attack Israel and the Jews. These are European leftists, American leftists, and American black radicals. For each of these groups, an anti-Semitic discourse serves a slightly different political purpose, though there is extensive overlap. We can add an improbable fourth anti-Zionist group that parrots some of the anti-Semitic rhetoric of the first three: politically progressive Jews in America, Europe, and even Israel. These Jews find it in their political interest to join the attack on the evil Zionist entity, a view that in the context of Jewish history has been tragically shortsighted.

Anti-Semitism and the European Left

The anti-Zionism and anti-Semitism of the European Left are extreme, more widespread, and easier to explain than the anti-Semitic and anti-Zionist rhetoric of other political forces. To put the matter simply, the anti-Semitism of the European Left is rooted in demographic and electoral considerations, namely, the presence of more than 15 million—possibly as many as 20 million—Muslims in Western Europe and the likelihood that this population will increase substantially during the next decade because of high Muslim birth rates and continuing Muslim emigration from war-torn Middle Eastern countries.[5] The Jewish population of Western Europe, by contrast, is only about 1 million and declining.

Between the creation of the Jewish state in 1948 and the 1967 Six-Day War, European socialists kept significant ties to Israel, whose Labor governments they found congenial and whose socialism they admired. Indeed, during this era, many European leftists spent summers in Israel working on kibbutzim.[6] How better to show one's commitment to the principle of collectivization than to spend a few months working on a collective farm? The European Left's enchantment with life on the kibbutz, however, diminished during the early 1970s, when Israel aligned its security policies with those of the United States and, from the Left's perspective, became a satellite of the American imperialists. In the view of the European Left, matters grew even worse after 1977 when the new Likud Party came to power in Israel. Since that time, Israel has been governed mostly by political conservatives like Benjamin Netanyahu, who looked to the American Republicans rather than European socialists for inspiration and support. And, of course, Israel's continuing occupation of the territories seized during the 1967 war and periodic military actions against the Palestinians and Lebanese continually angered and offended European leftists, as it did many American liberals. These international and partisan shifts brought about a cooling of the relationship between Israel and European leftists and paved the way for later events triggered by massive Arab immigration to Western Europe.

Beginning in the 1970s, millions of Muslims migrated from the Middle East and North Africa to France, Germany, England, Spain, the Netherlands, and other European countries. Initially, these immigrants were recruited to fill Western Europe's acute labor shortages. Subsequently, illegals, political refugees, and the children of immigrants added to Europe's Muslim population. Today, more than 5 million Muslims live in France, some 3 million in Germany, and 1.6 million in Britain; Spain and the Netherlands each host some 1 million.[7] Smaller Muslim communities exist in the remaining nations of Western Europe. In 2015–16, several European states, most notably Germany, welcomed Middle Eastern immigrants, even with the well-known problems of terrorism. This was the result of wars in Syria and Iraq, which created not only more refugees every day but also a refugee crisis throughout Europe and the Middle East.

The architect of Germany's open-door refugee policy was a conservative politician, Chancellor Angela Merkel, who saw the refugees as a solution to Germany's chronic labor shortages and a symbol of the new Germany's moral character. And, in France, the moderate Left has become alarmed by the ability of rightist parties to capitalize on antirefugee sentiment and has hardened its own stance on migration. French president Emmanuel Macron's 2017 speech denouncing anti-Zionism as a form of anti-Semitism, accompanied by an embrace of Israeli prime minister Benjamin Netanyahu, was, among other things, designed to signal that the forces of the center left were not anxious to welcome more Middle Eastern immigrants to France.

Traditionally, European conservatives have been hostile to refugees, while European leftists have shown Middle Eastern asylum seekers a welcoming face. For European socialists and other leftists, the ongoing influx of many poor Muslims offers an enormous political opportunity. Based on economic interest as well as their lack of ties to bourgeois European society, these growing Muslim communities are an important new electoral base for parties of the Left. If meticulously organized and mobilized, hundreds of thousands, even millions of Muslim adherents and voters may significantly enhance the political strength of socialist and other progressive parties. So socialist and other progressive groups have championed immigrant rights, the rights of asylum seekers, and the quick provision of the full benefits of the European welfare state to new arrivals. Indeed, the immigrant perpetrators of a vicious terrorist attack in Belgium received Belgian welfare checks even as they planned their murderous rampage.

The Left has also stood firmly against anti-Muslim sentiment resulting from Muslim terrorist activities. After the July 7, 2005, London Tube bombings, for example, left-wing former mayor Ken Livingstone addressed a huge throng of Londoners in Trafalgar Square and told them they should not start looking for "who to blame and who to hate."[8] Many European politicians voiced similar sentiments after the terror attacks by radical Muslims in France and Belgium in 2016. And as to Palestinian violence directed against Israelis, one noteworthy British periodical declared, "We must support Palestinian self-determination and decolonization without reservations and believe the movement's job is to support those goals, and not to impose its own standards on the means by which Palestinians free themselves."[9] In other words, Jewish deaths are not important.

The problem faced by the European Left, however, in looking to take advantage of the political opportunity offered by millions of poor Muslims, is that (leaving aside crime and terrorism) the values and beliefs of this potential Muslim mass base are often at odds with the Left's most cherished values: women's rights, gay rights, abortion, opposition to the death penalty, and separation of church and state. Even the matter of animal rights divides elements of the Left from the Muslim community; see, for example, the near riot that took place in the Italian town of Luino when animal rights activists tried to prevent local Muslims from carrying out a ritual slaughter of rams and lambs for an annual Islamic feast. The ritual requires the animals to be bled to death after their throats are slit, a practice that the defenders of animal rights find barbaric and outrageous.[10] Efforts by progressive politicians to appease Muslims on such matters as homosexuality, female circumcision, the wearing of veils in schools, and other beliefs and habits tend to alienate moderate-liberal European voters. These voters have shown an increasing inclination to support conservative parties that favor limits on further immigration and promote restrictions on the ability of Muslims to practice their religious customs in public places, exemplified by Switzerland's November 2009 constitutional referendum, which enacted a prohibition on the construction of minarets. Since 2014, several European states, including France, have sought to prohibit women from wearing the burka and other forms of Muslim garb in public. And, bowing to public pressure, even Angela Merkel proposed a ban on Muslim apparel in Germany in 2016.

At the same time, more radical Muslim leaders have not been particularly anxious to follow the leadership of, or even to make common cause with, secular leftist politicians. In Britain, for example, some radical Islamists refused to take part in demonstrations against the wars in Iraq and Afghanistan that were organized by the secular Left. Radical Islamists believed that Marxists and other secular radicals were trying to lure young Muslims into their fold and away from their own Islamic organizations. Radical Islamists urged young Muslims not to listen to "atheist Marxists" but, instead, to fight under a religious banner.[11]

To win the support of Europe's Muslims, progressives have tried to tolerate Muslim religious views and practices that might appear completely inconsistent with a secular leftist orientation. In Britain, for example, some leftist feminists have taken up the cause of the right of Muslim women to wear the hijab and burka. And in Germany, the feminist leader of the Green Party denounced as "immoral" a Baden-Württemberg state requirement that applicants for citizenship answer questions about their personal views. One of these allegedly immoral questions was this: "Where do you stand on the statement that a wife should obey her husband and that he can hit her if she fails to do so?"[12] On the hard Left, the expression of support for Muslim cultural and religious values and even terrorism is now seen as a properly Leninist strategy to be adopted by vanguard parties in order to draw the most progressive elements of the Muslim working class into the struggle against capitalism and imperialism. In this effort, acceptance of Muslim culture is a "litmus test of the capacity of revolutionaries to relate to the working class as it is, as opposed to what it was 30 years ago or in books that we have read."[13]

Of course, among the most prominent values espoused by Europe's Muslims is hatred of Israel and Jews. Throughout the Muslim world, anti-Israel and anti-Jewish oratory, newspaper and magazine articles, and radio and television broadcasts are commonplace. Millions of Muslims believe the *Protocols of the Elders of Zion*, which purports to unmask the secret Jewish plan for world domination and is referenced in the Palestinian Hamas Covenant of 1988.[14] Hamas also accuses the Jews of launching the French and Russian revolutions and the two world wars to promote Zionism. In 2002, the *Protocols* became a forty-one-part television series for Egyptian TV and then was sold to seventeen other Islamic television stations.[15] A similar series, produced by Syrian television in 2003, presents a close-up of the ritual murder of a Christian boy by two Jews.[16]

In a similar vein, Sheikh Husayn Fadlallah, who supplied the spiritual inspiration for Lebanon's Hezbollah movement, often declared that Israel was the expression of the corrupt, treacherous, and aggressive Jewish personality.[17]

Or take the views of former Syrian defense minister Mustafa Tlass, whose book *The Matzo of Zion* is known throughout the Arab world. According to Tlass, "The Jew can kill and take your blood in order to make his Zionist bread. Here opens a page uglier than the crime itself: the religious beliefs of the Jews and the perversions they contain, which draw their orientation from a dark hate toward all humankind and all religions."[18]

Following the 9/11 terrorist attacks in the United States, large segments of the Arab media declared that the destruction of the World Trade Center had been the work of the Jews. For example, the Syrian ambassador to Iran declared that "the Israelis have been involved in these incidents and no Jewish employee was present in the World Trade Center building on the day."[19] The Jews had purportedly received a secret directive from Israeli intelligence services warning them not to report for work.[20] In the Arab world, this became widely believed. Indeed, a Middle Eastern graduate student at my own university once assured me that the story of the "four thousand Jews" who stayed home from work on 9/11 was well known to be true.

The steady diet of anti-Semitic propaganda in the Muslim media both reflects and reinforces hatred of the Jews that is so prevalent in the Muslim Middle East. According to one recent survey, 74 percent of the residents of the Muslim Middle East harbored anti-Semitic views, while about 50 percent of Muslims resident in Western Europe shared similar views.[21] American audiences heard an example of the scope of Muslim anti-Jewish feeling when television host Greta Van Susteren famously broadcast a clip from Saudi state television in which a young Saudi child was asked what she thought of Jews. Likely, the three-year-old had never met a Jew but was certainly able to parrot what she was taught:

VAN SUSTEREN: Tonight, a disturbing message of hate from a source barely out of diapers, a three-year-old Muslim girl.

(BEGIN VIDEO CLIP)

BASMALLAH, TODDLER: Allah's mercy and blessing upon you.

DOAA'AMER, IQRAA-TV HOST: What's your name?

BASMALLAH: Basmallah.

'AMER: Basmallah, how old are you?

BASMALLAH: Three and a half.

'AMER: Are you a Muslim?

BASMALLAH: Yes.

'AMER: Basmallah, are you familiar with the Jews?

BASMALLAH: Yes.

'AMER: Do you like them?

BASMALLAH: No.

'AMER: Why don't you like them?

BASMALLAH: Because . . .

'AMER: Because they are what?

BASMALLAH: They're apes and pigs.

'AMER: Because they are apes and pigs. Who said they are so?

BASMALLAH: Our God.

'AMER: Where did he say this?

BASMALLAH: In the Koran.

(END VIDEO CLIP)

VAN SUSTEREN: It was part of an interview conducted by a Muslim woman magazine seen on Saudi Arabian television.[22]

Muslims living in Europe largely harbor anti-Jewish attitudes not so different from those manifested by their coreligionists in the Middle East. And, of course, if they forget to hate Jews, their mosques or hundreds of Islamist websites easily viewed anywhere in the world will remind them to do so. Muslim viewers in Europe can also watch Hamas and Hizballah television, both filled with anti-Semitic content and exhortations to violence against the Jews, over satellite television providers such as Saudi Arabia's Arabsat and Egypt's Nilesat.[23]

In the Muslim nations of the Middle East, of course, there are few Jews, so anti-Semitism is rhetorical. Western Europe, however, hosts about 1 million Jews, living mostly in France and England, along with synagogues and other Jewish institutions. As a result, Europe's Muslims can act out their hatred by attacking nearby Jews.

Thousands of incidents of anti-Jewish violence, mostly perpetrated by young Muslims, have taken place in France, England, and other European countries during the past several years.[24] In Germany, Muslim demonstrators chant, "Hamas, Hamas, Jews to the gas." In France, Muslims have attacked Jewish schools, firebombed synagogues, stoned buses carrying Jewish schoolchildren, and launched machine gun attacks against a kosher grocery store. Throughout Europe, Jews have been attacked and beaten.[25] Reluctant to point the finger of guilt at Muslims when reporting incidents of anti-Jewish violence, the European press usually limits itself to noting that Muslims are "overrepresented" among the perpetrators.[26] In 2014, Muslims were over-represented among the demonstrators who chanted, "Jew, Jew, cowardly pig, come out and fight," in violent protests throughout France and Germany sparked by Israel's attack on Hamas forces in Gaza. And, of course, in 2015 a Muslim terrorist raked a kosher supermarket in Paris with automatic weapon fire, killing four people.

To segments of the European Left, Muslim hatred of the Jews is a political opportunity rather than a moral problem. Opposition to Israel, and the Jews, is a vehicle through which European leftists can reach out to the Muslim community without much political risk. European liberals, who might be worried about the Muslim treatment of women or the seeming disdain for animal rights, have little use for Israel and, apart from the continent's few remaining Jews, little interest in the fate of the Jews. Indeed, levels of traditional European anti-Semitism are worryingly high, despite the murder of most of the Jews a couple of generations earlier.[27]

These political considerations are the backdrop for the anti-Semitic discourse of the European Left. Anti-Semitic rhetoric, participation in protests, demands for boycotts of Israel, and the like are a risk-free way of expressing solidarity with and reaching for the support of the millions of Muslims who now claim European citizenship or residence. Hence, in the demonstrations against Israel and the Jews organized in Europe in response to almost any incident of violence pitting Israel against the Arabs in the Middle East, the Left is very noticeable. In Belgium, these include the Belgian Socialist Party and the Belgian Green Party. In Germany, an official of the Free Democratic Party announced what was proper Palestinian violence against Jews. He said, "I would resist too, and use force to do so . . . not just in my country but in the aggressor's country as well."[28] In France, anti-Zionist demonstrations would not be complete without the participation of various trade union officials, the Revolutionary Communist League, the Greens, the French Communist Party, and the Human Rights League.[29]

Three elements of this progressive political outreach to Europe's Muslims are particularly worth noting. The first is a new form of Holocaust denial. Jews usually cite the Holocaust as a major moral and political justification for the creation of the state of Israel. In truth, no country would grant admission to the remnants of Europe's Jewish communities. Because Jews cite the Holocaust as a justification for Israel's creation, some Muslims, including the leaders of Iran and several Arab states, say Jews invented or exaggerate it. Europe's leftists, of course, know very well that the Holocaust occurred, but to express solidarity with Muslims they have looked to use the imagery of the Holocaust against its Jewish victims. Thus, in the leftist media, the Star of David is redrawn to resemble a Nazi swastika, Israeli soldiers are seen as goose-stepping Nazis, and the Palestinians are presented as the true victims of terror and repression. Preposterously, Israeli leaders are said to be worse than Hitler. Meanwhile, Israel is accused of conducting a "holocaust" against the Palestinians.[30] The Oxford poet Tom Paulin has compared Zionists to the Nazi SS, and Belgian Simon-Pierre Nothomb told newspaper readers that the West Bank was dotted with concentration camps.[31] Of course, the extreme Left takes these matters just a bit further, with some prepared to defend such Holocaust deniers as Robert Faurisson, who declares that the Holocaust is a historical lie designed to benefit the state of Israel at the expense of the Palestinian people.[32]

The second noteworthy aspect of the Left's effort to build bridges to Muslims is what might be called the Judaization of the antiglobalism campaign.[33] To many progressives, the loud and sometimes violent campaign conducted against the World Trade Organization (WTO), the World Bank, the International Monetary Fund (IMF), and other global economic institutions has always represented a form of outreach to the third world, which is allegedly victimized by these agents of Western economic imperialism. In recent years, the European Left, focusing its outreach on Muslims, has reframed the issue of globalization to emphasize the role of Jews in international banking and international financial institutions. Globalism's opponents cite such names as Summers, Greenspan, Wolfensohn, Fischer, Bernanke, and others to say to Muslims that financial globalization is part of the long-standing Zionist conspiracy to take control of the world. French antiglobalization activist José Bové explains that Israel is conspiring with the World Bank to integrate the Middle East into globalized production to exploit Palestinian labor.[34] To draw attention from this plot, the Israelis, according to Bové, have instigated anti-Semitic violence in France and other European countries. "The Israeli government and its secret services have an interest in creating a certain psychosis, in making believe that there is a climate of anti-Semitism in France, in order to distract attention from what they are doing."[35]

Many Muslims accept these ideas. Former Malaysian prime minister Mahathir Mohamad once complained that his country's economic problems were part of a Jewish "agenda" to weaken Malaysia's economy.[36] The 2008–9 global financial crisis added fuel for this view. Hamas spokesman Fawzi Barhum, for example, blamed the "Jewish lobby" for the crisis. He said this lobby "controls the U.S. elections and defines the foreign policy of any new administration in a manner that allows it to retain control of the American government and economy."[37] For his part, former Iranian president Mahmoud Ahmadinejad declared that the Jews dominate financial and monetary centers "in a deceitful, complex and furtive manner."[38] The notion that Jews use globalization to seize control of the world economy, of course, also resonates with the ideas of the Far Right and occasionally produces the green/brown alliances mentioned earlier. Neo-Nazis are eager to help their leftist compatriots shut down what they call the "Jew World Order WTO."

The third interesting element of the European Left's courtship of Muslims is the role of progressive intellectuals. Progressive political parties and factions see Muslims as potential supporters. Some left-wing intellectuals are active in the political arena or, at the very least, are eager to further what they see as anti-imperialist, anticapitalist, or third world causes. Others, though, particularly the university-based intellectuals who sign petitions to boycott Israeli universities, or men of letters like Tom Paulin or the late Portuguese novelist and Nobel laureate José Saramago, who accuses the Jews of committing crimes "comparable to Auschwitz," seem to find anti-Semitism intellectually titillating, an opportunity to be radically chic and to say what for so long was unsayable. Certain German intellectuals welcome the opportunity to accuse the Jews of perpetrating another Holocaust, a view that helps them overcome their own nation's past.[39] For these individuals, anti-Semitism seems more emotionally satisfying than politically useful. Yet the radically chic Saramagos, Paulins, and certain others supply the ideas and imagery that still others can use to further their own political goals.

Anti-Semitism and the American Left

Progressive forces in the United States are not oblivious to the possibility of building political alliances with America's Muslims, whom they view as a potentially radical and anti-imperialist force. And, as in Europe, one outgrowth of this effort has been an anti-Zionist and anti-Semitic discourse. However, the possibility of forging new political alliances is not the only factor leading America's Left liberals to express hostility toward Israel and the Jews.

The Muslim-Progressive Alliance

America's Muslim community is much smaller, more prosperous, and politically more conservative than Europe's.[40] And fewer American Muslims, moreover, hold overtly anti-Semitic views than is manifest among African Americans.[41] Many Muslim communities welcome interfaith dialogue and condemn attacks on Jews. Nevertheless, as the events of the past several years—particularly several terrorist incidents in 2016—have shown, some among America's Muslims gravitate to radical political activity. Moreover, radical religious and educational leaders, often funded by Saudi Arabia, have had some success convincing younger Muslims, including Muslim college students, to identify with their coreligionists in the Middle East and to regard Zionists and Jews as their mortal foes.

The precise number is open to dispute, but some 3.4 million Muslims of Middle Eastern background (with varying levels of religiosity) live in the United States, with the heaviest concentrations in Michigan, California, New York, Illinois, and New Jersey. Muslims in the United States have created several political organizations, such as the Council on American-Islamic Relations (CAIR), the Muslim Public Affairs Council (MPAC), the Muslim Students Association (MSA), and Students for Justice in Palestine (SJP). These and other Muslim groups work to create a positive public image of the Muslim community and to promote Muslim interests in the political arena. CAIR, MSA, and SJP are active on college and university campuses, where they have built alliances with several left-liberal and radical groups, including Jewish Voice for Peace, which together try to promote the global BDS agenda.

To be sure, not every supporter of BDS is an anti-Semite. However, calls for boycotts, divestment, and sanctions directed against Israel often make use of anti-Semitic caricatures, swastikas, and other Nazi iconography and references to Jewish greed and mendacity. At several schools, particularly in California, CAIR, MSA, SJP, and their campus activist allies—including the Worker Student Alliance, Students for a Democratic Society, and the Radical Student Union—regularly sponsor anti-Zionist and anti-Semitic activities, such as the annual celebration of "Israel Apartheid Week," a term coined in reference to Israel's allegedly racist policies. Apartheid Week, initially launched at the University of Toronto, takes place every March to coincide with the annual anniversary of the Arabs' 1948 defeat and the formation of the state of Israel. For its recent Apartheid Week campus presentations, MSA unveiled several colorful new posters mixing anti-Zionist and anti-Semitic images. One featured an image of a hooked-nose Hasidic Jew with a Star of David pointing a bazooka at an Arab carrying a slingshot. Another showed an Israeli helicopter emblazoned with a swastika dropping a bomb on a baby bottle.[42]

Generally, Apartheid Week and similar events feature speakers who denounce Israel and its supporters in the United States. One popular speaker is Amir Abdel Malik Ali, imam of an Oakland, California, mosque. Malik Ali is fond of declaring that Israelis staged the 9/11 terrorist attacks to give an excuse to wage war against Muslims around the world.[43] Another popular speaker is Affad Shaikh, civil rights coordinator of CAIR's Los Angeles office. Shaikh calls for an end to interfaith gatherings and on his blog has posted "DEATH TO ALL JUICE," which we can assume is not a reference to a citrus fruit. Speaking at the University of California, San Diego (UCSD), Shaikh compared the school favorably to the university's Irvine campus, which is known for the prevalence of anti-Semitic activities, where he had often spoken in the past. "It is critical that UCSD get credit," Shaikh declared. "UCI is not half as anti-Semitic as UCSD."[44]

Several of America's best-known Left liberals and radicals have been eager to prove their solidarity with the Muslim community. Some have taken part regularly in Israel Apartheid Week events and tried to promote other aspects of the BDS agenda. One popular Apartheid Week speaker is the infamous Ward Churchill, who explains that Jewish writers have paid a great deal of

attention to the European Holocaust to construct a "conceptual screen" behind which to hide Israel's ongoing genocide against the Palestinian people.[45]
Other popular Apartheid Week speakers include left-liberal anti-Zionist Jews
such as Norman Finkelstein and Ilan Pappé. In addition to those who speak
or lead panels at Apartheid Week events, other progressives wait in reserve
to denounce critics of Apartheid Week, whom they declare are intent on
promoting racism and curbing free speech. Among the most outspoken of
these individuals is the Canadian Jewish anti-Zionist Michael Neumann, a
left-liberal philosophy professor at Trent University, who once declared, "If
an effective strategy for promoting [the Palestinian cause] means that some
truths about the Jews don't come to light, I don't care. If an effective strategy
means encouraging reasonable anti-Semitism, or reasonable hostility to Jews,
I also don't care. If it means encouraging vicious racist anti-Semitism, or the
destruction of the State of Israel, I still don't care."[46]

Another expression of the effort by left-liberal activists to forge a relationship with Muslims is the campaign to encourage America's colleges and
universities—and occasionally other institutions such as church groups and
academic societies as well—to divest their holdings in companies linked to the
state of Israel. Patterned on the campaign to isolate South Africa that began
in the 1960s, a coalition of left-liberal and Muslim groups, including Students
for Justice in Palestine and the San Francisco chapter of the American-Arab
Anti-Discrimination Committee, launched the anti-Israel divestment movement at the University of California, Berkeley. The movement spread from
Berkeley to several other college campuses, including Harvard, MIT, Yale,
and the University of Michigan, where local coalitions of Muslims and Left
liberals organized under the umbrella of the Palestine Solidarity Movement
(PSM), incorporated later into the more general BDS movement. PSM and
BDS advocate nonviolent action to encourage awareness of the Palestine issue
but decline to condemn acts of terrorism against Israelis. At a 2017 conference
on divestment held at the University of Michigan—where Jewish students
were prevented from joining the discussion—one prodivestment delegate
repeatedly declared that "Jews are not a nation," insisting that "there's no nation called 'Judaism'" and asking, "Where on the map is there a country called
'Jews'?" He asserted that "Zionism is a dirty political ideology," that "most
Jews are Zionists," and that "any person who is a Zionist believes in the State

of Israel, even though it oppresses and kills millions of Palestinians—which I call terrorism."[47]

PSM and BDS efforts on several campuses touched off considerable controversy, with Harvard's former president Larry Summers denouncing calls for divestment as "anti-Semitic in their effect if not their intent."[48] The presidents and trustees of several schools explicitly rejected the idea of divestment, while most university administrators simply ignored the campaign. Thus far, boycott and divestment campaigns have claimed only one success. In February 2009, the now-defunct Hampshire College sold its shares in a mutual fund with ties to Israel. College administrators, however, deny that any political motivation prompted this sale and say that the school owns shares in several Israeli firms. The failure of the divestment campaign to influence university administrators and trustees led anti-Israel activists to organize a new effort aimed at college and university faculty members. This endeavor is the US Campaign for the Academic and Cultural Boycott of Israel (USACBI), organized in 2009 by a group of California professors. USACBI calls on American academics to sever all ties with Israeli universities. The USACBI advisory board includes several Muslim academics, such as Hamid Dabashi, professor of Iranian studies at Columbia, as well as several non-Muslim left-liberal academics, such as David Lloyd of the University of Southern California and James Petras of Binghamton University, a professor whose published work often attacks Israel and "Jewish power" in the United States.

As the foregoing examples suggest, efforts to build alliances between progressive political forces and Muslims in the United States mostly take place in and around university campuses, where the Far Left is strongest, but exist in varying degrees in other institutions. This alliance is important for both groups. The American Left's foundations are in activist organizations, a small number of church groups, certain segments of the media, and, of course, on a great many college and university campuses, where in the humanities and social sciences, Republicans and conservatives are scarce and where professors who are merely liberal Democrats run the risk of "dangerous reactionary" labeling.

College campuses are thus natural havens for activist organizations like CAIR, SJP, and MSA. Several schools enroll sizable contingents of Muslim students, including thousands from the Middle East itself. Saudi Arabia alone sends more than ten thousand students to the United States every year. These students are far more easily mobilized than American Muslims to take part in anti-Zionist rallies and protests, to disrupt Jewish events, to shout down pro-Israeli speakers, and to urge their non-Muslim classmates to take a harsher view of Israel and a more positive view of the Arab cause.

In some instances, expression of anti-Jewish sentiment is in the form of attacks on "Zionists," but often enough anti-Semitic speakers and vandals are happy to make their hatred more general and to point to the Jews as their targets. At the University of California, Irvine (UCI), for example, anti-Semitic speakers have informed their campus audiences that Jews need to be rehabilitated, that they suffer from a communal psychosis, and, ominously, that the Jews' days are numbered.[49] In 2020, the student council's vice president at the University of Southern California was subjected to a campaign of threats and abuse because of her support for Israel.[50] In 2017, at the University of California, Santa Cruz, demonstrators representing the Afrikan Black Coalition reportedly shouted anti-Semitic obscenities at Jewish students gathered for an Israel Independence Day celebration.[51] In a 2012 demonstration at the University of California, Davis, pro-Palestinian protestors prevented Jewish students from entering a classroom building, shoving them against a building window and threatening further physical violence.[52] And in August 2014, a Jewish student at Temple University in Philadelphia was punched in the face and reportedly called "baby-killer, racist, Zionist pig," and "kike" as he stood next to a table run by Students for Justice in Palestine.[53] The list is virtually endless.

In recent years, Jewish students on several campuses have begun to mobilize against anti-Zionist and anti-Semitic activities. In March 2017, Jewish students at Columbia looked to counter Israel Apartheid Week with a series of events of their own where Jews wore shirts emblazoned with the word *Zionist*. However, as Mitchell Bard has seen, Jewish students seem reluctant to engage in protests and demonstrations.[54] Pro-BDS groups, most notably Students for Justice in Palestine, have worked to isolate and ostracize those Jewish student groups willing to voice support for Israel. On several campuses, Jewish students and Jewish organizations supporting Israel are excluded from working with progressive groups on the extraordinary grounds that Jews have never faced and do not understand oppression. At the State University of New York at Stony Brook, SJP students went further, declaring that Jews were "oppressors" and demanding that the campus Hillel be replaced by a "proper Jewish organization" that focused exclusively on religious matters and did not support Israel.[55]

Often enough, college professors and administrators are the authors of anti-Semitic slurs. In 2016, the national news media reported that Oberlin College professor Joy Karega had posted on her website that Muslims were wrongly blamed for many terrorist acts perpetrated by Israeli intelligence services. These included the *Charlie Hebdo* attack, the downing of Malaysia Airlines Flight 17, and, of course, the September 2001 terrorist attacks in the United States. Karega, who was hired to teach social justice writing, also asserted that Jews controlled America's government and media. Oberlin's administrators were reluctant to act, citing free speech concerns, but had to terminate Karega's contract after college alumni and trustees expressed their serious concern. It turned out that Karega enjoyed considerable support on the campus, where several anti-Semitic incidents had already occurred during the previous two years.[56]

Exposure to anti-Israel ideas from student organizations and in the class-rooms of politically progressive professors is undoubtedly among the factors that have undermined support for Israel among younger Jews, since most of them have attended college. Among Jews over the age of fifty, more than 77 percent report strong or somewhat strong support for Israel. Among Jews between the ages of eighteen and twenty-nine, on the other hand, this level of support drops to 60 percent.[57] And, while older Jews support staunchly pro-Israel advocacy groups like the American Israel Public Affairs Committee (AIPAC), younger Jews are more likely attracted to groups like J Street that take a more "balanced view" of Middle Eastern matters. A small but vocal number sympathize with overtly anti-Israel Jewish groups like Jewish Voice for Peace.

On many campuses, including my own, politically progressive Jewish students flocked to the banner of Bernie Sanders in 2016 and again in 2020 before Sanders withdrew from the presidential race. For some of these students, Sanders stood for an ideal to which they might aspire. Sanders's mannerisms, voice, and Brooklyn origins marked him as a Jew, but he seemed to have transcended his parochial roots to become a nondenominational man of the Left—senator from a state with few Jews, married to a gentile, not supportive of Israel, and happy to make common political cause with Muslims. Sanders showed that such a Jew could lead the nation's progressive coalition. This was heady stuff for young Jewish progressives. But these young progressives might do well to remember that there have been other times and places, say the Soviet Union in the 1930s, when things did not turn out so well for Jews who thought they could lead coalitions that included large numbers of anti-Semites.

At any rate, the Muslim-progressive campus alliance, though limited in scope, has the potential to breed long-term consequences. College campuses also hold millions of impressionable American students who, on any given day, can be convinced of most anything. Even if each year only a comparatively few find it persuasive that Israel is a vicious, racist, apartheid, fascist state, supported by a Zionist conspiracy (in other words, Jews), who manipulate the press and Congress, the numbers can arithmetically grow on any campus. Indeed, a 2016 survey showed that support for Israel among Americans born between 1981 and 1998, a group that includes recent college graduates, has been declining, while support for the Palestinians is rising sharply.[58] And not wishing to have their progressive credentials challenged, some Jewish students have joined the anti-Israel chorus through such groups as Jewish Voice for Peace and Open Hillel. In the meantime, the main consequence of anti-Zionist activity on college has been a growth in anti-Semitic rhetoric as well as some anti-Semitic violence on several of America's campuses.

Anti-Semitism and Anti-Imperialism

Intersectionalism and coalition politics are not the only sources of the American Left's anti-Zionist rhetoric. Some on the Left also find an anti-Zionist or anti-Semitic discourse to be a useful instrument with which to attack the legitimacy of US foreign policy by unmasking the Zionist cabal that has hijacked America's policy-making processes. A posture of anti-Zionism allows progressives to claim the patriotic high ground usually occupied by their opponents in foreign policy debates.

Since the Cold War, progressive forces in the United States have denounced American foreign policy as overly aggressive and an expression of America's imperialist designs. Progressives, of course, strongly opposed US military endeavors in Korea, Indochina, the Persian Gulf, Afghanistan, and elsewhere. In general, Left liberals asserted that America was needlessly squandering its blood and treasure, alienating much of the world, and pursuing an agenda defined by defense contractors, multinational corporations, and politicians looking to divert the public's attention from America's own social inequalities. This commentary was most marked during the Bush years but continued in more muted terms during the Obama presidency, especially considering Obama's continual use of drones to conduct targeted assassinations of individuals suspected of leading militant groups in various parts of the Middle East.

The progressive critique of American foreign policy was not without a measure of validity. Several of America's military ventures were ill-advised, to say the least. American interests were hardly advanced by toppling Saddam Hussein's regime in Iraq. Nevertheless, opponents of American military interventions typically found themselves charged with lacking patriotism and showing undue solicitude for the nation's foreign foes. Often Americans told progressives to love America "or leave it!" And even when the public at large eventually tired of a particular war, seldom were the original left-liberal naysayers credited for their prescience. Instead, their patriotism remained in question. The same had, ironically, been true of the leftists who had been among the first to urge opposition to Nazism in the 1930s. Rather than receive the nation's kudos for having been quick to sound the alarm, they found themselves, during the postwar period, accused of "premature antifascism" by congressional red hunters.

Progressives found themselves in a particularly precarious political position after the 9/11 terrorist attacks, which sparked American military campaigns in Afghanistan and Iraq. From the perspective of the Left, the Bush administration had seized an opportunity to launch two wars designed to expand American hegemony in the Middle East and to ensure privileged American access to Middle Eastern oil supplies. However valid this argument and the accompanying political refrain "No blood for oil" was, outside of the left-liberal camp, Americans considered it unpatriotic, which further increased the American Left's political isolation at the time.

This backdrop helps explain a second element of the American Left's anti-Semitic discourse. This is the charge that American foreign policy, especially

American military campaigns in the Middle East, is the product of an effort by American Jews, led by the Israel lobby and a cabal of "neoconservative" Jewish officials, to promote Israeli goals at the expense of the United States. The great political value of this accusation, from the Left's perspective, is that it allows progressives—usually impugned for lack of patriotism—to present themselves as the true defenders of American interests. A similar argument, of course, was made during the 1990s by right-wing anti-Semites like paleoconservative commentator Pat Buchanan, who famously called Congress "Israeli-occupied territory." In some respects, the Left's embrace of Buchananism seems odd. Buchanan has consistently argued that foreign policy should be based on the national interest. America's liberal Left, on the other hand, usually favors a foreign policy tied firmly to principle and morality rather than naked self-interest. Nevertheless, the notion of Jewish conspirators shedding American blood to serve Israeli purposes has become an essential element of the progressive critique of American foreign policy, especially so since the 2007 publication of the well-known book *The Israel Lobby and U.S. Foreign Policy* by John Mearsheimer of the University of Chicago and Stephen Walt of Harvard. As the title shows, the book is a controversial argument by professors at two major universities, once limited to the academic fringes.[59]

Like its counterpart in Europe, the American Left initially became disenchanted with Israel during the early 1970s, when Israeli security policies aligned with those of the United States. The Left's antipathy toward Israel increased with the Jewish state's ongoing occupation of territories captured in the 1967 war and the emergence of the conservative Likud bloc, which displaced Labor as Israel's dominant political force. This disenchantment only increased with the policies of successive Netanyahu governments in Israel, which expanded Jewish settlements and avoided negotiations with the Palestinians. From the 1970s onward, American progressives, including some Jewish Left liberals, attacked Israel often as an aggressive agent of American imperialism, a brutal occupying power, and a declared racist toward Arab residents of the occupied territories and Israel proper.

These criticisms intensified in response to what was considered harsh Israeli suppression of the first and second Palestinian intifadas during the 1980s and 2000 as well as various Israeli military operations against Fatah, Hamas, and Hezbollah militias. Israel's elaborate security wall, designed to inhibit Palestinian suicide bombers from reaching their targets in Israeli cities, dubbed an "apartheid fence," became for progressives a symbol of Israeli racism. Progressives were unmoved by the Israeli government's assertions that it had a duty to protect its citizens from terrorists, suicide bombers, and rocket attacks.

Historically, the mainstream US media had been overwhelmingly sympathetic to Israel, and in their coverage of both the 1967 and 1973 Middle East wars, presented Israel as a victim of Arab aggression. During the later 1970s and 1980s, however, more liberal periodicals such as the *New York Times* began to cover the Middle East from a more "balanced" perspective, presenting Israel and the Palestinians as equally blameworthy, locked in a self-perpetuating cycle of violence for possession of land to which both lay claim.

Gradually, with the help of their American supporters, the Palestinians learned to improve their own media image at the expense of the Israelis. Israel had always gained from casting itself as a "David" standing up to Arab "Goliaths." The Palestinians learned how to reframe this story so as to present themselves as a defenseless people victimized by a brutal Israeli military occupation.[60] Making use of this new media frame, Palestinians were, for example, able to convince large segments of the American and international press that a 2002 battle in the Palestinian town of Jenin that had resulted in the deaths of fifty-two Palestinians and twenty-three Israelis had been a "massacre" in which hundreds, perhaps thousands, of Palestinian civilians had been butchered.[61]

In a similar vein, in June 2010 Palestinians staged an effort to undermine Israel's blockade of Gaza by dispatching a ragtag flotilla of vessels crewed by Palestinians and their various supporters to bring supplies to the Hamas-controlled enclave. The goal of the flotilla was to provoke an Israeli military response, announced to the world as another example of Israel's barbarism. The Israelis understood the Palestinian strategy but were determined to keep their blockade. When Israeli commandos armed mostly with nonlethal weapons boarded the vessels, individuals wielding clubs and knives attacked them. In the ensuing melee, several Israelis were injured, and various supporters including Turkish activists killed and injured. As expected, liberal opinion throughout Europe condemned Israel, and the incident led to violent anti-Israel demonstrations and boycotts in France and elsewhere.[62] Similarly, in

2014 when Israel responded to hundreds of rockets fired from Gaza by Hamas with a ground invasion, liberals focused their attention on Palestinian civilian casualties. Many dismissed as irrelevant Israel's claims that it was acting in self-defense.

Before September 2001, whatever sympathy for the Arab cause might have occurred in the United States, outrage over the murder of thousands of American civilians by Arab terrorists on 9/11 tempered it. In response to the attack, the Bush administration launched major military campaigns against the Taliban regime in Afghanistan and Saddam Hussein's government in Iraq. Both wars were initially popular. As is often the case, however, the public soon tired of the costs and casualties inevitably associated with military operations. The Bush administration came under fire for having underestimated (the president might have said "misunderestimated") the difficulties involved in simultaneously suppressing major insurgencies in two nations. At the same time, critics questioned the Bush administration's explanation for having launched an invasion of Iraq in the first place. Bush had asserted that the Iraqi regime was developing weapons of mass destruction (WMDs) that would pose a danger to the United States. American forces searched every nook and cranny in Iraq for these WMDs but to no avail. The weapons had never existed, and the entire story appeared fabricated by the administration to supply a pretext for the American invasion.

This revelation offered progressives an opportunity to give their own Judeo-centric explanation for the invasion of Iraq and, indeed, for American policy in the Middle East more generally. In a host of books and articles, published mostly during Bush's second term, progressives as well as several Muslim authors (and right-wing anti-Semites too) pointed to the prominence of Jewish neoconservatives in the Bush administration. The list included government officials like Paul Wolfowitz, Richard Perle, Elliott Abrams, Kenneth Adelman, Douglas Feith, and Lewis Libby; journalists like William Kristol and Charles Krauthammer; and several academics and other pundits. Progressives borrowed from the Buchananite Right the notion that these neocons, working closely with the pro-Israel lobby in Washington, were able to gain control over US foreign policy. The result, as Mearsheimer and Walt put it, was the emergence of a foreign policy that "was a significant source of anti-Americanism in the Middle East and a source of tension with key strategic allies." Mearsheimer and Walt went on to suggest that the neocons and Israel lobby bore much of the responsibility for the war in Iraq, "a strategic disaster for the United States."[63]

Other progressives assert that Jews continue to conspire to lead the United States into wars in the Middle East. For example, the leftist sociologist James Petras, author of several anti-Zionist tracts, writes, "The American Jewish lobby [has led] a large-scale, intensive, and partially successful campaign to demonize Iran and Syria." At the top of the Jewish lobby's agenda, according to Petras, is "a new war against Iran on behalf of Israel."[64]

It is certainly true that the Israel lobby and many, if not all, neocons have been concerned with Israel's security and are hostile to the radical Muslim regimes of the Middle East, which they continue to view as threats to American military and economic interests. Nevertheless, attributing responsibility for America's actions in the Middle East to the machinations of Jewish lobbyists, pundits, and officials seems far-fetched. At the very least, this line of argument gives insufficient weight to the brute fact that the key policy makers behind the Iraq debacle had the names of Bush, Cheney, and Rumsfeld—not a Jew among them. And while Bush may have been unduly influenced by Cheney and Rumsfeld, these two worthies had far too much confidence in their own abilities and were congenitally incapable of listening to anyone.[65]

Nevertheless, attacking the Jewish neocons and the Israel lobby provides Left liberals with a patriotic critique of American foreign policy. Rather than rail against US militarism and imperialism and thereby commit themselves to political isolation, groups on the Left can attack the Jews for hijacking American foreign policy and committing the nation to an imperialist agenda designed to serve Israel's interests. Elaboration of this anti-Semitic thesis has become a cottage industry in recent years, with left-wing and some right-wing authors vying with one another, in an ersatz green/brown competition, to develop ever more lurid titles. My personal favorite is *The Host and the Parasite: How Israel's Fifth Column Consumed America.*[66]

This left-liberal discourse, to be sure, has thus far been unable to produce any general increase in anti-Semitic attitudes in the American populace, where anti-Semitic views have varied within a narrow 12 to 15 percent range for several years. However, the notion of Israel as a malign influence seems to have seeped from the left-liberal fringe into the general consciousness of the

Democratic Party. Recent surveys indicate that while 75 percent of Republicans believe Israel is an ally of the United States, only 55 percent of Democrats agree.[67] In addition, more than half of Democrats recently surveyed expressed equal levels of sympathy for Israel and the Palestinians, a substantial shift from previous surveys.[68] It is certainly possible to be suspicious of Israel without being in the least bit anti-Semitic, but, again, for reasons discussed earlier, one often gives rise to the other.

Black Anti-Semitism

A second source of anti-Semitic discourse on the American political Left is within America's black community. In recent years, several African American politicians and public figures have made anti-Semitic comments and speeches. One notable example is a former US representative from Georgia and 2008 Green Party presidential candidate, Cynthia McKinney. When McKinney was defeated for reelection in 2002, her father, a veteran Georgia state legislator, declared that the "J-E-W-S" were to blame. When McKinney lost another race in 2006, the head of her security detail confronted a reporter whom he took to be Jewish. "Put on your yarmulke and celebrate," he told the reporter. In 2008, the Israeli navy took McKinney into custody as she took part in an attempt to penetrate the naval blockade of the Gaza Strip. McKinney called Israel's activities in Gaza "full-scale, outright genocide."[69] In 2016, McKinney declared that Israel was behind terrorist attacks in France and Germany usually blamed on Muslims. Not to be outshone by McKinney, Hank Johnson, a black congressman from Georgia who succeeded her in the House, referred to Jewish settlers in the West Bank as "termites." Johnson made his remarks while attending an event sponsored by a group calling itself "The U.S. Campaign to End the Israeli Occupation."[70]

More recently, African Americans have been prominent among those claiming that Jews had been responsible for police misconduct and for the COVID-19 pandemic. One black member of the Washington, DC, city council claimed that a snowmaking machine controlled by the Rothschilds had been responsible for bad weather in the nation's capital. But balancing this nonsense was the white nationalist claim that a space laser controlled by the Rothschilds caused California's forest fires.

Jews are often outraged and surprised by anti-Semitic rhetoric on the part of blacks because the Jewish community recalls the significant role it played only a few decades ago in the civil rights movement. During the 1950s and 1960s, Jews were prominent in most, if not all, of the nation's major civil rights organizations. Stanley Levinson, a Jewish attorney, was Dr. Martin Luther King's chief adviser. Kivie Kaplan, a retired Jewish businessman from Boston, served as president of the National Association for the Advancement of Colored People (NAACP) and was also one of King's major fund raisers and financial contributors. Attorney Jack Greenberg headed the NAACP Legal Defense Fund after President John F. Kennedy named future Supreme Court Justice Thurgood Marshall to the Second Circuit Court of Appeals. At the same time, Jewish intellectuals, and the journals of opinion they controlled, spoke out forcefully on issues of civil rights, Jews contributed most of the funds available to civil rights groups, and Jewish organizations such as the American Jewish Committee and the Anti-Defamation League supplied financial, legal, and organizational support for civil rights groups.

Its involvement in the struggle for black civil rights, to be sure, involved a measure of self-interest on the part of the Jewish community. Jewish organizations recognized that the civil rights movement's goal of outlawing discrimination in such areas as education and employment would serve the desire of Jews for fuller inclusion in American society. By supporting African Americans in the battle for civil rights, Jews were fighting to demolish the barriers that stood in their own way as well.[71] But self-interest is not everything. Jews also had a strong moral commitment to the civil rights cause. Indeed, some Jews risked their lives as well as their resources in the struggle. More than half the lawyers who made their services available to civil rights demonstrators in the South were Jews. A certain majority of the whites who accepted the danger of service as freedom riders were Jews, as were some two-thirds of the whites who went into the South during the violent Freedom Summer of 1964. These, of course, included Michael Schwerner and Andrew Goodman, who, along with their black colleague, James Chaney, were murdered by racist thugs in Mississippi.

This alliance between blacks and Jews has not entirely evaporated. In 2021, a black candidate and a Jewish candidate ran in tandem to win the runoff elections in Georgia that gave Democrats control of the Senate. In 2008, a solid majority of the whites in Democratic presidential candidate Barack Obama's inner circle were Jews, as were several of President Obama's key appointees. Nevertheless, relations between blacks and Jews have deteriorated significantly in recent years. Most surveys show that African Americans are in general the most anti-Semitic segment of the American-born populace, with about 28 percent of black respondents, more than double the national average, showing some measure of antipathy toward Jews. In 2014, blacks were more likely than almost any other group of Americans to blame Israel for the Gaza War. Black anti-Semitism predates the emergence of a sizable contingent of Muslims within the black community, though this development certainly has not reduced anti-Jewish feeling among blacks.

Several prominent African American political and intellectual figures commonly voice anti-Israel and anti-Jewish views and accuse Jews of conspiring against blacks. Louis Farrakhan, Jesse Jackson, and Al Sharpton have often used coarse anti-Semitic language. And, while former president Barack Obama courted Jewish support, his former pastor and confidant, Jeremiah Wright, was a vociferous critic of Israel. Wright blames the Jews for Obama's reluctance to keep his formerly close ties with the minister. In an interview, Wright said, "Them Jews ain't going to let him [Obama] talk to me. . . . He's got to do what politicians do. And the Jewish vote, the AIPAC vote that's controlling him, that will not let him send representation to the Darfur Review Conference, that's talking this craziness on Israel because they're Zionists, they will not let him talk to somebody who calls a spade what it is. Ethnic cleansing is going on in Gaza—the ethnic cleansing of the Zionists is a sin and a crime against humanity."[72]

The existence of a substantial reservoir of anti-Semitic sentiment in the black community may encourage black political figures to believe that anti-Semitic comments will find a receptive audience among their constituents. At the same time, the anti-Semitic rhetoric of black public figures most certainly serves to legitimize and encourage hostility toward Jews within the larger African American community and America at large. With good reason, American progressives view blacks as America's most victimized group. This gives African Americans a special moral standing and confers upon them the right to say what others will or will not say, without fear of criticism. And, once blacks say it, others can more safely follow their lead.

What motivates some black public figures to engage in an anti-Semitic discourse? To begin with, African Americans have reason to feel a sense of sympathy for the Palestinians, whom they view as dark-skinned people victimized by whites. The parallels to their own history, while not precise, are nevertheless compelling for some. Beyond this, however, today's black anti-Semitism is, in part, an ironic and unforeseen outgrowth of the success of the civil rights alliance between blacks and Jews.

The civil rights movement brought about the enfranchisement of millions of African Americans once denied the right to vote. Voting rights significantly enhanced the importance of African Americans in American political life and, particularly, in the Democratic Party coalition, which became heavily dependent on black electoral support. The increased political weight of African Americans, in turn, encouraged members of the black political stratum to seek greater influence, more significant political offices, and a larger share of the public expenditures controlled by the Democrats. In many instances, this effort led to conflicts with other groups in the Democratic coalition.

Blacks came to be especially resentful that Jews, a much smaller group, seemed to hold more prominent positions and exercised more power within the Democratic Party than African Americans. As recently as 2000, for example, it angered some black Democrats when Al Gore chose a Jew, Connecticut senator Joseph Lieberman, as his vice presidential running mate rather than an African American, as many had hoped. Lee Alcorn, president of the Dallas NAACP chapter, said he opposed "any kind of partnership between the Jews at that kind of level because we know that their interest primarily has to do with, you know, money and these kinds of things."[73] The chairman of the *Amsterdam News*, Wilbert Tatum, suggested that the only reason Gore had chosen Lieberman was that "Jews from all over the world will be sending bundles of money."[74]

The development of an anti-Semitic discourse in the African American community is also related to the emergence of several cohorts of ambitious young African American politicians, eager to supplant existing black notables and assume leadership positions. Those like Barack Obama or Massachusetts governor Deval Patrick who aspired to national leadership developed an inclusive rhetoric and were careful to keep good relations with the existing political establishment. On the other hand, younger political notables who looked primarily to gain prominence within the black community believed that anti-Semitic or in some cases anti-Zionist rhetoric could be a useful weapon against the members of that establishment. In a variety of different contexts, insurgent forces within the African American community charged that incumbent leaders were the paid puppets of whites, and Jews in particular. Precisely because established black leaders had worked closely with Jews in the civil rights movement, and often were dependent on Jewish funding, they were quite vulnerable to this charge.

The first major black politician to successfully use this tactic was Malcolm X. Malcolm denounced established black politicians who had allied with and been dependent on white support as collaborators who had sold out the black community. Because the most prominent white allies of black causes were usually Jews, Malcolm's rhetoric often had anti-Semitic or anti-Zionist references. In this way, Malcolm underscored the difference between himself and the "kept" black politicians, especially black members of Congress who received financial and other forms of help from Jewish organizations and, in exchange, gave their support to Israel and other Jewish causes. Thus Malcolm accused the Jews of sapping "the very life blood of the so-called Negroes to maintain the state of Israel." In another speech Malcolm dismissed a question about the Holocaust by criticizing those who became "wet-eyed over a bunch of Jews who brought it on themselves."[75]

Malcolm's successor, Louis Farrakhan, adopted the same tactic and gained considerable notoriety by referring to Judaism as a "gutter religion." When traditional black leaders looked to repudiate such comments or to remind blacks of the support Jews had given to the civil rights movement, they, in effect, supplied ammunition for their more radical foes, buttressing charges that they had sold out to whites. Later, based on the same political calculus, Jesse Jackson and his protégé Al Sharpton made use of anti-Semitic slurs in their own bids for prominence in the black community. Subsequently, several black political figures, like Cynthia McKinney, continued to make use of anti-Semitic rhetoric to show their racial bona fides. Others, like former Maryland congresswoman Donna Edwards, make a major point of criticizing Israel, though eschewing more overt anti-Semitism. And, as noted above, BLM protests in 2020 castigated the Jews as oppressors of people of color at home and abroad.

Still one more role played by black anti-Semitism is in support of efforts by African Americans to forge alliances and coalitions with other groups that may have their own reasons for supporting expressions of antipathy for Jews. Some African Americans have, for instance, sought ties with groups in Africa and the Middle East, and some, like McKinney, have been alleged to receive considerable funding from Muslim groups in the United States.[76] Identification with third world forces allows American blacks to see themselves as participants in a worldwide struggle against oppression. Most third world participants in this struggle, of course, strongly oppose Israel, and hence anti-Zionism can be a crucial element of third world solidarity for African Americans, as it is for Western European socialists. Hence delegations of American blacks often attend international conferences where condemnation of racism, imperialism, and Zionism happens. The expectation is that African American participants will give their support to these resolutions, and usually do so with enthusiasm.

In 2009, the Congressional Black Caucus (CBC) was sharply critical of the Obama administration for boycotting the second UN conference on racism. At the earlier conference in 2001, delegates had voted to declare Zionism a form of racism. The 2009 conference, featuring a keynote address in which Iran's president, Mahmoud Ahmadinejad, declared that the Holocaust was merely a pretext for Israeli aggression, also focused on the alleged crimes of the Jewish state. Cynthia McKinney was especially outraged that the United States would not be attending. McKinney had led the CBC in demanding American participation at the 2001 conference and was forced to go "toe to toe" with the Anti-Defamation League and Jewish members of Congress.[77]

An anti-Semitic discourse has also helped radical and left-liberal blacks achieve a more prominent position on the American Left. Through the 1960s, blacks were a subordinate group on the Left, especially within the Communist Party, which Jewish intellectuals dominated. Harold Cruse, a black Communist, described this situation in his well-known 1967 work, *The Crisis of the Negro Intellectual*. Jewish Communists, said Cruse, always looked to ensure their complete political and ideological power over their black allies. Jews sought to dominate the field of "Negro studies" and made sure that Jews always held the top Communist Party posts in the black community.[78] Through a posture of anti-Semitism, blacks simultaneously link themselves to non-Jewish leftists, most of whom are anti-Zionist, if not anti-Semitic, while intimidating Jewish leftists, who are, in effect, accused of being insufficiently militant in their support for third world causes, perhaps even of being closet Zionists. Trying to disprove this implicit or explicit charge is one reason that some Jewish leftists have become vehemently and outspokenly anti-Zionist.

Thus left-liberal blacks add their voices to the anti-Semitic discourse of the contemporary Left. Jews find black anti-Semitism particularly galling in view of the contribution made by the Jewish community to the civil rights cause not so long ago. Politics, however, is about interests, not gratitude. And some black public figures, most recently Congresswoman Ilhan Omar, are likely to continue to find that anti-Semitic rhetoric serves their political interests.

In recent years, black anti-Semitism has taken a violent turn, particularly in the New York area. In December 2019, for example, two African American gunmen killed four Jews in a kosher grocery in Jersey City. The shooters were affiliated with an anti-Semitic group called the Black Hebrew Israelites. In January 2020, a black man who burst into a Hanukkah party hosted by a rabbi in Monsey, New Jersey, stabbed five Jews. Attacks by African Americans against easily identifiable Hasidic Jews in New York have become so commonplace that even Mayor Bill de Blasio, no friend of the Jews, was compelled to assign more police to Jewish neighborhoods in Brooklyn.

Jewish Anti-Zionism and Anti-Semitism

A final important source of anti-Semitic discourse on the political Left consists of European, American, and even Israeli Jews whose criticism of Israel and those Jews who support Israel has become so vehement as to constitute a form of Jewish anti-Semitism. At first glance, the notion of Jewish anti-Semitism may seem improbable. Indeed, an essay by the Indiana University English professor Alvin Rosenfeld accusing several prominent Jewish intellectuals of promoting anti-Semitism generated considerable controversy.[79]

Yet, just as there are Americans who hate their country enough to take up arms against it—the "American Taliban," to take one recent example—there have always been Jews who, for whatever reason, reject their own community in favor of some other religious or social identification. The Jewish community castigates such individuals as "self-hating Jews," a term that suggests a psychological aberration. Often cited as an exemplar of a deeply disturbed, self-hating Jew is Otto Weininger, mentioned earlier, a young turn-of-the-century Viennese Jewish intellectual. Weininger converted to Christianity in 1902 and in 1903 published a book titled *Sex and Character*, in which he characterized Judaism as a cowardly, feminine religion that lived as a parasite on its masculine host nations.[80] Weininger killed himself soon after his book's publication but was later praised by Adolf Hitler and other Nazis.[81] Psychological explanations might also be useful in understanding the behavior of various American neo-Nazis such as Davis Wolfgang Hawke, aka Andy Greenbaum, who have turned out to be Jewish.[82]

Does this Jewish self-loathing explain the anti-Zionism of several left-liberal Jewish intellectuals and political activists such as Jacqueline Rose, Judith Butler, Noam Chomsky, Richard Falk, Michael Neumann, the late Tony Judt, Ilan Pappé, and Norman Finkelstein—or even the outright anti-Semitism of a Gilad Atzmon? To an extent, certainly. Butler and Finkelstein begin talks with "I am a Jew but . . . ," a shamefaced effort to distinguish themselves from other Jews.

But psychological explanations certainly do not tell the whole story. The anti-Zionism of some leftist Jewish intellectuals seems related more to Israel's place in the international system than to self-hatred. Between 1948 and the 1967 war, Israel was a small and beleaguered socialist country whose chief international sponsor was France. Israel's Arab foes during these decades were feudal monarchies and military dictatorships that trumpeted quasi-fascist ideologies. Most Jewish leftists had no difficulty reconciling their political orientation with a favorable view of Israel. During the late 1960s and early 1970s, however, Israel's international position had been transformed. Israel became a regional superpower, an occupying power no less, led by a succession of conservative governments whose security policies aligned with those of the United States. At the same time, several of the Arab states along with the Palestinians aligned themselves with radical states and liberation movements in the third world and labeled the Israelis imperialists, brutal occupiers, and racists.[83]

These changes in Israel's place in the world have made it increasingly difficult to be both pro-Israel and a member in good standing of the left-liberal community. Intellectuals and activists have felt compelled to make choices. For some Left liberals, identification with the Jewish community and with Israel outweighed any attachment to the political Left. A number of today's neoconservatives began their movement from the socialist camp to the Democratic Party because of Soviet anti-Semitism, and then became Republicans when they lost confidence in the Democratic Party's security policies, including its willingness to defend Israel.[84] Other Jewish leftists and liberals continue to resist the pressure to choose or have sought to carve out an increasingly shaky middle ground where they can be both politically Left and pro-Israel. Some of these individuals are in such organizations as Americans for Peace Now or J Street and write for periodicals such as *Tikkun*, which are sharply critical of Israeli policies but in general supportive of Israel's existence as a nation.

A third group of Jewish Left liberals, currently represented by such organizations as Jewish Voice for Peace, has decided that it was risky not to protect its bona fides on the political Left by offering any support to Israel. To a certain extent, this decision reflects a particular moral and political commitment including sympathy for the Palestinians, whom they see as victims of a brutal occupation. But other social factors are at work as well. A pro-Israel stance means alienating friends and associates in the progressive community. On some elite university campuses, being insufficiently opposed to Israel may lead to a professor being labeled a "right-winger" and ostracized from polite academic society. Self-loathing may play some part here too. As Edward Alexander has noted, some left-liberal Jewish intellectuals express a sense of embarrassment or even shame at the idea that they might be identified with Israel.[85] Thus Jacquelyn Rose writes of her shame at Israeli actions.[86] Similarly, the late NYU history professor Tony Judt declared that because of Israel, "non-Israeli Jews feel themselves exposed to criticism and vulnerable to attack for things they didn't do. . . . The behavior of a self-described Jewish state affects the way everyone else looks at Jews."[87] Some progressive Jewish intellectuals have gone so far as to publicly renounce their "right of return" to Israel, hoping this will help their friends and colleagues to avoid confusing them with the Zionists.

In their books, articles, speeches, and other presentations, these anti-Zionist Jews have little to say that is different from the utterances of other anti-Zionist progressives. One group, exemplified by Ilan Pappé, asserts that from its very founding the state of Israel was committed to a program of "ethnic cleansing."[88] A group led by Noam Chomsky views Israel as an agent of US imperialism.[89] Another group, exemplified by Michael Neumann, accuses Israel of practicing genocidal policies against the Palestinians.[90] Still another group, exemplified by Norman Finkelstein, declares that the Holocaust, if not exactly a myth, is exaggerated and misused by Zionists as a justification for the existence of the state of Israel.[91]

Some Jewish progressives, most often JVP members, specialize in using their Jewish background and knowledge of Jewish ritual to turn sacred Jewish texts and observances against Israel. In 2013, for example, JVP declared Tisha B'Av—a day when Jews fast in remembrance of the destruction of the Temple—a "Day of Action" against Israel. JVP activists said that henceforward they would recite newly crafted Palestinian lamentations in place of the traditional Jewish texts.[92] This mockery of Jewish ritual follows a pattern begun by Nazi propagandists in such films as *Der Ewige Jude* (1940), where Jewish religious practices were presented in a manner calculated to demean the Jews.

The anti-Zionist Jewish progressives add little to the substance of the discussion about Israel. What they say, others say too, whether gentile progressives or Muslims. The contribution of the Jewish anti-Zionists is political rather than intellectual. When Muslims or gentiles denounce Israel, their motives might be suspect, and their assertions taken with a grain of salt. The Muslim might simply be advocating for Palestine, and the gentile might harbor some ill will toward Jews. When Jews denounce Israel, though, they claim a special status as truth tellers. Some begin their denunciations by citing their own childhood Torah study or work on a kibbutz or parents who survived the Holocaust. Judith Butler, indeed, cites her own Jewish upbringing as the source of her moral authority to absolve the other progressive anti-Zionists of the charge of anti-Semitism.[93] When individuals such as these denounce Israel, the casual or credulous listener is more likely to assume them to be credible. They play the role of "experts" who hawk products in television commercials. No wonder, America's most media-savvy Nazi, David Duke, found much to praise in the work and courage of Chomsky, Finkelstein, and the others.[94] A clever fellow, Duke recognized a group of kindred spirits who, in their own way, were working to promote his cause. In the old Soviet Union,

Westerners who naïvely sympathized with the Soviet cause were sometimes known as *polezniye duraki* (полезные дураки), or "useful fools." The term might apply to the Jewish anti-Zionists as well. How else would one describe Jewish LGBTQ+ groups that take anti-Zionist positions and declare Israel to be guilty of practicing a "reductive" version of gay rights?[95] Reductive? Could they be unaware of the brutality inflicted on gay people in much of the Muslim world? Or how should we characterize the Jews, under the banner of "If Not Now," who rallied in Washington in 2016, claiming that there existed an "inextricable" linkage between the demands made by the Black Lives Matter movement and the Palestinian cause? Is this intersectionality or merely *narishkeit* (foolishness)?[96]

And speaking of *narishkeit*, in 2017 the Democratic Socialists of America (DSA) voted to support BDS in a meeting scheduled for a Saturday to make a point about not caring what the Jews thought. The DSA is a venerable organization. In its nineteenth-century heyday, it was led by Jewish socialists and was among the foremost groups on the American Left. The DSA has practically disappeared on the ash heap of history, as Marxists like to say. Yet there was something sad about watching the members of this group, with its strong Jewish roots, chanting, "From the river to the sea, Palestine will be free." Didn't they realize that many Palestinians who chant these words envision a time when there will be no Jews between the Jordan and the Mediterranean? Didn't they think about how such a *judenrein* Palestine would come about?

So, suppose the Jewish anti-Zionists win. Further suppose that Israel is erased from the map. Would the Muslim and other anti-Zionist friends of the anti-Israel Jews love and respect them for their efforts? My suspicion is that the traditional Yiddish saying would apply: *Es vert sie nisht helfen* (It won't help them).

3

Why the Jews Persist

BENEATH THE THIN disguise of anti-Zionism and anti-Israel sentiments, anti-Semitism has strongly reasserted itself in Europe and on US college campuses and even within the Democratic Party, home to most liberal, university-educated, and upper-middle-class American Jews. Why should anti-Zionism be mushrooming, strangely, at the very heart of Jewish loyalties and political identity?

Ironically, few American Jews have ever been Zionists in the literal sense of the term or plan to live in Israel—that is, few have ever given serious thought of "making Aliyah" and emigrating from the US to Israel. Indeed, few American Jews are fluent in Hebrew or know much about Israeli culture or politics. Even fewer subscribe to English-language newspapers such as the *Jerusalem Post*, which offers day-to-day coverage of events in Israel. It is also ironic for American Jews that since the founding of Israel, the relationship between Israel and them has not been without tensions. So, why are American Jews unable to separate themselves from anti-Zionism or indeed from the policies of Israel?

Despite their opinion of Zionism, American Jews have a natural kinship with Jews in Israel and a commitment to Israel's security and well-being, in part based on tradition and on Israel's martial prowess. For American Jews, Israel's military success has been a notable source of pride and a counter to the myth that Jews do not fight, as alleged during the Holocaust. American Jewish support for Israel is also based on something that Jews will admit to one another but seldom to non-Jews: the fear that, as has occurred so often in Jewish history, Jews might someday find themselves compelled to leave America and seek refuge elsewhere. Among other things, Israel, to many Jews, is an insurance policy against a major upsurge of anti-Semitism in the United States.

The Jews, we might note, are the last of America's nineteenth-century immigrant groups to preserve their social and religious identity. The Irish, Germans, Scandinavians, and Italians, for instance, long ago faded into America's melting pot. Jews, however, are perennial outsiders and suffer anti-Semitism for it. So, the question lingers, given their history, why do Jews choose to remain members of a distinctive community, when they have always had other options in America? At this point in American history, Jewishness would seem to be voluntary, just as it was during certain periods of European history when Jews could convert to Christianity and, by so doing, end the various constraints under which they lived. Recall that it was his father's conversion to Christianity that paved Benjamin Disraeli's path to political leadership in nineteenth-century England. In America today, there is virtually nothing to prevent a Jew from changing his or her name, marrying a gentile, joining a church, or abjuring religious practice altogether, and simply vanishing into American society. In this case, there would also be no need for Zionism. This course of action is almost certain to protect a Jew in America from discrimination, from anti-Semitic slights, and even from the possible reemergence of anti-Semitism as a potent political force in the future.

Of course, some Jews do follow this path. Indeed, every year Jewish organizations express alarm over the threat posed by assimilation to the long-term prospects of the Jewish community in America.[1] Millions of Jews, however, refuse to surrender their Jewish identification, despite the rewards for defecting and the real or potential penalties for keeping a Jewish identification. While Jewish organizations express dismay about the number of Jews who leave the community, the real puzzle is why more do not. Given the attractiveness and openness of American culture and institutions, it is, indeed, remarkable that there are any Jews left at all. It is the solution to this puzzle that explains the peculiar character of the Jew in modern history.

The Jewish Government-in-Exile

Hannah Arendt argued that Jews were always marginal in gentile society and eventually sought the protection of the gentile state because they had no state of their own (a source of their allegiance, for example, to the Democratic Party today, discussed in a later chapter).[2] This, however, is only part of the story. Israel is, of course, identified as the Jewish state. However, everywhere that there is a sizable Jewish community, there also exists a complex of religious, educational, communal, and other institutions that collectively serve as a Jewish government-in-exile, regulating the affairs of the Jewish community.

Often Jews created these institutions or transplanted them in response to anti-Semitism and discrimination. However, as is true for any other government, this government-in-exile developed a stake in perpetuating itself by keeping its constituency as a separate and distinct group. Whether or not Jews need Jewish institutions, these institutions certainly need Jews if they are to survive. The survival of Jewish institutions depends on the continued existence of the Jews as a separate and distinct group. Hence these institutions and their leaders promote a doctrine of separatism beginning with a religion that emphasizes the Jews as God's "chosen people," and a version of history that emphasizes the danger posed by non-Jews.

What these institutions fear even more than anti-Semitism is Jewish assimilation and disappearance—search the internet for the alarm presently raised by the entire Jewish communal establishment about the increasing rate of mixed marriage. Quite naturally, Jewish leaders presume that the welfare of Jewish individuals and the preservation of the Jewish people as a group go hand in hand. But this presumption is open to question. Intermarriage hurts exactly whom? Are there data to show that Jews who marry gentiles suffer more emotional or physical distress than Jews who marry other Jews or remain single? Obviously, the potential victims of intermarriage and assimilation are not individual Jews so much as the Jewish community and the institutions that serve it.

The beginnings of this government-in-exile or diaspora can be traced to the Babylonian exile more than 2,400 years ago. Following the Babylonian conquest of Jerusalem in 597 BCE, a large segment of the population of Judah was deported to the Babylon Empire intact. Brought to the capital, commoners, scribes, priests, and members of the nobility were left on their own and allowed to function as a community. It was during this period that the Jewish leadership began to learn how to keep its authority and the allegiance of its followers without the customary institutions and powers of a national government.

As part of this effort, scribes recorded and copied Jewish secular law, history, and oral tradition and incorporated them into Jewish religious ceremonies. For two thousand years thereafter, as Jews practiced their religion, they read and studied the laws of the Jewish state, though that state, itself, no longer had a physical existence. To help ensure that their followers kept a separate communal identity while in exile, the Jewish leadership strongly emphasized the importance of ritual circumcision, creating an ineradicable distinguishing mark, and organized a major religious ceremony around it. To keep the coherence and distinctiveness of the community, new emphasis was given to the weekly Sabbath and many other festivals.[3] Using these and other techniques, Jewish governments-in-exile have continued to function throughout the world to the present time.

It is the government-in-the-diaspora that has kept Jewish identification, despite the temptation faced by Jews to defect. This complex of lay and religious leaders and institutions, making use of secular techniques of governance as well as religious rituals and laws, keeps the Jewish community together. The Jewish philosopher Ahad Ha-am concluded, "More than the Jews kept the Sabbath, the Sabbath kept them."[4] Expanding this observation, Jews do not create Jewish institutions so much as these institutions create the Jews and work to ensure their continued existence.

Through the eighteenth century, a communal authority, or *kehillah*, governed the European Jewish communities. This regulated a community's religious, cultural, and political affairs according to the *halakhah*, the Jewish legal system based on the divine revelation of the Torah. The *kehillah*, in fact, functioned as a Jewish government-in-exile within the boundaries created by the gentile authorities. The *kehillah* and *halakhah* maintained the Jews as a nation apart. During the nineteenth century, emancipated Jews were given political rights in Europe, leading to a reduction in *kehillah* authority and its eventual abolition as national governments ended most corporate bodies that stood between them and their citizens.

Jews never brought the *kehillah* to the United States. However, even without the *kehillah*, contemporary Jewish communities support institutions that preserve Jews as an entity apart. Virtually all Jewish groups and organizations, secular as well as religious, are united on the importance of this goal, though how best to ensure the survival of a distinctive Jewish community is a matter of intense controversy. Indeed, even what might seem to be theological disputes among the different branches of Judaism are at heart really debates about how to best preserve Jewish identity. Orthodox Jews, for example, say that strict adherence to Jewish law and religious precepts is essential for keeping the integrity of the community. The leaders of the Reform community assert that Jewish practice must be more consistent with the secular life led by Jews to persuade them to remain in the community.

The Jews are undoubtedly the most, if not always the best, organized communal group in the United States. At the heart of every Jewish community is a synagogue, presided over by a rabbi who usually serves as both its spiritual and its secular leader. In addition to religious services, larger synagogues have a religious school that may involve anything from a rudimentary Sunday morning series of classes to a day school with instruction in all subjects in addition to religious classes. Many synagogues run elaborate cultural and social programs catering to various segments of the Jewish community, such as dances for Jewish singles, programs for Jewish senior citizens, social clubs and activities for Jewish children and teenagers, adult educational programs, lectures, and so forth. Most synagogues also sponsor sisterhoods as a basis for women's activities and men's clubs for men's activities. Synagogues typically also arrange for the burial of their members in a Jewish cemetery or a reserved section of a general cemetery, with the proper Jewish burial service. Often the synagogue also serves as the base for other Jewish cultural, social, and political organizations in the community.

Beyond the synagogue is a network of often overlapping and affiliated organizations and agencies that undertake religious, educational, cultural, social, economic, and political tasks. The *American Jewish Year Book* lists more than 400 national Jewish organizations, which each year collectively raise and spend more than $2 billion for communal purposes.[5] In addition, the American Jewish community supports some 180 local welfare boards, federations, or community councils; approximately 184 daily, weekly, or monthly periodicals focusing on Jewish issues; some 80 political action committees that, together, contribute millions of dollars to candidates for political office; and last, but not least, a complex of schools that enroll nearly half a million students (a hundred thousand of these in Jewish day schools) with an annual budget that may approach $1 billion.

The most important Jewish organizations include the American Jewish Committee and American Jewish Congress, which concentrate on the protection of the civil and religious rights of Jews throughout the world; the Anti-Defamation League, which focuses on combating anti-Semitism; the Conference of Presidents of Major American Jewish Organizations, an umbrella group that works to maintain American support for Israel; the National Jewish Community Relations Advisory Council, which coordinates the 11 national and 114 local Jewish community relations agencies; and the Simon Wiesenthal Center, which seeks to preserve the memory of the Holocaust and sponsors research and education on the Holocaust.

Others include the American Jewish Joint Distribution Committee, which supplies aid to Jewish communities throughout the world; the Hebrew Immigrant Aid Society, which gives aid to Jewish immigrants primarily in Israel and the United States; the United Jewish Appeal, which raises funds for social and humanitarian programs in Israel and elsewhere; the B'nai B'rith Hillel Foundation, which offers cultural, social, religious, and educational programs for Jewish college students; the Council of Jewish Federations, which is involved with community organizing, fund-raising, and welfare planning for more than two hundred local federations throughout the United States; the American Israel Public Affairs Committee, or AIPAC, which lobbies on behalf of American aid for Israel; the Center for Learning and Leadership, which sponsors adult leadership education; the Center for Jewish Community Studies; the Jerusalem Center for Public Affairs, a Jewish think tank modeled after the Brookings Institution; and Hadassah, a women's organization promoting cultural ties between American Jews and Israel. Another prominent, if controversial, Jewish organization is J Street, a left-liberal Jewish group that lobbies on behalf of its idea of a fair solution to the Israeli-Palestinian conflict. (Established Jewish organizations regard J Street as insufficiently supportive of Israel and in 2014 rejected J Street's bid for membership in the Conference of Presidents of Major Jewish Organizations.)

In addition, each of the major Jewish religious denominations and their many affiliates sponsors a variety of organizations to promote proper religious practices and offer religious education and training. For example, the Jewish

Reconstructionist Federation coordinates the Reconstructionist Rabbinical Association and the Reconstructionist Rabbinical College. At the other end of the Jewish spectrum, the Merkos L'Inyonei Chinuch (the Central Organization for Jewish Education) is the educational arm of the Lubavicher movement and looks to stimulate interest in Jewish education and observance and supports a network of offices, schools, camps, and Chabad-Lubavitch Houses. The Rabbinical Alliance of America is an organization of Orthodox rabbis. The United Synagogue of Conservative Judaism is an organization of 850 Conservative congregations throughout the United States.

The organizations and agencies in this enormous complex assert that they exist to serve the needs of the Jewish people. And, of course, they do. They work to combat anti-Semitism, deliver social services, offer educational opportunities, ensure religious training, resettle immigrants, protect Israel's interests, and the like. A major goal, however, of most if not all of these organizations, agencies, and institutions is what Jonathan Woocher has called "sacred survival."[6] That is, they work to ensure the continuity of the Jewish people as a distinctive group both by struggling against enemies seeking to destroy the Jews and by struggling to prevent the assimilation of the Jews into the larger society.

Thus, on the one hand, Jewish organizations are forever vigilant against all manifestations of anti-Semitism, believing that the eventual aim of every anti-Semite is the annihilation of the Jewish people. On the other hand, frightening as annihilation may be, Jewish organizations are equally worried about the danger that Jews will disappear because of assimilation. Major Jewish organizations have made the fight against assimilation a primary goal of their activities.

Through their cultural and educational programs, Jewish groups emphasize three major points. First, Jews today have a debt to their forefathers to pass on their Jewish heritage to their children. To fail in this duty is to betray the millions of Jewish martyrs who fought and died for their faith over the past four thousand years. Second, Jews as a people have made an enormous contribution to civilization through the philosophical ideals and scientific principles they have introduced. Thus, Jews have an obligation to humanity to keep their distinctive identities, "because we are struggling to teach men how to build a better world for all men," as one Jewish leader put it.[7] Finally, only as self-conscious members of the Jewish community, the Jewish leadership avers, can Jews lead meaningful lives.

In these ways, the leadership of the Jewish community justifies its efforts to combat Jewish assimilation. Obviously, the leaders of Jewish religious and secular organizations are not inherently cynical and do not oppose assimilation merely to preserve the organizations they lead. Instead, they see themselves precisely as they portray themselves: individuals fighting on behalf of noble and transcendent goals, preserving Jewish heritage and welfare.

However, as students of social organizations know, the leaders of such organizations and institutions convince themselves that whatever serves their interests also promotes their members' well-being and society in general.[8] So the enormous complex of organizations and institutions that try to govern the Jewish community must battle against intermarriage and assimilation because they need committed Jews to continue. It follows that intermarriage and assimilation are social evils.

The great key to Jewish survival over the centuries has been a government-in-exile, struggling to preserve the identity and integrity of its people. Also, this is a government-in-exile that has had centuries to perfect three instruments to foster a Jewish community: law and religious practice, education, and communal mobilization.

Law and Religious Practice

A central precept of Jewish law and religion is the distinctiveness, or "chosenness," of the Jewish people. Jewish religious practice, moreover, serves to reinforce this distinctiveness by keeping community unity and separation from the gentile community. Jews have their own rituals, their own holidays, their own dietary codes, and so on, justified as the special duties of Jews stemming from their special relationship with God. The effect of these practices is to remind the Jewish practitioner—and the gentile observer—that Jews are distinctive, separate from the influence of gentile society.

The notion of the Jews as a people chosen by God begins with God's covenant with Abraham: "I will maintain My covenant between Me and you, and your offspring to come, as an everlasting covenant throughout the ages, to be God to you and your offspring to come. I assign the land you sojourn in to you and your offspring to come, all the land of Canaan, as an everlasting holding I will be their God."⁹

Exodus renews the covenant, which suggests that the Jews, as God's chosen people, have a special mission: "You have seen what I did to the Egyptians, how I bore you on eagles wings and brought you to Me. Now then, if you will obey Me faithfully and keep My covenant, you shall be My treasured possession among all the peoples. Indeed, all the earth is Mine, but you shall be to me a kingdom of priests and a holy nation."¹⁰

This idea of a special relationship made by God with the Jews continues in Deuteronomy: "For you are a people consecrated to the Lord your God; of all the peoples on earth, the Lord your God chose you to be His treasured people."¹¹ Even suffering and misfortune are attributed to the distinctive character of the Jews and their special relationship with God. In the words of the prophet Amos, "You alone have I singled out of all the families of earth—that is why I will call you to account for all your iniquities."¹²

Chosenness implies a special mission. And what is the mission of a "kingdom of priests and a holy nation"? Jews are chosen to bring all people of the world to an acknowledged sovereignty of God and to accept the values God has revealed. According to Rabbi Abba Hillel Silver, Jews are chosen by God to work toward the establishment on earth of a universal brotherhood under God.¹³ Through the work of the Jews, "all the families of the earth shall bless themselves."¹⁴

The chosenness of the Jews and their special mission, in turn, can require them to remain apart from other nations. "To carry out successfully the task assigned to it," says Silver, "Israel found it necessary to live in the world but apart from it."¹⁵ As Balaam puts it in the book of Numbers, "There is a people that dwells apart, not reckoned among the nations."¹⁶ The book of Leviticus makes a similar point: "I have set you apart from other peoples to be Mine."¹⁷ Similarly, the prophet Jeremiah compares Israel to an olive tree, in that other liquids readily mix with one another while olive oil refuses to do so and keeps separate.¹⁸ Speaking through the prophet Ezekiel, God declares, "And what you have in mind will never come to pass—when you say, 'We will be like the nations, the families of the lands, worshipping wood and stone.'"¹⁹

From the beginnings of Jewish history, as Silver says, God admonished Jews to separate themselves from the customs of the people around them and to follow their own moral precepts and way of life.[20] As the book of Leviticus puts it, "You shall not copy the practices of the land of Egypt, where you dwelt, or the land of Canaan, to which I am taking you; nor shall you follow their laws."[21]

The injunction to Jews to keep themselves separate from the people around them is a critical part of Jewish law as expressed in the Mishnah and later in the Talmud. The Mishnah, a six-part code of laws formulated under the authority of Judah the Patriarch, the head of the Jewish community of Palestine at the end of the second century CE, has many provisions regulating and restricting the relations between Jews and gentiles and warns Jews of the dangers inherent in associating with gentiles. For example:

> They do not leave cattle in Gentiles' inns, because they are suspect in regard to bestiality. And a woman should not be alone with them, because they are suspect in regard to fornication. And a man should not be alone with them, because they are suspect in regard to bloodshed. An Israelite girl should not serve as a midwife to a gentile woman, because she serves to bring forth a child to the service of idolatry.[22]

Similarly, according to Talmudic law, Jews were forbidden to eat food cooked by non-Jews, to engage in sexual relations with non-Jews, or to eat bread baked by non-Jews—all to prevent unnecessary contact with them. Jews were likewise forbidden to marry non-Jews unless the latter converted.

Of course, in the contemporary world, only certain Orthodox Jews keep these Talmudic laws. Indeed, most Jews are probably unaware of many of the prohibitions governing their relationships with non-Jews and cheerfully eat gentile-baked bread, drink gentile-handled wine, and perhaps even leave their cattle in gentiles' inns, oblivious to the risks involved in so doing.

However, even if they do not deliberately refrain from interacting with gentiles, to the extent that they practice their religion, Jews separate themselves from the gentile community in important ways. The Jewish Sabbath and Jewish religious holidays, for example, take place on different days from gentile religious holidays. Jews are, thus, celebrating their religious beliefs when the community around them is engaged in its normal affairs. As all Jewish children who absent themselves from public school on Rosh Hashanah and Yom Kippur know, this has the effect of reminding the Jew that he is different from his neighbors and reminding those neighbors of the difference too. As one authority puts it, "By staying out of school on these days, the child is taught to assign priority to his religious commitments and to assert his Jewish self-respect in an overwhelmingly non-Jewish society."[23]

Similarly, Jewish dietary laws, if followed, inhibit social interaction between Jews and gentiles. Observant Jews find it difficult to eat in their gentile neighbors' homes, difficult to attend business luncheons with gentile colleagues, and difficult to join gentile friends or associates for dinner in a restaurant. If they wish to adhere to the dietary restrictions prescribed by their religion, Jews find it much easier to associate with their fellow Jews than with non-Jews, even if they have no personal desire to avoid gentiles.

Similarly, when Jews do not take part in gentile religious observances, they remind themselves and their non-Jewish neighbors of their distinctiveness. Jewish children who refrain from singing Christmas carols in school and decorating a Christmas tree at home like those of their neighbors mark themselves in the eyes of their friends and, even more important, in their own minds, as members of a different group.

Some Jewish groups, of course, have tried for decades to end public forms of religious expression precisely to diminish the discomfort and sense of difference they feel when confronted by gentile religious observances. Ironically, their very success has reduced the overt sense of distinctiveness that Jews feel and thus eroded the barriers to assimilation that many of these groups fear even more than anti-Semitism.

Education

Hundreds of thousands of Jewish children attend Jewish educational institutions of various sorts every year, ranging from Jewish day schools and Hebrew schools to morning Sunday schools. These schools offer a variety of different curricula. In the Jewish day schools, a great deal of instruction is in the Hebrew language and in Jewish law and history. In the afternoon Hebrew schools, some of which meet only once a week, less time is available, and the curriculum, abbreviated. Weekly Sunday schools offer only two or two and a half hours of instruction each week and an extremely limited curriculum.

The differences among these schools are instructive. As instructional time is reduced and curricular content abbreviated, usually training in the Hebrew language is the first subject to be eliminated. Next to go is the study of Jewish law. Next is training in prayer and ritual. What is left when everything else is dropped from the curriculum? The irreducible minimum, conceived to be more important than law, religion, or language, is the inculcation of Jewish communal identity and loyalty. In other words, even where children are taught next to nothing about the substance of Jewish belief and practice, an effort is made to teach them to be Jews and, indeed, to take pride in their difference from other people.

For example, one very well-written and beautifully illustrated text aimed at primary school children recounts the tale of Jeroboam, from the book of Kings.[24] Jeroboam, of course, ruled Israel after the death of Solomon and the division of his kingdom into Israel and Judah. He encouraged idolatry—worship of a golden calf—and introduced several major changes in religious practice. The story of Jeroboam is fascinating from both a religious and a political perspective. Some of Jeroboam's religious reforms appeared to call for a more direct relationship between worshipper and deity rather than one mediated by a hereditary priesthood. These religious reforms had a political purpose. Jeroboam was interested in changing the character of Jewish religious practice to reduce the political influence of his rival Rehoboam, king of Judah, who controlled Jerusalem and the established holy places.[25]

Yet the story of Jeroboam as presented by this text discusses neither the religious nor the political issues. Instead, the story emphasizes the importance of Jewish distinctiveness. "Why were so many Israelites willing [to obey Jeroboam] and bring sacrifices to the altars of the golden calves?" the text asks.[26] Though the Torah offers no clear answer to this question, the author of the text has no problem finding one.

> Even before Jeroboam commanded his people to worship the golden calves, some Israelites may have been wishing that they were not different from all the other nations. Only they worshiped a god who could not be seen. And only their god cared how people behaved … . And why might some Israelites have wanted to be the same as everyone else? Because being different is often very hard. Many think that there

is something wrong with people who are not the same as everyone around them. And even those who are different may come to believe that there is something wrong with themselves, only because they are different. Sometimes people laugh at the "different" ones and call them strange; sometimes they even hurt them … . Perhaps such treatment made some Israelites wish they were the same as everyone else.[27]

It is obvious that God would punish those Israelites who were afraid to recognize their distinctiveness from other people, who failed to understand that other nations could worship golden calves. This is, of course, the message of the text. Politics and even religion are, at most, secondary. Identification and distinctiveness should be the Jew's primary concerns.

Jewish identification and distinctiveness are also the themes of the three holidays that form the foundation and pillars of Jewish children's education: Passover, Purim, and Hanukkah. As religious purists often note, two of these three celebrations are not remarkable events in the Jewish religious calendar. In terms of their significance in Jewish law and ritual, Yom Kippur, Rosh Hashanah, and several other festivals are certainly more important than Purim and Hanukkah. Nevertheless, Jewish schools emphasize chiefly Passover, Purim, and Hanukkah. Not only are these cheerful holidays, emphasizing triumph over adversity, believed to appeal to childish sensibilities; they also help teach three fundamental concepts to Jewish children: chosenness, distrust of gentiles, and the danger of assimilation.

Passover and Chosenness

The major emphasis of the Passover celebration is, of course, the chosenness of the Jewish people, though a secondary theme is the ingratitude and duplicity of gentiles. The events celebrated in the Passover ritual are those described in the books of Genesis and Exodus. Joseph, sold into slavery by his brothers, manages by virtue of superior foresight and administrative acumen to become chief adviser to Pharaoh and the governor of Egypt and to save the country from a severe famine. From his exalted position, Joseph can bring his family to Egypt, where the Jews quickly become powerful and prosperous. The Egyptians, however, soon become jealous of the Jews' success and fearful of their power. After Joseph's death and the accession of a new pharaoh, the Egyptians turn on the Jews and enslave them.

For three centuries, Egyptians subject Jews to many trials and tribulations, and eventually they cry out for help. God remembers his covenant with Abraham and sends Moses to liberate the Jews from bondage. Pharaoh initially refuses to heed the demands of God as reported by Moses but is compelled to obey when God kills the firstborn child of every Egyptian household. To save their own firstborn, God orders the Jews to clearly mark their doors with the blood of lambs or (goat) kids. The willingness of the Jews to distinguish themselves allows God to discriminate between them and the Egyptians and to spare the Jews while smiting the Egyptians. Thus, only by clearly and publicly displaying their distinctiveness from the surrounding peoples are the Jews able to save themselves and win their freedom.

Subsequently, when the Jews reach Sinai, God tells them that so long as they obey him and keep his covenant, they, out of all people, will be his personal possession. He then singles them out by granting to them, of all people, his Ten Commandments. The Jews, God's special "kingdom of priests and holy nation," are entrusted with special knowledge of God's Will—knowledge not given to any other nation.

Initially, the Jews seem unworthy of this gift. Indeed, they show their lack of worth by abandoning God and fashioning and worshipping a golden idol like the Egyptians and other peoples worshipped, living licentiously like them too. Inevitably, when they forget that God has especially chosen them to be his people and receive his commandments—that is, when they try to be like other people—the Jews are severely punished. Moses has more than three thousand of them killed on the spot, and God promises to punish the others for their sins by abandoning them. Moses, however, intercedes and reminds God that if he truly wishes the Jews to be a people "distinguished … from every people on the face of the earth," he must go with them to the land he has promised them.[28]

God relents and renews his covenant with the Jews. But, in renewing his covenant, God sets a few conditions. The first of these is that the Jews must remain separate and distinct from all the people among whom they live. He says:

> I hereby make a covenant. Before all your people I will work such
> wonders as have not been wrought on all the earth or in any nation

and all the people who are with you shall see how awesome are the Lord's deeds which I will perform for you. Mark well what I command you this day. I will drive out before you the Amorites, the Canaanites, the Hittites, the Perizzites, the Hivites, and the Jebusites. Beware of making a covenant with the inhabitants of the land against which you are advancing, lest they be a snare in your midst … . You must not make a covenant with the inhabitants of the land, for they will lust after their gods and sacrifice to their gods and invite you, and you will eat of their sacrifices. And when you take wives from among their daughters for your sons, their daughters will lust after their gods and will cause your sons to lust after their gods.[29]

The clear condition for God's favor—the condition for being God's chosen people—is that the Jews keep themselves separate and distinct from all others.

Thus, what are the themes of the Passover celebration? First, the angel of death spared, or "passed over," the Jews because they were willing to appear clearly and distinctly different from the Egyptians. Second, and central, God chose the Jews to be his special people, to receive his commandments, and to live in his promised land. Third, a condition for God's continuing favor is to remain separate and distinct from surrounding peoples and customs.

Each year in the Passover seder, a ritual attended by more than 85 percent of all Jews, families and guests recite portions of the story of the exodus from Egypt, emphasizing the Jews' special status as the recipients of God's exceptional favor.[30] Adults ask children to imagine that they, themselves, were delivered from bondage in Egypt and brought to the Promised Land by the hand of God. "In every generation," says the Passover Haggadah, "one ought to regard oneself as having personally come out of Egypt." "Tell thy son," the Haggadah continues, "that this is what the Lord did for *me* when *I* went forth from Egypt."[31]

A "wicked son" will hear a special warning. That is, the child who questions the ceremony and, by extension, the distinctive customs and traditions of the Jewish people is cast out, stripped of his chosenness, and punished by God. "Tell him," orders the Haggadah, "that if *he* had been [in Egypt] he would not have been redeemed."[32] To question the ceremony is, in effect, to refuse to mark one's door with lambs' blood, to refuse to distinguish oneself from the gentiles, and, by so doing, to incur God's wrath. The first seder night, of course, concludes with the cry, "Next year in Jerusalem," reminding Jews that they are outsiders, living in the lands of strangers, not in their own land.[33]

Purim and the Duplicity of the Gentiles

If the Passover celebration tells Jews that God has chosen them for a special purpose, the Purim celebration teaches them that gentiles are untrustworthy. For they are jealous of the Jews and their accomplishments, suspicious of the Jews' distinctive culture, and may, if given an opportunity, viciously try to murder them.

The events celebrated by the Purim festival involve a Jew, Mordecai, who served as an official in the court of King Ahasuerus (Xerxes) of Persia, and Mordecai's ward, Esther, a member of Ahasuerus's harem who has hidden her Jewish identity. Mordecai earns the enmity of a Macedonian Greek named Haman who is his superior in the royal chancellery. Haman is furious because Mordecai, in keeping with Jewish custom, refuses to bow and prostrate himself before him. Haman resolves to kill not only Mordecai but all his people as well. He approaches King Ahasuerus to secure permission for the annihilation of the Jews in the Persian realm. The reason he gives is their unwillingness to assimilate and become like other subjects of the empire. Haman says to the king:

> There is a certain people, scattered and dispersed among the other peoples in all the provinces of your realm, whose laws are different from those of any other people and who do not obey the king's laws; and it is not in Your Majesty's interest to tolerate them. If it please Your Majesty, let an edict be drawn for their destruction, and I will pay ten thousand talents of silver to the steward for deposit in the royal treasury.[34]

The king agrees to Haman's request and tells the Greek courtier that he may dispose of the Jews as he sees fit. Haman issues an edict signed in the name of the king ordering the killing of Jews. Couriers dispatch written instructions to all of the king's provinces, to destroy, massacre, and exterminate all the Jews, young and old, children and women, in a single day … and to plunder their possessions.[35]

Fortunately, Mordecai can communicate the news of the royal decree to Esther in the harem. He asks her to remember that though she lives in the royal palace she is still a Jew, and her fate is the same as that of her people. "Do not imagine," says Mordecai, "that you of all the Jews, will escape with your life by being in the king's palace."[36] Esther risks her life by approaching the king without a royal summons (a capital offense), reveals that she is a Jew, and begs Ahasuerus to spare her people. Esther's entreaties move the king, and he orders Haman executed, Mordecai promoted to a position of great power in the empire, and the Jews spared. With the support of the crown, the Jews of Persia turn on their enemies and slaughter tens of thousands of their erstwhile foes.

The story of Esther is a fascinating account of court politics and political intrigue in ancient Persia alone. It was common for Persian kings to rely on educated foreigners as administrators and advisers, and Jews and Greeks were often among those vying for power within the royal court. Often, when ministers came from different minority ethnic or confessional communities, it was not unusual for them to try to turn their Persian masters against other communities as threats to the crown. In the book of Esther, both Mordecai and Haman use this tactic. Haman first persuades the king that the Jews flout Persian law and represent a threat to the stability of the realm. Later, however, Mordecai can convince Ahasuerus that Haman planned, according to some versions of the book of Esther, "to transfer the Persian empire to the Macedonians."[37]

In this case also, one minister, Mordecai, can use his connection to one of the king's favored concubines to undermine his rival, Haman. This was certainly not an unusual tactic in Middle Eastern court politics. Indeed, there is another well-known example in Jewish history. In eleventh-century Fatimid Egypt, the Jewish merchant prince Abu Saed Ibrahim al-Tustari became the power behind the throne and a man who could make and break viziers and other ministers.[38] The source of his enormous influence was Tustari's close and continuing relationship with one of his former Sudanese slave girls, whom he had sold to the royal harem. Within a few short years, this concubine gave birth to the heir to the throne, became Queen Mother, and later was named regent for her son when he succeeded to the caliphate in 1036 while still a child. During her regency, this former slave relied extensively on her onetime master, Tustari, as her confidant and agent.

Struggles among courtiers often ended with the murder or execution of one or another of the rivals as well as the massacre of his followers, kinsmen, and political supporters. If, as was often the case, the courtier was from a minority ethnic community, his conationals or coreligionists might also be at risk, suspected of having ties to the fallen courtier, who, typically, would have used his power to provide them with patronage, favorable treatment, and government jobs.

As a result, during political struggles between courtiers from different ethnic communities, each might look to mobilize the support, especially the armed support, of his own confessional community. Thus court politics often resulted in communal violence. In the Tustari case, political rivals from other ethnic communities often made use of anti-Jewish appeals to mobilize and incite their own followers against him. After Tustari fell from favor and was executed, many of his followers were killed and violence was directed toward Jews, who had enjoyed his protection and patronage. While this did not get out of hand, Jews came to enjoy a less favorable position than they had under the protection of their powerful coreligionist.

Thus, stripped of its religious and allegorical trimmings, the biblical tale of Esther is an interesting but typical account of court intrigue in the ancient Middle East. But what do Jewish children learn from this story? What emphasis lies in the account that makes Purim one of the pillars of a Jewish religious education? The first point is that among the gentiles are many vicious murderers who are extremely eager to turn on their Jewish neighbors. In retaliation for what is a minor slight by Mordecai, Haman resolves to murder every Jewish man, woman, and child in Persia. And he does not seem to have any trouble finding Persians to help him carry out his plans. Large numbers of gentiles, it seems, are extremely happy to have license to turn on and murder their Jewish neighbors.

The second point of note is the behavior of the good gentile, King Ahasuerus. The king appears to have no ill will toward the Jews and is enamored of a Jewish woman. However, even this good gentile is prepared to stand by and watch Jews slaughtered. Indeed, although the king does not himself raise his hand against the Jews, he is indifferent to their fate and is perfectly happy to acquiesce in their murder. Thus the two major gentile figures in the story, Haman and Ahasuerus, are a murderer and a man indifferent to murder. Gentiles either want to murder Jews or, even if they do not want to do it themselves, are perfectly willing to stand by and see Jews murdered.

Third is the loyalty to the Jewish people. Esther is a fully assimilated member of the royal household, and no one knows she is a Jew. Nevertheless, during the crisis, she risks her life to save her people. The lesson here is that when the crisis comes, Jews can rely only on other Jews to help them. The other lesson here is that Jews should not think that assimilation and passing as gentiles will save them.

Thus this festival that serves as the second pillar of a Jewish child's religious education commemorates what? One small victory against the unrelenting efforts of the gentiles to murder the Jews. As one popular Jewish children's history text puts it, "The story of Esther is an old, old story. But to the Jews it stays ever new. For other Hamans have appeared in their long history, even in recent years. And the story of Esther reminds them, Hamans may come, but they are destroyed in the end, while the Jews continue to live on through the ages."[39]

Hanukkah and the Danger of Assimilation

The third pillar of Jewish religious education in America is the Hanukkah celebration. The emphasis that Hanukkah receives in America is mostly a function of its fortuitous timing. Hanukkah, of course, falls conveniently near Christmas. It thus allows Jewish parents to inundate their children with gifts and, in this way, to prevent their children from feeling envious about the gifts that their Christian friends receive or feeling left out of the holiday festivities. Hanukkah is an antidote to the lure of gentile and culture religion and the danger of assimilation. In addition, though, the Hanukkah story is itself an allegory about the danger of assimilation and the importance of Jews remembering that they are Jews.

The events commemorated by the Hanukkah celebration are in the First and Second Books of Maccabees. These tracts are not parts of the Tanakh or Hebrew scriptures; they are preserved only in Greek, though a Hebrew original of the Greek text may have existed. Nevertheless, excerpts from the books of Maccabees are a staple of the volumes of Bible stories used in Jewish schools for the edification of children.[40]

In the second century BCE, the Hebrew kingdoms had become quasi-autonomous states within the part of the Alexandrian Empire ruled by Antiochus Epiphanes, a descendant of one of Alexander's generals. To keep and bolster his authority within the realm, Antiochus had embarked on a process of Hellenization. Encouraged to abandon their own religions and cultures, only then would subjected people be welcomed into the Greek religious and cultural community, while those who refused faced several restrictions and penalties.

Hellenistic culture, which attracted substantial numbers of Jews, was the dominant culture of the era and opened to Jews a world of knowledge, opportunity, power, and wealth that was foreclosed by their own culture's strict religious codes and constricted worldview. The First Book of Maccabees reports the result:

> It was then that there emerged from Israel a set of renegades who led many people astray. "Come," they said, "let us ally ourselves with the Gentiles surrounding us, for since we separated ourselves from them many misfortunes have overtaken us." This proposal proved acceptable, and a number of people eagerly approached the king, who authorized them to practice the Gentiles' observances. So, they built a gymnasium in Jerusalem, such as the Gentiles have, disguised their circumcision, and abandoned the holy covenant, submitting to Gentile rule as willing slaves of impiety.[41]

This apostasy, however, brings nothing but grief to the Jews who look to abandon their own culture and religion for that of the Greeks. Jewish resistance fighters, led first by Mattathias and then by his son Judas the Maccabee, try to throw off Greek rule. They launch a holy war against the apostates, killing them, seizing their property, and forcibly circumcising their sons. This holy war was a necessary and proper part of throwing off the yoke of Greek tyranny. When Mattathias is invited to give his support to Antiochus and refuses, he happens to meet an assimilated Jew offering a sacrifice to Zeus as required by royal decree. Mattathias, seeing this, is moved to righteous fury: "He was fired with zeal; stirred to the depth of his being, he gave vent to the depth of his legitimate anger, threw himself on the man and slaughtered him on the altar."[42] For good measure, Mattathias kills the royal commissioner who had come to invite him to forsake Judaism and adopt Greek ways.

The apostates, for their part, had become traitors and informers helping the Greeks kill their own people and ravage their own country. A group of apostates goes to the new Greek king, saying:

> We were content to serve your father, to comply with his orders, and to obey his edicts. As a result our own people will have nothing to do with us; what is more, they have killed all those of us they could catch, and looted our family property … . Unless you forestall them at once … you will never be able to control them.[43]

Of course, the Greeks did not trust the despised Jewish apostates either. The apostates had been left without friends, without a country, and without honor. "Setting no store by the honors of their fatherland, they esteemed Hellenic glories best of all. But all this brought its own retribution; the very people whose way of life they envied, whom they sought to resemble in everything, proved to be their enemies and executioners."[44]

Only by adhering to the law, to belief in God and to the people of Israel, can honor and dignity be preserved. As the Greeks and their apostate allies kill and torture faithful Jews, the latter are moved to reaffirm their commitment to God and the Torah even at the point of death. Thus Eleazar, a teacher of the law, refuses to eat pork despite the threat of death by torture because he is determined to set a good example for the young. Similarly, rather than taste the forbidden pork as commanded by the Greeks, a mother and her seven sons willingly accept death. As the last son dies, he says, "I too, like my brothers, surrender my body and life for the laws of my ancestors."[45] In the end, of course, the strength of their faith and commitment to the Jewish people allows the Maccabees to overcome the Greeks and their allies and to regain the Jewish patrimony.

The lessons of Hanukkah are that the apostate betrays his people and dishonors himself. In the end, the hope of assimilation is chimerical, for the apostate is never accepted by the community he hopes to enter. Honor alone requires adherence to the faith and loyalty to the Jewish people.

As Steven Cohen has shown, a major impact of Jewish education is to stimulate a sense of communal identification among Jewish children.[46] Obviously, a Jewish education does not guarantee that a child will forever identify with the Jewish community. However, in this as in so many other areas, those treated to several years of indoctrination can never fully escape its effects. It is mainly because of the Jewish educational process that even many of the most assimilated Jews—Jews who seem to regard themselves completely as Americans—at some level never really do.

Communal Mobilization

The making of Jews does not end with religious practice and the education of Jewish children. The organizations and institutions forming the Jewish government-in-exile employ a third mechanism for keeping the identity and distinctiveness of their followers. This technique, called *communal mobilization*, involves the use of campaigns, meetings, books, rallies, and outright propaganda to present Jews with issues and problems that will remind them of their Jewish heritage and induce them to take part in communal affairs—and, most important, by contributing time and money to the organizations charged with managing those affairs.

The two most important, though certainly not the only, topics currently used for communal mobilization are, of course, Israel and the Holocaust. Indeed, these two matters have become the central objects around which Jewish communal life, fund-raising, political activity, and even religious observance have become organized. These are central to the efforts of Jewish institutions to create and keep Jewish identity. In recent years, of course, both the state of Israel and the Holocaust have also become major topics in most Jewish schools and in Jewish religious observance.

Israel

Unlike with individual American Jews mindful of Jewish history, for American Jewish institutions, Israel has been more than a future insurance policy. To the Jewish government-in-exile, Israel has been the key to survival in the present. In the period following World War II, American Jewish organizations supported the creation of a Jewish homeland as a place where Jewish refugees from Europe could go other than to the United States. American immigration policy was too restrictive to allow the acceptance of more than a small number of homeless Jews, and American Jewish groups were not eager to engage in a battle to try to liberalize these policies. Moreover, there was concern among American Jews that an influx of "unassimilated" Jewish refugees from Europe could heighten anti-Semitic sentiment in the United States.[47]

Despite these reasons to support the creation of a Jewish state in Palestine, some American Jewish leaders, and major organizations such as the American Jewish Committee, were less than enthusiastic about the enterprise. The existence of a Jewish state might raise questions in America about the loyalty of American Jews. Moreover, a Jewish state in Palestine might pose a threat to the primacy of the institutions forming the "Jewish state" in America. In a sense, the rebirth of a Jewish state in Israel represented as serious a threat to the leadership of the American Jewish community as the return of Christ represented to Dostoyevsky's Grand Inquisitor.

In the immediate aftermath of Israel's creation, a fierce struggle developed between the fledgling Israeli government and the American Jewish leadership over primacy in the Jewish world. David Ben-Gurion, Israel's first prime minister, in effect claimed leadership of the entire Jewish world by declaring that all Jews belonged in, and hence to, the state of Israel. Abba Hillel Silver, leader of the American Zionist movement, asserted that Jews everywhere had a special relationship to Israel and, therefore, had the right to exert influence over the decisions of the Israeli government. Silver's position, in other words, was that American Jewish organizations had a right to intervene in Israeli policies and politics. Ben-Gurion's famous response was that no one "could sit in Cleveland and give directions to Tel Aviv." He invited Silver to move to Israel and exert as much influence as he could through the Israeli political process.[48]

In the early 1950s, the Jewish state in Israel and the Jewish state in America reached an accommodation. The Israeli government agreed to stop embarrassing American Jews and undermining the American Jewish leadership with declarations that Israel was the only true home for a Jew. The American Jewish leadership, for its part, agreed to supply financial and political support for Israel but to refrain from trying to meddle in Israeli policies. In the aftermath of this accommodation, previously non-Zionist American Jewish organizations like the American Jewish Committee became staunch supporters of Israel.[49]

The position developed by American Jewish organizations and given the blessing of Israeli leaders was that American Jews had a religious and moral commitment to support Israel but no obligation to come to Israel to live. Indeed, some prominent Jewish leaders in America argued that American Jews could best fulfill their moral obligation to Israel by staying in America, where they could use their political influence and organizational strength to assure Israel of American financial and military support. By this strained logic, even the most ardent American Zionist should remain in America and strongly support American Jewish organizations rather than move to Israel.[50]

The threats posed by the state of Israel to the Jewish state in America instead became an opportunity. American Jewish vacationers, taking part in guided tours arranged by Jewish organizations in the United States, began to visit Israel in large numbers and to return to America with a strengthened sense of Jewish consciousness and solidarity. Jewish students went on free "birthright" trips to Israel. This made them more willing to take part in and contribute to Jewish affairs in New York, Chicago, Cleveland, and Baltimore. Through participation and charitable contributions, one could be a good Jew and still live comfortably in the United States.

Beginning in the late 1950s after Israel's victory over Egypt in the Suez War, and heightened after Israel's spectacular victory over all the Arab nations in the 1967 Six-Day War, Israel became the central focus of American Jewish life. Support for Israel became the major theme around which American Jewish institutions organized their communal, political, and fund-raising efforts. As Jews became less religious and more secular, Jewish institutions found that Israel, and especially pride in the military prowess and achievements of the Jewish state, was a more effective rallying point for their fund-raising and membership activities than religious observances and themes. Indeed, as Israelis often charged, during the 1960s and 1970s American Jewish organizations invoked Israel as a vehicle for fund-raising activities even though many of the funds raised were spent in the United States.[51]

The Holocaust

After the Likud bloc came to power in Israel during the mid-1970s, and especially after the 1983 Israeli invasion of Lebanon and the continuing occupation and settlement of the West Bank by Israelis, Jewish organizations began to feel that support for Israel on the part of some American Jews had weakened. Their response was to reduce Israel's role (at least marginally) in their fund-raising activities and turn to other rallying points. Support for Israel was, of course, never abandoned. However, many left-liberal American Jews have become critical of Israeli policy, and some have begun to take part in the anti-Zionist discourse that has become so prominent on the political Left. To avoid alienating liberal Jews who oppose the policies of conservative Israeli administrations, Jewish organizations have looked to develop other, less controversial, mobilizing themes. The most important of these has been remembrance of the Holocaust.[52]

Through the 1960s and 1970s, the annual United Jewish Appeal spring fund-raising drive, conducted through direct solicitations and telethons in every Jewish community in the nation, focused mostly on the need to help Israel. Solicitation letters and calls emphasized Israel's military needs, housing needs, desert reclamation, children's programs, and so forth. By the 1980s and 1990s, faced with some unease among more liberal American Jews about Israel's right-wing political leadership and treatment of Arabs, the annual campaign moved toward a policy of reduced emphasis on Israel and greater emphasis on other issues. Most important among these was the Holocaust. During the actual Holocaust, American Jewish organizations, politicians, and high-ranking Jewish government officials had been shamefully silent, more concerned with anti-Semitism at home than with the fate of millions of Jews in Europe.[53]

Indeed, when Joseph Proskauer became president of the American Jewish Committee (AJC) in 1943, his acceptance speech, which dealt with the problems American Jews were likely to face in the postwar period, made no mention whatsoever of the ongoing slaughter of European Jews or of any possible rescue efforts.[54] Similarly, the "Statement of Views" adopted by the AJC's 1943 annual meeting has no mention of the Germans' ongoing efforts to destroy the European Jews, something that was already known by all American Jewish leaders at that time.[55]

In the years following World War II, moreover, Jewish organizations mostly ignored the Holocaust, and the few Holocaust survivors to reach the United States were led to understand that they should remain silent about their experiences. I can personally recall that when my parents and I arrived in America, after several years in a displaced persons camp, our relatives cautioned my parents not to talk about their experiences during the war. "Nobody wants to hear about those things," said one cousin.

American Jewish leaders were embarrassed about the cowardice they themselves had shown, eager to avoid charges of inaction, and were never anxious to link themselves in any way to the benighted Jews of Europe. One source of shame, of course, was the seeming absence of Jewish resistance to the Germans. American Jews often felt contempt for their European brethren who, the Americans thought, had "allowed" Germans to kill them. The Americans resented being associated with people who seemed not only to confirm but to give new meaning to the stereotype of Jewish timidity. Jews, it appeared, had been too spineless to fight even when herded into the gas chambers.[56] The truth, of course, was that Jews had fought bravely in many ways, especially through their service in the Soviet Army.[57] American Jews were unlikely to embrace this fact during the 1950s.

During the 1970s, however, a new generation of Jewish leaders appeared who had no complicity in the events of the war years and who could, indeed, use the inaction of the established leaders of the Jewish community during the Holocaust to discredit and displace them. The story of the Holocaust, moreover, became a useful parable on the dangers of assimilation and the evil of which even the best gentiles were capable. For had not the Jews lived in Germany for centuries and regarded themselves as Germans first and Jews second? Yet their German friends and neighbors turned on them in a murderous rage.

During the 1970s, this version of the story of the Holocaust began to join or even to replace Bible stories as mechanisms through which to teach American Jews—especially American Jewish children—to be wary of identifying too closely with the world of gentile America. American Jews might think of themselves as Americans, but as with German Jews, there might be a brutal reminder of their real identity. One history of the Holocaust written for American Jewish children points out that even "Jews who did not consider themselves to be Jews were sought out by the Nazis and forced to wear the badge. Some startled Christians found they had Jewish blood from some grandfather or grandmother. They also had to wear the star."[58]

As Jewish organizations began to make the Holocaust an increasingly central focus of their organizational and fund-raising activities, Holocaust survivors were honored rather than told to be quiet. Holocaust studies became a major focus of activity for the young, and Holocaust memorials, museums, and commemorations became central parts of the agenda of all Jewish institutions. The Holocaust even entered the Jewish liturgy as a special day of prayer and remembrance. Conservative and Reform Jews added Yom HaShoah to the religious calendar, though most Orthodox synagogues did not.

Rare today is the fund-raising appeal from a Jewish organization that does not remind the potential donor of the Holocaust and of contemporary efforts by neo-Nazi "revisionists" to claim that the Holocaust never took place—efforts that, they say, must be countered by cash contributions. Rather than feel shame over the alleged lack of Jewish resistance to the Germans, American Jewish organizations now celebrate the Warsaw ghetto uprising, which held the Germans at bay longer than the entire Polish Army had been able to do in 1939.

A book subtitled *A History of Courage and Resistance* is a popular history of the Holocaust used in Jewish schools throughout the United States. Of its twenty-two chapters, close to half focus on themes of Jewish defiance and heroism. Chapter titles include "A Leader in the Underground," "Women Fighters," and "The Doctor Warriors." A young student reading this or one of several similar texts might easily conclude that everywhere in Europe rag-tag bands of Jewish partisans fought the *Wehrmacht* to a standstill. Two full chapters recount the tale of the Warsaw ghetto uprising, concluding with the obligatory observation, "The Jews in the ghetto with their pitiable weapons, held out longer against their Nazi enemies than the Poles had held out when the Germans attacked Poland."[59] As I have shown elsewhere, the Jews did play a key role in the defeat of Nazi Germany as weapons engineers, cryptanalysts, and soldiers in the Soviet and American armies, but historical accuracy does not seem to be relevant in this context.[60]

The prominence currently given to the story of the Warsaw ghetto tragedy is especially ironic given the lack of a response among American Jewish leaders to the uprising when it occurred. In April and May 1943, as the Germans liquidated the ghetto, Jewish resistance fighters made a series of dramatic broadcasts and desperate calls for help over their clandestine radio station. On April 22, the station broadcast, "Gun salvos are echoing in Warsaw's streets. Women and children are defending themselves with bare hands. Come to our aid!" On May 25, the BBC reported listening to a broadcast telling of Jews killed by firing squads and burned alive. Yet many American Jewish organizations had other priorities during this period and gave little attention to the grim news from Warsaw.[61]

4

The Benefits of Philo-Semitism and the Costs of Anti-Semitism: Genesis 12:3

THROUGHOUT AMERICAN HISTORY, Jews played a vital role in building a prosperous land. In the book of Genesis, God declares to Abraham: "And I will make thee a great nation ... . And I will bless them that bless thee, and him that curseth thee I will curse."[1] This promise is unequivocal. God says those who treat the Jews well, he will bless, while those who abuse them are accursed.

God does not explain precisely how his blessings and curses might manifest themselves. Yet to many religious individuals the point is clear enough. Millions of Bible-believing American evangelical Protestants, for example, sometimes called Christian Zionists, often aver that God has commanded them to support the Jewish people and, specifically, to defend the state of Israel. A failure to heed this commandment, they insist, could lead to dire heavenly punishment for America. One prominent evangelical leader and Christian Zionist spokesman, the late Reverend Jerry Falwell, said, "If this nation wants her fields to remain white with grain, her scientific achievements to remain notable, and her freedom to remain intact, America must continue to stand with Israel."[2]

Before the Civil War, America's Jewish community was small—some fifty thousand individuals. Small groups of Sephardim had arrived in the South during the seventeenth century, and German Jews settled in the North in the eighteenth century. Both groups sought religious freedom, and America was mostly hospitable to them. In the South, by the nineteenth century, members of the early Sephardic families had become intellectuals, professionals, and important merchants. Though the total number of Jews in the antebellum

South was small, so too was the South's merchant and professional class. Hence Jews figured prominently within this stratum and achieved a measure of acceptance within Southern society.

Several German Jews of the North also achieved considerable success and prominence in the nineteenth century. The period following the Civil War was one of great industrial and commercial expansion in the United States. Americans made huge fortunes in banking, railroad construction, and manufacturing; among the largest fortunes were those made by German Jewish bankers, financiers, industrialists, and merchants. The most prominent included the manufacturer Philip Heidelbach; the bankers Joseph Seligman, Lewis Seasongood, and Solomon Loeb; the railroad magnates Emanuel and Mayer Lehman and Jacob Schiff; and the Warburgs, the Lewisohns, and the Guggenheims.[3]

Joseph Seligman was the most important member of this group. During the Civil War, Seligman had made a great deal of money helping create a secondary market for US government bonds. When the conflict began, the major European financiers who normally handled government loans had little confidence in the ability of the American national government to win the war and were reluctant to take part in loans to the federal treasury. In response, the national government turned to domestic bankers who were able to sell more than $2 billion in federal securities within the United States itself. This effort gave American financiers a great deal of marketing experience and a much stronger financial base than they had previously known.[4] The Civil War, in effect, created a new class of powerful American financiers, among them a group of New York German Jewish bankers.[5]

After the war, these same Jewish financiers became actively involved in US government bond sales, industrial expansion, and railroad construction. With their connections to Jewish banking houses in Europe, the Seligmans and other German Jewish financiers became valuable agents in government securities transactions. And with participation in government finance came political influence. When President Ulysses S. Grant took office in 1869, he offered Joseph Seligman the position of secretary of the treasury. Though Seligman refused the offer, the Grant administration continued to consult him on the refunding of the public debt, currency stabilization, and methods for strengthening US credit abroad. Along with Jacob Schiff, Seligman also played a key role in the construction and expansion of railroads. Schiff financed the expansion of the Union Pacific and Pennsylvania Railroads, while Seligman financed several western lines. Seligman was also among the chief financiers and political backers of the Panama Canal project undertaken during the administration of Theodore Roosevelt.

Jewish Quotas and Restrictions

In the late nineteenth century, America's Jewish population increased markedly by a flood of Jewish refugees fleeing pogroms in Russia and eastern Europe. Largely because of immigration, the United States was home to more than 1 million Jews by the turn of the century and as many as 3 million by the 1920s. America, unfortunately, was not as hospitable to these new Jewish immigrants as it had been to their forebears. Nativism, spearheaded by such groups as the Immigration Restriction League and directed at Jews and Catholics, had become a major political force in the United States in the late 1800s. One of the league's most important intellectual spokesmen was Edward Ross, a pioneer of American sociology. In his widely read 1914 work, *The Old World and the New*, Ross explained the importance of protecting Anglo-Saxon Americanism against pollution through immigration. As "beaten members of beaten breeds" come to America, the "immigrant blood" of morally inferior races was polluting "American blood." Ross was particularly vehement in his denunciation of the Jews and seemed especially perturbed that Jewish college students "always want their grades changed."[6]

The rise of nativism led not only to the imposition of restrictions on immigration but also to the exclusion of American Jews from upper-class American society and its clubs, hotels, schools, and resorts. The tony Grand Union Hotel in Saratoga Springs, New York, famously denied Joseph Seligman admission in 1877. Seligman had often been a guest at the hotel, but the management decided on a policy of exclusivity.

The most damaging to the Jews was the imposition of a system of Jewish quotas for university and professional school admission, first at the elite East Coast schools and later at lesser institutions. University administrators claimed to be concerned about "excessive" Jewish enrollments. Meeting at

Princeton in May 1918, the Association of New England Deans, including representatives of Bowdoin, Tufts, Brown, MIT, and Yale, held lengthy discussions about the Jewish problem. The following year, Columbia, led by President Nicholas Murray Butler, introduced new admissions procedures designed to reduce the number of Jews in its classes. The new application process required a psychological test mostly designed to measure character but included a form that asked for religious affiliation. Quickly, the number of Jews was halved.[7] At Harvard, President A. Lawrence Lowell called for a reduction in the number of Jewish students. This created a controversy on campus and among the alumni, and the president was nominally rebuffed. However, new discriminatory admissions policies, which achieved the same goal, were quietly introduced.[8] By the late 1920s, only Chicago, Cornell, Brown, and Penn among the elite schools remained open to Jews. Yet even in these institutions, the professional schools kept anti-Jewish quotas.[9]

This system of restrictions and quotas, particularly in America's colleges and universities, began to erode in the 1930s and had all but disappeared by the late 1960s. In the 1930s, of course, Jews became notable members and leaders of the Roosevelt coalition. From this period going forward, it became more difficult for colleges and other institutions to engage in discriminatory practices against Jews, while the civil rights movement of the 1950s and 1960s, a movement strongly supported and funded by American Jews, finally made it close to impossible.

The End of Discrimination and America's Brain Gain

With the gradual end of anti-Jewish discrimination, America's Jews—whether the descendants of earlier immigrants or more recent arrivals—found an opportunity to use their talents fully. The result was an efflorescence of Jewish achievement that was an enormous brain gain for the United States. For example, Jewish scientists, including refugees from Nazi Germany, have been the nation's leaders in physics, information science, medicine, and virtually every other scientific field. In the field of physics, of course, Jews like Albert Einstein, Richard Feynman, Murray Gel-Mann, and others were at the forefront of scientific theory. These and other Jewish scientists translated theory into practical applications that put the United States at the forefront of technological development in the late twentieth century. For example, Leo Szilard was the principal developer of the nuclear reactor. Hyman Rickover pioneered the use of nuclear reactors to power ships. Felix Bloch was a pioneer in the development of semiconductors—one of today's core technologies. Theodore Maiman built the first laser. The process of MRI diagnostic imaging is based on technology discovered by I. I. Rabi. Jews currently constitute more than 40 percent of the scientists elected to the divisions of physics and applied physical sciences of the US National Academy of Sciences.[10]

In the related field of computer science, Jews have played a dominant role; Jewish computer scientists make up 40 percent of the individuals elected to the Computer and Information Science Division of the National Academy of Sciences.[11] The contribution of Jews to American preeminence in this field is extraordinary. The logical architecture of close to all modern computers is based on the work of John von Neumann, while Dan Bricklin and Robert Frankston designed the computer spreadsheet. Marvin Minsky, Herbert Simon, and John McCarthy (McCarthy had a Jewish mother, while Simon had a Jewish father and half-Jewish mother) founded the field of artificial intelligence. Paul Benioff, Richard Feynman, and David Deutsch invented quantum computing, while Leonard Adelman developed DNA computing. The Monte Carlo method, which is the basis for computer simulation, was devised by Stanislaw Ulam and John von Neumann, while George Dantzig helped develop the main linear programming algorithm used in engineering and economics. Abraham Wald devised statistical decision theory, and Amos Joel developed the switching technology that made cellular telephone networks possible. The six main inventors of the internet included Leonard Kleinrock, Paul Baran, and Robert Kahn. Two of the others, Vinton Cerf and Lawrence Roberts, had Jewish mothers. Sergey Brin and Larry Page (Page's mother was Jewish) designed the world's major internet search engine, Google. This list barely scratches the surface of Jewish American contributions to the realm of computer science.

Similarly, in the field of medical science, American Jews have played a commanding role in bringing about America's preeminence. Note that 40 percent of America's Nobel Prizes in medicine have been won by Jews and that more than one-third of the scientists elected to the life sciences division of the US Academy of Sciences are Jews.[12] Individual Jewish contributions to American medicine include the development of streptomycin by Selman Waksman and Albert Schatz; the development of warfarin therapy by Shepard Shapiro; the development of polio vaccines by Jonas Salk and Albert Sabin; and the creation of the hepatitis B vaccine by Baruch Blumberg and Irving Millman. In addition, American Jewish contributions include the development of modern chemotherapy by Louis Goodman, Alfred Gilman, and Sidney Farber; the development of a cure for childhood leukemia by Gertrude Elion; a cure for testicular cancer by Barnett Rosenberg; the invention of modern radiation oncology by Henry Kaplan; the invention of gene splicing by Stanley Cohen; the invention of the sonogram by Robert Rines; and the invention of the cardiac defibrillator, external pacemaker, and cardiac monitor by Paul Zoll. As in the cases of physics and computer science, this list barely scratches the surface of the Jews' role in America's dominance in this field.

Another major realm in which America has gained from Jewish talent is economic innovation. Jews have pioneered everything from the world's most important internet search engines to the world's leading chain of coffee shops. Indeed, Jewish entrepreneurs have developed businesses that employ tens of millions of Americans and have contributed enormously to the US economy. To cite just a few of many examples, Jews built virtually all the major Hollywood studios—Paramount, Universal, MGM, Warner Brothers, Twentieth Century Fox—and built the modern motion picture industry.[13] Jews built the radio and broadcast television industries, including the NBC, CBS, and ABC networks. Jews built many of America's major retail chains, including Macy's, Saks, Bloomingdale's, Sears, and Neiman Marcus. Jews pioneered such industries as television retailing (QVC and the Home Shopping Network). Jewish entrepreneurs even developed America's ubiquitous weight-loss plans: Weight Watchers, Nutrisystem, and SlimFast. Jews developed the auto-leasing industry with Hertz Rent-a-Car. Jews built many of the major American financial services companies, such as Goldman Sachs. A Jew created the world's largest coffee chain, Starbucks. And Jewish entrepreneurs, looking to create markets that others did not know existed in the realm of computers and technology, devised Facebook, Dell, Oracle, Google, and others. This has been America's Jewish brain gain that has not been followed, yet, by the usual Jewish brain drain of history.

The Logic of Genesis 12:3

The principles and consequences of Jewish brain gains and brain drains are anticipated in the Bible—namely, in God's words to Abraham in Genesis 12:3. To secular intellectuals, including most academics, the Bible is often an odd text with tales of patriarchs who lived hundreds of years and miraculous events and conversations between humans and God. Among such intellectuals, indeed, the Bible is mostly viewed as mythological and allegorical—not so different from, say, Tolkien's *Lord of the Rings*, to which I have heard it compared unfavorably at the faculty club. In many intellectual gatherings, those who take the Bible seriously are treated with polite disdain, while those like Falwell, who believe that the Bible is the literal word of God, provoke secular intellectuals' scorn.

There are, however, some considerations that might induce even the most committed skeptic to hesitate before completely dismissing the concept if not the claim of divine intervention, embodied in Genesis 12:3. Let us begin with the late Nobel Prize–winning economist Simon Kuznets's observation that states will benefit from allowing Jews the "utmost freedom." Left alone, the Jews are likely to advance science, promote commerce, create new industries, and pioneer ideas and perspectives that contribute to the vibrancy of a nation's culture and politics. One might say that giving the Jews opportunities is likely to result in a "brain gain."

To extend Kuznets's idea, if those same states turn against the Jews, limiting, say, Jewish access to the universities and key occupations or, as has often occurred, inducing or compelling the Jews to flee, the result is a "brain drain" and loss of Jewish talent. Often, the states to which Jews later immigrate find themselves the beneficiaries of their own brain gain as they employ Jewish talent. In some instances, indeed, states offering refuge to Jews are very much aware of their opportunity to profit at the expense of their rivals. Take the Ottoman Empire, for example: The Ottomans welcomed many Jews forced to leave Spain in the fifteenth century. Sultan Bayezid II reportedly marveled at the foolishness of the Spaniards for expelling such useful and talented subjects. Or, to cite a more recent case, the British and Americans welcomed the Jewish nuclear physicists who fled Nazi Germany during the 1930s. The immediate result was that America and not Germany came to have the atom bomb.[14]

Jews, to be sure, are neither uniformly talented nor the world's only source of intellectual capital. The nations of Asia have done quite nicely in recent years despite the absence of Jews, and the nations of northern and western Europe, while profiting from Jewish literacy, numeracy, and intellectual ability, were able to develop or import other sources of talent. Nevertheless, in such realms as commerce and science, Jews have notably been represented at the intellectual forefront, contributing mightily to the economic, scientific, and even military prominence of their host nations.

Viewed from this perspective, the blessings and curses affirmed in Genesis 12:3 embody a truth that does not depend on biblical exegesis. Given an opportunity, Jews can make a major contribution to their host country. If that same country then turns against them, the consequences can be damaging both for the Jews and for their erstwhile hosts. This secular explanation, of course, should by no means upset those who believe in the literal validity of God's promise to Abraham. God, as is well known, works in his own mysterious ways.

The matter of brain gains and brain drains also sheds light on the great mystery and tragedy of Jewish history. This is the recurring pattern of rise and fall. Repeatedly, Jews rise to positions of wealth or power only to find themselves attacked, tormented, exiled, or worse. Spain, Germany, and Soviet Russia come to mind at once, but many other examples stretch back some two millennia, and even longer if one wishes to give credence to the account of the rise and fall of the Jews of Egypt as presented by the book of Exodus. Recall that Joseph saved the Egyptians from famine, became a powerful official in Pharaoh's court, and was able to secure sanctuary in the Egyptian realm, under favorable conditions, for his brothers and their many dependents. Eventually, though, a new pharaoh came to power who "knew not Joseph." The Jews lost their privileges as their hosts enslaved them and compelled them to engage in "wracking labors" in Pharaoh's fields, mines, and construction sites. Indeed, as the first known account of anti-Semitism, the story of Joseph can serve both as a metaphor for and as a prologue to the later millennia of Jewish history.

Many explanations abound for the frequent rise and equally frequent fall of the Jews. I wrote on this topic in my 1993 book, *The Fatal Embrace: Jews and the State*, where I argued that Jews in the diaspora typically sought security in alliances with rulers and regimes, offering service in exchange for protection. Initially, at least, Jews often gained from the state's embrace, hence their rise to power and wealth. The eventual fall came when their friends lost power—pharaohs arose who knew not Joseph—or when their erstwhile allies jettisoned the Jews to bolster or safeguard their own positions.[15] After reflecting on this issue for another two decades, I have concluded that what I wrote in 1993 is true but incomplete. The relationship between Jews and states is an important part, but only a part, of the story.

To understand the ebb and flow of Jewish history fully, let us begin with the Jews themselves. Among them are found so many unusually talented, industrious, and intelligent individuals. Some have argued that this is a matter of cultural predispositions, while others, like Charles Murray, have asserted that sheer genetics is the explanation for Jewish success.[16] One "secret" of Jewish success, particularly in such fields as politics, academics, and journalism, is social marginality. The Jews are, to a greater or lesser extent, outside society, as Hannah Arendt put it.[17] Marginality can expose the Jews to suspicion, hostility, and discrimination. At the same time, though, talented marginals may see politics and society with clearer eyes and from a better vantage point than those fully immersed in their own culture. The marginal may envision possibilities others do not see and undertake courses of action others are unwilling to do. Of course, Jews who keep themselves completely outside society—the ultra-Orthodox—may know little about the country in which they live. It is the more assimilated Jews who are in a position to observe, criticize, and innovate.

Arendt's exemplar of the brilliant, assimilated, half-Jewish marginal, Benjamin Disraeli, famously rejected the accepted wisdom of his political party and social class to assert that, if enfranchised, British industrial workers would become champions of the established order. Disraeli proved to be correct. "In the inarticulate mass of the English populace, he discerned the Conservative workingman as the sculptor perceives the angel prisoned in a block of marble," said the *London Times* after Disraeli's death.[18]

Whatever the ultimate explanation or set of explanations, wherever there is freedom and opportunity, certain Jews excel in science, commerce, the arts, and other intellectual endeavors. Indeed, in various places and times, Jews have also been leaders in athletic pursuits such as fencing, boxing, competitive swimming, and even basketball.[19]

A second point to make is that states that allow the Jews the freedom and opportunity to develop and express their abilities secure the benefit of Jewish talent too. Simon Kuznets asserted, "Given the kind of human capital that the Jews represent, the majority in any country, if it wished to maximize long-term economic returns, should not have only permitted the Jewish minority the utmost freedom, but in fact should have subsidized any improvement in the economic and social performance of promising individual Jews." This would be "a high-yield investment," whereas discrimination against the Jews, said Kuznets, constituted "extreme economic irrationality."[20]

Unfortunately, the explanation for what Kuznets saw as irrational conduct is, in its own way, quite rational. Jews contribute to a nation's collective interest by increasing the general level of economic, scientific, and other achievements. At the same time, however, what is good for the general society may not serve the interests of certain groups. Thus Jews may strengthen a nation's economy, but competition from Jews may not be good for gentile merchants and bankers and might trigger the envy of those who feel that more of the wealth should have been theirs. As Werner Sombart noted, when medieval Jews revolutionized business practices to the benefit of the German and French cities where they lived, local gentile merchants, whom they drove out of business, disliked their innovations.[21]

Similarly, Jews may advance a nation's science, but those pushed aside often resent Jewish talent. In Germany during the 1930s, for example, the remarkable achievements of Jewish physicists were denounced as *Judenphysik* by some gentile scientists who could not quite grasp the complexities of relativity and quantum theory.[22] These individuals argued for the superiority of what they called "Aryan science," which dealt with readily observable phenomena that could be understood by scientists like themselves.[23] In a contemporary echo of this phenomenon, Kevin MacDonald, former professor of psychology at California State University, Long Beach, has called for the imposition of quotas limiting the admission and employment of Jews at universities. MacDonald believes quotas are needed to protect other ethnic groups from the unfair advantages Jews accrue from their "verbal intelligence" and "aggressiveness."[24] Jews, at any rate, may produce any number of extremely useful collective goods, but one or another social group or political movement may find it useful to promote or appeal to suspicion of the Jews—suspicion that can be heightened by Jewish prominence and success—to advance their own interests and enhance their own power.

Thus, rather than represent irrationality, as Kuznets thought, discrimination against the Jews is a rational, if an unfortunate, example of narrow, isolated costs becoming politically more salient than greater, diffused benefits.[25] Those who feel aggrieved by Jewish prowess have far more incentive to assail the Jews than the general and often unwitting beneficiaries of their broader accomplishments. Indeed, the higher the Jews rise, the more enemies they can make and the more dangerous their position can become. Thus the rise-and-fall pattern manifest in Jewish history follows a certain logic.

The position of the Jews in many societies can be particularly tenuous because of their lack of full social integration. Jews tend to become allied and socially integrated with segments of the social and political elite but not larger society. This pattern was true in Spain, Germany, and Soviet Russia and is quite clear in the United States. This lack of comprehensive social integration makes Jews vulnerable if the elite stratum with which they are aligned comes under attack or, as is sometimes the case, decides it can do better without the Jews. In the 1930s, most Germans had never met a Jew and were willing to believe the most outlandish things about them. One wonders how many Americans in the nation's heartland have knowingly had dealings with Jews.

Of course, we might predict that rulers and governments, the entities nominally focused on national rather than sectoral interests, would be most likely to see the virtues of hardworking, talented Jewish citizens and to protect them from attack. Historically, many rulers and ruling groups saw their interest in doing precisely what Kuznets advocated, encouraging the Jews and protecting them from mistreatment. Thus the wiser English kings and German princes, among others, protected the Jews, who drove their economies and whose taxes and loans were a considerable part of their royal incomes. Take the medieval bishopric of Speyer. During the eleventh century, the Jews of Speyer asked the ruling prince-bishop to grant them a charter of privileges and to build a defensive wall around their quarter. Because the Jews were economically valuable and he wished to induce more to settle in his city, the bishop agreed. Subsequently, the bishop protected the Jewish community from rioting crusaders, going as far as to hang the ringleaders of the mob that sought to attack the Jewish quarter.[26]

Partly because of this historical experience, Jews often continued to look to the state for protection even when it was the state itself that was the source of their problems. Thus, in his famous work *Shevet Yehuda*, written in the wake of the Jewish—and his personal—expulsion from Spain, Solomon Ibn Verga sought to portray the rulers of Spain, including Ferdinand and Isabella, who ordered the expulsion, as allies of the Jews.[27] In a similar vein, as Hannah Arendt and others have observed, to the very end many German Jews could not believe that the German state would fail to protect them from the excesses of Nazi fanatics.[28] The historical dependence of Jews on the state also gave rise to a Jewish philosophical tradition, beginning in the seventeenth century with Spinoza and continuing through the *maskilim* of the eighteenth and nineteenth centuries, and perhaps some Jewish liberals today, in which the state is seen as a source of protection from an unruly and dangerous society.[29]

Unfortunately, however, while they have incentives to pursue collective interests, rulers also have personal preferences and private interests that may override their other concerns. Stalin, for example, fully understood the importance of Jews to the Soviet state and economy. He nevertheless regarded Jewish Communists as dangerous rivals and purged them from the higher ranks of the party and state. During World War II, of course, when the state's existence was at stake, Stalin ended the purges and welcomed Jewish comrades back into the fold. After the war, with the existential threat to the Soviet state averted, the purges resumed. In some instances, too, as in the cases of Spain and Nazi Germany, rulers find attacks on the Jews such useful tools for intimidating opponents and increasing their own power that they are willing to give vent to their personal hatreds despite the ensuing loss of talent to the general society.[30]

There is, nonetheless, nothing inevitable about an anti-Semitic trough following in the wake of a successful Jewish peak. Displaced or aggrieved groups may grumble about the Jews, but their muttering may come to nothing in the absence of some precipitating event—depression, war, a rise in popular religious or nationalistic fervor—that gives such groups an opportunity to mobilize supporters in the general populace. Some have argued that the nationalism and populism unleashed by the 2016 Trump campaign opened such a possibility. In this respect, at least, the idea that there is something exceptional about the United States is dreaming. During American history, there have certainly been efforts to exclude and expel the Jews, and it has only been during the past few decades that American Jews have not faced quotas in the universities, barriers in the professions, and overt attacks in many public forums.

In the United States today, two groups that compete with Jews for positions and influence grumble quite a bit about them. African American politicians, who compete with Jews for influence within the Democratic Party, sometimes give voice to anti-Semitic sentiments.[31] In addition, some members of the gentile liberal bourgeoisie—a group that competes with Jews in the universities, business, government, and the professions—grumble about the state of Israel. Anti-Zionism can serve as a genteel vehicle for the expression of anti-Semitic thoughts.

Brain Gains and Brain Drains

During the Middle Ages, and as early as the eighth century, Jews became key factors in the realm of international trade, with commercial networks extending throughout Europe, the Middle East, and the Near East.[32]

The Jews were ideally suited for this role. To begin with, Jews were everywhere after the diaspora yet kept a common language, a sense of communal identity and distinctiveness, and an adherence to a common Talmudic law governing business transactions. As cosmopolitans rather than parochials, the Jews were able to assess and match the needs of one nation with the goods available in a second, including rival Christian and Muslim states whose native merchants could not easily trade with one another directly. Jews in one country, moreover, could trade goods with Jews in another country under an established set of Talmudic rules recognized by all participants.

The law of the Talmud was particularly conducive to international exchange among Jews by providing for impersonal credit arrangements.[33] Under Talmudic law, as opposed to medieval Christian law, debts were transferable, becoming a form of liquid assets. This meant that sellers were more willing to extend credit to buyers, knowing that they would be able to sell or transfer the indebtedness to a third party if they wished or the need arose. This simple Talmudic provision eased the granting of credit and significantly promoted trade. According to Werner Sombart, the idea of debt as an impersonal rather than personal obligation was a distinctly Jewish innovation and formed the basis for modern systems of credit.[34]

The Talmud, moreover, supplied sets of rules governing contracts, torts, trade regulations, and the like that allowed settlement of business disputes among Jews by rabbinical authorities.[35] Just the existence of international arbitral panels to resolve disputes promotes trade, so the existence of rabbinical courts interpreting Talmudic rules assured trading partners that those potential disagreements could be impartially settled. This assurance, in turn, encouraged Jewish traders to enter into contracts with one another and smoothed the flow of international commerce.

These considerations help explain why the innovative Jews would become important in international trade and investment and influential globally—and how Jewish prowess bolstered countries and empires where they lived, leading to Jews gaining tremendous wealth and power in the diaspora. Yet an uglier side continued, as old as the Bible itself, where the distinctive yet vulnerable Jews saw their prosperity and influence evaporate through anti-Semitism. This age-old cycle was characterized by brain gains and drains until the founding of modern Israel. The Jews would thrive in a country, adding to its prosperity; then anti-Semitism would force them to flee (the luckier ones), and the country would become less prosperous. Several factors promoted anti-Semitism, not least of which was jealousy and distrust of a distinctive minority. It became evident, too, that anti-Semitism was costly, a fact first outlined in the book of Exodus and predicted in Genesis 12:3. (See the appendix for earlier cycles of philo-Semitism and anti-Semitism, and brain gains and drains, during the Carolingian and the Holy Roman Empires and in England, France, and Spain in the Middle Ages and after.)

Classic Brain Gains and Brain Drains: Germany and Russia

Germany

One of the most notable modern cases of brain gain followed by a brain drain is that of Germany. Jews in small numbers had lived in the German lands since Roman times, with a trickle of newcomers arriving after the expulsion from Spain. Jews were active as merchants, tradesmen, craftsmen, pawnbrokers, and moneylenders, and their lot was not always a happy one, with periods of prosperity often followed by expulsions from one or another German principality. Nevertheless, a small number of Jews were able to accumulate considerable wealth, as became clear during the Thirty Years' War (1618–48), which embroiled most of the states of central Europe and needed, among other things, enormous expenditures for the maintenance of armies.

In central and eastern Europe, the savings of Jewish merchants and traders represented one of the few sources of liquid capital. Jewish financiers could mobilize this capital and provide monarchs with loans to underwrite war making and state building. Thus, in central Europe, so-called court Jews served as administrators, financiers, and military provisioners.[36] The Hapsburg emperors of Austria relied on Jews for these purposes from the late sixteenth century and, in return, provided Jews with protection from riots and pogroms. For example, when a mob attacked Frankfurt's Jewish quarter in 1614, Emperor Matthias moved forcefully against the rioters and hanged their leaders.[37]

After the Thirty Years' War broke out, the Hapsburg emperor, Ferdinand II, turned to the financier Joseph Bassevi of Prague to finance the war effort. Bassevi had an alliance with the most powerful figure at the imperial court, Karl I, Prince of Liechtenstein, and with General Albrecht von Wallenstein, commander of the imperial armies. In exchange for loans to finance the war, Emperor Ferdinand leased the imperial mint to Bassevi, Liechtenstein, and Wallenstein. The three men recouped their investment by debasing the coinage.[38] Bassevi also set up a network through which to supply the imperial armies with food, fodder, arms, and ammunition. During and after the Thirty Years' War, most of the major states in central Europe and Scandinavia found it necessary to make use of the resources and talents of Jews to compete with their rivals. The Hohenzollern rulers of Prussia relied initially on Israel Aaron and then on the Gomperz family. The Behrends served the court of Hanover and the Lehmans, Saxony, while the Fuersts served Schleswig-Holstein, Mecklenburg, and Holstein-Gottorp.[39]

Jews continued to serve German states in these ways through the nineteenth century. The most prominent of these Jews, of course, were members of the Rothschild family, whose name came to be synonymous with international finance. The founder of the dynasty, Mayer Amschel Rothschild of Frankfurt, was the chief financial agent for William IX, elector of Hesse-Cassel. During and after the Napoleonic Wars, Mayer dispatched his sons to the major financial capitals of Europe, London, Paris, Vienna, and Naples. Nathan Rothschild, who headed the London branch of the family, saved William IX's fortune by investing it in England and served the British government by transferring millions of pounds in gold to the British Army in Spain.

In the decades after the wars, governments became increasingly dependent on foreign borrowing, an activity that the Rothschilds came to dominate. Between 1818 and 1832, Nathan Rothschild handled 39 percent of the loans floated in London by such governments as Austria, Russia, and France. Similarly, the Vienna and Paris branches of the family raised money and sold bonds for the Hapsburgs, Bourbons, Orléanists, and Bonapartes. By midcentury, the entire European state system was dependent on the international financial network dominated by the Rothschilds.[40]

In the 1860s and 1870s, another Jewish financier, Baron Gerson von Bleichröder, was a principal figure in the creation of a united German state. Bleichröder helped Otto von Bismarck obtain loans for the war against Austria after the chancellor could not secure financing from the Prussian parliament. Subsequently, Bismarck entrusted Bleichröder with negotiating the future indemnity France paid after its defeat in the Franco-Prussian War in 1871 (on the French side, the Rothschilds conducted negotiations). During Bismarck's tenure as chancellor of a united Germany, Bleichröder continued to serve as his chief confidant and fiscal adviser.[41] Sombart summarized these events by asserting, "When speaking of modern statesmen and rulers we can hardly do so without perforce thinking of the Jews … . Arm in arm the Jew and the ruler stride through the [modern] age … . Jews furnished the rising states with the material means necessary to maintain themselves."[42]

Many of these same Jewish financiers were also responsible for Germany's extraordinarily rapid industrial development during the late nineteenth century. The House of Rothschild, the Bleichröders, and the House of Oppenheim of Cologne, as well as the Jewish-owned Deutsche Bank and Dresdner Bank, financed the construction of railroads, shipyards, and steel mills and the overall expansion of Germany's industrial base. Bleichröder and the Oppenheims, for example, were the chief financiers of the construction of the German rail system in the middle to late nineteenth century.[43]

Of course, only a handful of German Jews were industrialists or financiers or "walked arm in arm" with the likes of Bismarck. Most Jews worked in their traditional trades and crafts, with a small number fortunate enough to gain access to the universities and the professions. This situation changed gradually in the late nineteenth and early twentieth centuries when the universities, but not the professions, opened their doors to Jews. In the years before World War I, in both Germany and Austria, Jewish students were able to gain access to higher education; indeed, the proportion of the population attending universities was far greater among Jews than any other group. In Prussia, the largest German state, the percentage of Jews receiving a university education was ten times greater than the percentage of Protestants and Catholics. At the same time, however, the Prussian civil service mostly barred Jewish university graduates from careers that attracted many of their fellow students. Moreover, those Jews who pursued academic careers found that anti-Semitism pervaded German universities, too, and limited their opportunities to secure professorial appointments. Before World War I, close to 20 percent of the part-time and temporary teaching staff at German universities were of Jewish origin. However, less than 7 percent of the full professors were Jews. At the most prestigious university, Berlin, there was not a single Jewish full professor. Many examples of the difficulties faced by Jewish scholars are noteworthy. The University of Strassburg denied Georg Simmel, one of Germany's most brilliant sociologists and philosophers, a full professorship until four years before his death at the age of sixty. Similarly, Ernst Cassirer, Germany's leading neo-Kantian philosopher, could secure a professorship only at the new and struggling University of Hamburg.[44]

This situation changed dramatically after World War I with the collapse of the monarchy and the creation of the liberal Weimar regime. Before the war, German Jews had largely been supporters of liberal political parties and politicians. Jews had been particularly important in the liberal press. Jews owned and edited two of the most important liberal newspapers, the *National-Zeitung* of Berlin and the *Frankfurter Zeitung*. Of the twenty-one daily newspapers published in Berlin during the 1870s, Jews owned thirteen and a further four had important Jewish contributors. All three newspapers specializing in political satire were Jewish run.[45] In the aftermath of World War I, Jews strongly supported the creation of the liberal Weimar Republic. Indeed, Hugo Preuss, a Jewish socialist who served as minister of the interior in the provisional government created after the collapse of the monarchy, was primarily responsible for drafting the Weimar constitution. Throughout the life of the Weimar regime, Jewish businessmen, journalists, and politicians were among its most active and ardent supporters.

Through their commercial and banking activities, Jews contributed to the substantial economic development and reconstruction that took place during the Weimar era. Jewish firms accounted for close to 80 percent of the business done by department and chain stores, 40 percent of Germany's wholesale textile firms, and 60 percent of all wholesale and retail clothing businesses. Jews also created close to half of all private banks and the largest and most successful of the credit banks. The most important was Arthur Salomonsohn's Disconto-Gesellschaft, which helped to revive and rebuild Germany's heavy industry and merchant navy after World War I. Eugen Gutmann directed the equally important Dresdner Bank until his death in 1925, followed by Henry Nathan. The Darmstädter and Nationalbank, directed by Jakob Goldschmidt, was significantly responsible for obtaining major loans of working capital for German industry from Holland, Sweden, and the United States.[46]

Continuing the pre–World War I pattern, Jews were influential in the liberal press of the Weimar Republic. Jews owned three of the nation's most important liberal newspapers, the *Berliner Tageblatt*, the *Vossische Zeitung*, and the *Frankfurter Zeitung*. Jews also built the two largest publishing houses in Germany, the Ullstein and Mattes concerns, as well as many smaller publishing firms.

In addition, Jews were extremely important in the professional, intellectual, and cultural life of Weimar Germany. Even though doors had only recently begun to open to Jewish professionals, some 11 percent of Germany's physicians and 16 percent of its lawyers were Jews. Jewish academics, intellectuals, and artists were the leading figures in German and Austrian theater, literature, music, art, architecture, science, social science, psychology, and philosophy during the Weimar era. Jews were also the most influential critics of drama, art, music, and books as well as the owners of the most important art galleries and theaters.[47]

Even more lasting, late nineteenth- and early twentieth-century Germany became a world leader in the natural sciences thanks in no small part to the work of its Jewish scientists. The most famous of these were, of course, such physicists as Albert Einstein, James Franck, Max Born, Hans Bethe, and a host of others—many of whom had struggled against professional and academic restrictions before Weimar—who helped make Germany the unquestioned world leader in the field of physics at the beginning of the twentieth century. Other German Jewish scientists included, to name but a few, Fritz Haber, who won the 1918 Nobel Prize in Chemistry for developing a method for synthesizing ammonia that became indispensable both to Germany's agriculture and to its war industries. The bacteriologist August von Wassermann developed the Wassermann test, which, for decades, was the standard test for syphilis. Paul Ehrlich, another German Jewish Nobel Prize winner, developed the first treatment for syphilis as well as the first treatment for diphtheria. Though Jews never constituted even 1 percent of the German population, they won a third of the Nobel Prizes awarded to German scientists.[48]

Their main place in the economy and cultural life of Weimar Germany gave Jews a major stake in the liberal regime. The commitment of the Jews to this regime was, of course, hugely increased by the rise of the Nazis and other anti-Semitic movements looking to overthrow the Weimar Republic. The virulent anti-Semitism of these groups provided Jews with a strong incentive to fight for the survival of the republic.

Although Jews had taken part in the creation of the German Communist party (Kommunistische Partei Deutschlands, or KPD), the overwhelming majority of German Jews backed parties and politicians who supported the republic against its enemies on both the Left and Right. Most Jewish voters identified with the moderate Democratic Party. A smaller number belonged to the Social Democratic Party (Sozialdemokratische Partei Deutschlands, or SPD), which had mostly abandoned its more radical prewar stance and given its support to the liberal regime. Many important Jewish politicians were liberals independent of party ties. These included Walter Rathenau, the minister of the interior whom right-wing extremists assassinated in 1922, and Curt Joël, the leading figure in the Reich ministry of justice from 1920 to 1931.

Because Jews constituted only 1 percent of Germany's population, their electoral weight was slight. Jews, however, were important financial contributors to liberal parties, and the political influence of the Jewish legal establishment, press, publishing industry, and other media was large. Jews were a major source of financial support for liberal parties, including the Center, Democratic, and Social Democratic Parties as well as the Bavarian People's Party. As the militancy of the Nazis and other anti-Semitic parties on the political Right grew after 1930, Jews also helped fund the paramilitary "Reichsbanner" units formed by the Social Democrats to defend against violent attacks from right-wing thugs and paramilitary groups.

The Jewish legal establishment, too, played a role in opposing right-wing opponents of the Weimar Republic. Politicians of the Right specialized in arousing their followers with inflammatory speeches that often provoked violence. Lawyers funded by the Jewish Centralverein (Central Association of German Citizens of Jewish Faith) adopted the tactic of pressing charges of disorderly conduct or slander against such speakers and their followers. As a result of this technique, several prominent right-wing politicians, including Julius Streicher, Gregor Strasser, and Pastor Ludwig Münchmeyer, paid fines or served short jail terms.[49] Jewish journalists, writers, dramatists, and intellectuals were among the most determined opponents of the institutions and forces associated with the antirepublican political Right. Writers like Kurt Tucholsky and Ernst Toller enraged conservatives by mounting fierce attacks on the Junkers (members of the landed nobility) and the army—the twin pillars of the old regime. Similarly, Jewish journalists were relentless in their criticism of the right-wing political parties and politicians that arose after the war. In the end, of course, the exertions of the Jews on its behalf were not sufficient to save the Weimar regime. Their strong identification with and defense of the Weimar Republic, moreover, helped make the Jews an inviting target for the new republic's foes.

Anti-Semitism played an important political role in Weimar Germany. Hatred of Jews was a political theme that could unite the disparate conservative and populist opponents of the liberal regime who had little else in common. Jews were quite visible in the political, cultural, and intellectual life of the Weimar era, and as a result, many Germans associated Weimar government with the Jews. Its foes, in fact, often derisively called the Weimar regime a "*Judenrepublik.*" Some forces in Germany had never been able to reconcile themselves to the defeat and dismemberment of the empire, while others joined the ranks of Weimar's opponents in the wake of Germany's economic collapse in the 1920s. The republic's various enemies found that they could effectively attack it by attacking the Jews.

Opponents of the regime included traditional conservatives such as Prussian Junkers, army officers, and Ruhr industrialists, who feared the influence of socialists in the government and feared that the regime was too weak to control the forces of the radical Left. In general, these groups supported such conservative parties as the DNVP (Deutschnationale Volkspartei, the Nationalist Party). A second set of the regime's foes consisted of middle- and lower-middle-class Germans undermined by the defeat and disintegration of the empire and the collapse of the German economy in the 1920s. These included former officials of the imperial regime as well as demobilized army officers, ruined smallholders, small businessmen, and students. These groups formed the base of support for parties of the radical Right such as the Freiheitspartei, the Deutsche Erneuerungsgmeinde, and the Deutsche Arbeiterspartei as well as the Freikorps and other paramilitary groups. Several hundred radical right-wing parties of this sort, many of them emphasizing anti-Semitic appeals, appeared in Germany in the chaos following World War I. The Nazi party, like the others, appealed primarily to members of the dispossessed lower middle class.

The Nazis were unique, however, in one respect. Unlike the others, the Nazis were able to mobilize significant support among working- and upper-class forces as well. As to the working class, during the late 1920s, the Nazis developed a network of factory cells and attracted the votes of large numbers of unemployed workers. Their ability to secure working-class support was a function of the Nazis' organizational skill and the appeal of their methods to some workers. In contrast to worker-established Social Democratic leaders, the Nazis did not speak of complex, long-term solutions to the problems faced by the working class. Instead, the Nazis engaged in direct and violent action against immediate and visible targets—the Jews. Indeed, to a far greater extent than even other parties of the radical Right, the Nazis exulted in acts of violence—in beatings, riots, desecrations, pogroms, and murders. As Peter Pulzer has concluded, the simplicity of Nazi ideology and the ferocity of their tactics had an enormous allure for desperate and angry workers.[50]

The ability of the Nazis to appeal to the working classes, in turn, led traditional conservative and upper-class forces to view Hitler as a useful instrument through which they might link themselves to a broader popular base. Moreover, the Nazis appeared to pose less of a threat to traditional elites than other radical populist forces. Most radical Right parties appealing to the dispossessed presented platforms calling for a variety of social and economic reforms in addition to whatever anti-Semitic appeals they might make. The Nazis, however, focused almost exclusively on the issue of the Jews. In Nazi ideology, other social and economic reforms were virtually irrelevant. As Hitler put it, "There are no revolutions except racial revolutions: there cannot be a political, economic, or social revolution."[51]

While traditional conservatives were uneasy about all the rabble-rousers, the political and economic condition of Weimar Germany made them desperate. From the perspective of the upper classes, the Nazis' exclusive focus on issues of race meant that Hitler and his followers might be potential links to the masses who had little interest in and posed little threat to their own economic concerns. The resulting support the Nazis received from conservative forces led by the DNVP's Alfred Hugenberg, as well as the financial backing they received from industrialists like Thyssen and Stinnes, was critical to the Nazis' ultimate success. Significantly, though Hitler welcomed this support, conservatives were the junior partners in the Nazi coalition. Indeed, the Nazi party admitted few individuals drawn from traditional elites into its upper ranks or, later, to positions of power in the Nazi state, with the partial exception of the military.

Thus the Nazis were able to use anti-Semitism and especially systematic violence against the Jews to build a coalition of upper-, lower-middle-, and working-class forces against the Weimar regime. With the total collapse of the German economy during the Great Depression, this coalition was able to take control of Germany.

Once in power, the Nazis organized a violent campaign against the Jews of Germany and introduced several legal measures designed to drive Jews from the universities, the professions, the civil service, and the general economy in what became the first act of the "Final Solution." One of the early anti-Jewish enactments was the 1933 Law for the Restoration of the Professional Civil Service. Among other things, this measure, and later amendments, followed by the Law Against the Overcrowding of German Schools and Institutes of Higher Learning, drove Jews from the universities by design. Thousands of Jewish professors lost their posts, and many, particularly the most eminent, soon sought positions abroad. What ensued was an enormous transfer of intellectual capital from Germany and its allies, such as Hungary, to the United States and, to a lesser extent, Great Britain. Soon, scientific research and teaching in Germany lost its prewar momentum, with a loss of some three thousand teachers and researchers and a 65 percent decline in the number of students in physics and mathematics.[52] Asked by the German education minister if his department had suffered because of the departure of the Jews, the head of the mathematics faculty at the University of Göttingen replied, "Suffered? It no longer exists."[53] Of special importance were the great German Jewish and Hungarian Jewish physicists who stood at the forefront of this realm of science in the early twentieth century. It can be argued strongly that the departure of these individuals from Germany was the greatest transfer of human capital during such a brief period in the history of the world.

The list of émigrés includes the greatest names in physics as well as chemistry and other natural sciences, including thirty-three present or future Nobel Prize winners: Hans Bethe, Felix Bloch, Konrad Bloch, Max Born, Ernst Chain, Peter Debye, Max Delbrück, Albert Einstein, Enrico Fermi, James Franck, Dennis Gabor, Fritz Haber, Gustav Hertz, Gerhard Herzberg, Victor Hess, Bernard Katz, Hans Krebs, Rita Levi-Montalcini, Fritz Lipmann, Otto Loewi, Salvador Luria, Otto Meyerhof, Wolfgang Pauli, Max Perutz, Josef Rotblat, Erwin Schrödinger, Emilio Segrè, Jack Steinberger, Otto Stern, Georg von Hevesy (George de Hevesy), Eugene Wigner, and Richard Willstätter. Other scientific luminaries included Leo Szilard, Edward Teller, Stanislaw Ulam, and John von Neumann.[54] Some of these scientific refugees fled to Great Britain, where the newly formed Academic Assistance Council helped them find positions.[55] Most, however, found their way to the United States, where university positions were found for them by the Emergency Committee in Aid of Displaced Foreign Scholars, a private organization funded mainly by the Rockefeller Foundation.[56] The scientists were soon followed by other prominent German Jewish intellectuals and academics, who found positions in American universities and made America a dominant force in philosophy, psychology, and the social sciences. Some of these individuals, such as the social theorist Theodor Adorno, US intelligence agencies hired during the war to analyze German intentions and capabilities.

A major result of the transfer of scientific talent from Germany to America was, of course, that it was the United States, not Nazi Germany, that developed the atomic bomb. In 1939, Szilard and Einstein, in consultation with fellow Jewish refugees Edward Teller and Eugene Wigner, sent a letter to President Franklin D. Roosevelt in which they described the possibility of a new type of weapon of unprecedented power, based on the principle of nuclear fission. Such a weapon, they said, might potentially destroy an entire city with one blast. Moreover, the letter went on to say, there was reason to believe that Germany had already begun work on a nuclear bomb. Roosevelt received the famous Einstein-Szilard letter a few days after the German invasion of Poland and was sufficiently concerned to authorize the creation of an advisory committee that, in turn, funded the first stages of work on what would become an atomic bomb. Over the ensuing years, for the Jewish scientists, both native-born and refugee, who joined the project, the defeat of Nazi Germany was an overriding goal. "After the fall of France," Hans Bethe wrote, "I was desperate to do something—to make some contribution to the war effort."[57] And as J. Robert Oppenheimer wrote, "I had a continuing, smoldering fury about the treatment of Jews in Germany."[58]

It turned out that a German atomic bomb was a misplaced fear. Absent the Jewish physicists, such a project had few advocates in a Germany whose leaders had other obsessions. Nuclear theory, moreover, smacked of "Jewish science," which was to be supplanted by a purer "Aryan science." The leaders of this Aryan science included two once-eminent but now-superannuated German physicists, Johannes Stark and Philipp Lenard, who were unable to make much sense of newer ideas, which they dismissed as *Judenphysik* and "kabbalistic" in origin. The Nazis accused Germany's leading gentile nuclear physicist, Werner Heisenberg, of being a "white Jew" and came close to arresting him for his ideas and Jewish associations.[59]

Russia and the Soviet Union

Tsarist Russia had a large Jewish community. Some Jews had settled in what became Russia as early as the fourth century, but most derived from Jews who had settled in eastern Europe in the fourteenth century in territories later absorbed by the Russian Empire. In what was a landlord-peasant society,

Jews found a niche and worked as estate managers, traders, moneylenders, and so forth. Beginning with the eighteenth-century reign of Catherine II, the government allowed the Jews to settle only in the "Pale of Settlement," which included Lithuania, Poland, and Ukraine. Typically, Jews were excluded from the universities and hence from the professions and were often persecuted through officially sanctioned pogroms. A small number of Jews, nevertheless, accumulated some wealth and played a role in Russia's nineteenth-century economic development. Thus, for example, Evzel Gintsburg, Abram Zak, Anton Varshavsky, and other Jewish bankers and financiers helped fund the construction of much of Russia's railroad system, its chemical industry, its gold-mining industry, and its oil-processing industry.[60]

As unique victims of tsarism, Jews were also among the government's most vehement opponents. Several Jews, most notably Paul Axelrod and Lev Deutsch, were among the founders of the Social Democratic Party in the 1890s. In addition, the Jewish Socialist Bund organized tens of thousands of workers in the Pale and played a key role in the unsuccessful 1905 Revolution. During the period leading up to the 1917 Revolution, Jews were active in both the Menshevik and Bolshevik leaderships.[61]

After the revolution, among the first official acts of the victorious Bolsheviks was outlawing the pogroms and anti-Semitic movements that Russian Jews had feared for centuries. In a radical break with the Russian past, moreover, the new regime provided Jews with the opportunity to take part fully in government and society. They quickly came to play a significant role in the ruling Communist Party and Soviet state. Jews were among the few supporters of the revolution with a modicum of education and literacy. Thus they soon assumed positions of leadership in areas requiring such skills as foreign affairs, propaganda, finance, and administration.

Three of the six members of Lenin's first Politburo—Leon Trotsky, Lev Kamenev, and Grigory Zinoviev—were of Jewish origin. In addition, Trotsky, as commissar of defense, organized and commanded the Red Army during the civil war that followed the October Revolution. Kamenev and Zinoviev became members of the triumvirate (along with Stalin) that ruled the Soviet Union just after Lenin's death in 1924. Other prominent Jews in the early Soviet government included Yakov Sverdlov, president of the Communist Party Central Committee; Maxim Litvinov, commissar for foreign affairs; and Karl Radek, who served as press commissar. In later years, Jews continued to play major roles throughout the Soviet state. Lazar Kaganovich, for example, was one of Stalin's chief aides, commissar of heavy industry during World War II, and a member of the Politburo. Jews were also important in the Red Army. In addition to Trotsky, prominent Jewish generals included Yona Yakir, who was a member of the Communist Party Central Committee; Dmitri Schmidt, a civil war hero and commander of the Kiev area; and Yakob Kreiser, a hero of the defense of Moscow during World War II.[62] In what must constitute one of the most unsavory chapters in Jewish history, Jews were also a major element in the leadership of the Soviet secret police and other security forces.

The 1917 Revolution also opened educational and career opportunities to talented Jews who had been for the most part excluded from both under the tsarist regime. Jewish students flooded into the universities, including the excellent engineering schools in Moscow, Leningrad, Kiev, and Kharkov, where they quickly formed sizable percentages within the overall student population. Though less than 2 percent of the overall populace, between 1929 and 1939 Jews constituted 11 percent of the students in Soviet universities. This included 17 percent of all university students in Moscow, 19 percent in Leningrad, 24 percent in Kharkov, and 35.6 percent in Kiev.[63]

From the universities, Jews streamed into the professions, especially those needed by the new regime. These included science and engineering, particularly in such fields as aircraft design, industrial production, and transport. Indeed, Jewish engineering graduates became major figures in the Soviet armaments industry, designing and producing the tanks, aircraft, and artillery without which the USSR could not have defeated Nazi Germany. For example, several of the Soviet Union's most prominent aircraft designers were Jews. These included Semyon Lavochkin, a 1927 Moscow State Technical University graduate, who developed the La series of fighter planes, which became the mainstay of the Soviet air force, and Mikhail I. Gurevich, designer of the famous MiG fighters. After the war, Jews continued to be major figures in Soviet science and in the Soviet Union's nuclear program. By the 1930s, Jews had also become the backbone of the Soviet bureaucracy; constituted a sizable percentage of the nation's physicians, dentists, pharmacists, and other professionals; and were close to 20 percent of the scientists and university professors in such major cities as Moscow and Leningrad.

The importance of Jews in the Communist Party and Soviet state did not prevent, and in some ways prompted, a revival of anti-Semitism. During the struggles that followed Lenin's death in 1924, anti-Semitic appeals to the Communist Party's rank and file were among the weapons used by Stalin to defeat Trotsky, Zinoviev, and Kamenev and to seize party leadership. Indeed, much of the invective designed and used by Stalin in the intraparty battles of this period appealed to anti-Semitic sentiment inside and outside the party. For example, the label "left oppositionist," used by Stalin to castigate his enemies, was a euphemism for *Jew*. In a similar vein, Stalin's advocacy of the doctrine of "socialism in one country" was with certainty designed to limit the influence of foreign Jewish Communists, who often had ties to Jewish Communists in the Soviet Union itself.

During the 1930s, Stalin moved to fortify his power by intimidating, jailing, or killing all potential sources of opposition within the Communist Party, the army, the secret police, and the administrative apparatus. Jews exercised a great deal of influence within all these institutions and, as a result, formed the largest and most important group of victims of the Stalinist purges. Jews constituted about 500,000 of the 10 million purge victims of the 1930s and formed a majority of the politically most prominent victims.[64]

In a series of show trials during this period, the Communist Party and Soviet state accused key Jewish officials of plotting against the revolution and executed them. These included Kamenev, Zinoviev, Radek, and Alexei Ivanovich Rykov. Important Jewish military commanders such as Yakir and Schmidt also faced liquidation. Often, Jews led the secret police forces used to implement these purges. Later, Stalin purged them, too, until the influence of Jews within the secret police was sizably diminished.

Stalin's purges continued during the 1940s. At the 1941 party conference, for example, Stalin demoted Jews Maxim Litvinov and Naum Antselovich from full to candidate membership on the Communist Party Central Committee and expelled G. D. Vainberg and Vyacheslav Molotov's Jewish wife, Polina Zhemchuzhina. In 1939, Jews had been 10 percent of the membership on the Central Committee. A decade later, they formed barely 2 percent of the committee's members. This not only gave Stalin total control of the

Communist Party apparatus but also allowed the regime to broaden its political base by increasing the representation of other nationality groups in the party leadership.[65]

During World War II, Jews played prominent roles in the Soviet government, particularly in the realms of propaganda and foreign relations. After the war, however, the regime confronted an upsurge of popular anti-Semitism, most notably in German-occupied areas. The populations of these areas, who had often cooperated with the Nazis, feared that returning Jews would seek restoration of their homes, property, and positions. Nationalist movements, notably in Ukraine and Lithuania, sought to exploit this popular anti-Semitism to attack the Soviet regime.[66]

Stalin, who disliked and distrusted the Jews, responded to the nationalist threat by embarking on a new anti-Semitic campaign of his own. The Soviet press began to impugn the loyalty of Jews and to suggest that they might betray the socialist motherland. Also accused were several of the leading figures of the wartime Jewish Anti-Fascist Committee (JAC) of plotting to transform the Crimea into a Zionist republic to serve as a base for American imperialism. The KGB murdered Shlomo Mikhoels, JAC head and director of the Moscow State Jewish Theater, in January 1948. By the early 1950s, Jews were in effect barred from the Soviet foreign service, from foreign trade institutes, from positions of military command, and from senior positions in the bureaucracy as well as from positions of leadership within the party itself. Not only Russians but also members of many minority nationality groups in the USSR replaced Jews in these positions, part of the regime's effort to curb nationalist opposition to the USSR and expand its political base.

Because Jews constituted the best educated and most talented group in the Soviet populace, the regime could not completely dispense with their services in the professions, in scientific research, or in the civil service. The government, however, relied on a policy of intimidation to check Jewish influence. This was one factor behind the arrest of some of the Soviet Union's leading Jewish physicians in 1953. In the case of the so-called doctors' plot, authorities charged several Moscow physicians with conspiring with American intelligence services to destroy the Soviet leadership. Dismissed from their posts were also hundreds of Jewish doctors throughout the USSR, saved from execution only by Stalin's sudden death.

After Stalin's death, the Soviet regime continued its efforts to placate the nation's various nationality groups by increasing their representation in the civil service, in the professions, and in institutions of higher education. This was done often at the expense of the Jews, who then found themselves relegated to marginal positions in the bureaucracy, the education system, and the economy. Many Jews became alienated and began to look for ways to leave the Soviet Union.

In the 1970s, bowing to American economic pressure in the form of the 1974 Jackson-Vanik Amendment, which tied trade to the USSR's willingness to allow emigration, the Soviet government for the first time allowed large numbers of Jews to emigrate. Because of the fear of a serious brain drain, Soviet authorities were initially reluctant to allow Jewish emigration. One KGB report found that while Jews constituted less than 1 percent of the Soviet population, "in terms of absolute numbers of people employed in scholarship and research Jews occupy third place after Russians and Ukrainians. Among those with PhDs they occupy second place after Russians."[67] Initially, the Soviet government imposed a "diploma tax" on would-be educated emigrants, sometimes amounting to twenty years' salary, to deter a brain drain. American economic pressure, however, forced the Soviets to rescind the tax.

Following the enactment of Jackson-Vanik, more than 1 million Jews left the Soviet Union and its successor states. Most emigrated to Israel or the United States, with smaller numbers choosing other destinations. Those who left the Soviet Union included tens of thousands of Jewish scientists and engineers, who constituted a large segment of the Soviet scientific and technical elite. These Russian Jewish scientists and engineers have helped make Israel a leading actor in such realms as computer engineering, aerospace engineering, genetics, biomedical engineering, and pharmaceuticals.[68] According to one estimate, as many as 90 percent of the major specialists in Israel's "military-industrial complex" are former Soviet citizens.[69] At the same time, Russian Jewish scientists who immigrated to the United States have enhanced America's standing in physics, chemistry, mathematics, and biology. NASA alone employed more than a hundred former Soviet space scientists. One American scientist said, "If you go around the Harvard campus Russian is the second language. The same is true for the University of California at Berkeley and some other universities."[70]

As to Russia itself, its scientific research has shown a marked decline for the past several decades.[71] Some 40 percent of Russia's top-level theoretical physicists and about 12 percent of its top experimental physicists left the country along with large numbers of biologists, chemists, engineers, economists, and physicians. The result, according to Russian experts, is a threat of the "disintegration of research teams and schools including those having advanced knowledge in the most progressive areas of research and development."[72]

5

The Myth of American Exceptionalism

GIVEN THE EPIC rise and fall of Jews throughout history, there have been three ways the fall happens, and America, so far, has not been an exception. First, when the Jews' allies decide that they no longer need to share power with them and use anti-Semitic discourse to drive the Jews out of institutions and positions of power. Second, when the Jews' allies find themselves under attack by opponents who accuse them of being associated too closely with or, indeed, being little more than puppets of the Jews. Third, when the elite stratum that Jews occupy is weakened or overthrown, crippling the Jews along with their allies.

The first of these possibilities, a ruling elite's decision that it no longer wishes to share power with Jews, is exemplified by Stalin's attack on the Jews of the Soviet Union during the 1920s and 1930s. The Jews had been a major force within the Bolshevik Party, and, in the aftermath of the revolution, they were an extremely important element in the coalition that ruled the Soviet regime. During the 1920s, however, Stalin and a group of non-Jewish Bolsheviks decided to enhance their own power by driving their Jewish allies from leadership positions in the Communist Party and the Soviet state. To seize party leadership, Stalin and the non-Jewish members of the Soviet elite made use of an anti-Semitic discourse to discredit Bolshevik Jews such as Trotsky, Zinoviev, and Kamenev, who were eventually murdered or summarily executed. Also killed were such formerly powerful Jewish officials as Yagoda, Pauker, Slutsky, and the Berman brothers.[1] Stalin himself designed much of the invective during the intraparty struggles of the 1920s to enhance and appeal to anti-Semitic sentiments in the nation. Today, contemporary denunciations of Zionists by Left liberals have eerie Stalinist overtones, if not usage, of Stalin's exact words.

For the second possibility, Hungary, Ukraine, and England are cases where allies who had been accused of allowing themselves to become Jewish puppets jettisoned the Jews. In pre–World War I Hungary, Jews allied themselves closely with the Magyar governing class, which dominated business and the professions, extending Magyar influence in the provinces. During the nineteenth century, with the government's encouragement, Jews built banks, factories, railroads, and a host of commercial enterprises. These efforts hugely contributed to Hungarian economic modernization. Indeed, according to the historian C. A. Macartney, "the capitalist development of modern Hungary ... has been almost entirely of their [the Jews'] making."[2] At the same time, their participation in Hungary's economy gave the Jews considerable wealth and economic power. By the latter years of the nineteenth century, an astonishing 85 percent of the owners and directors of Hungarian financial institutions were Jewish, as were 62 percent of all the employees in commerce. Twenty extremely wealthy Jewish families, according to Andrew Janos, controlled as much as 90 percent of Hungary's banking system and industrial plants.[3] For example, the Hatvany-Deutsch family controlled sugar production as well as Hungary's five largest banks; the Weiss family built a huge munitions company; the Brull family dominated the grain trade; the Buday-Goldbergers were the major force in the textile industry.[4] In these endeavors, Jews worked closely with the Magyar aristocracy, who provided the political influence necessary for successful Jewish enterprise and often helped themselves to a handsome share of the profits.[5] So close was the relationship between the Jews and the Magyar elite that William McCagg has called the Hungarian Jews of the nineteenth century a "feudalized bourgeoisie."[6]

In addition to wealth, their partnership with the Magyar elite gave the Jews an important measure of political freedom and security. Aristocratic governments made the Jews Hungarian citizens in 1868 and, over the next decade, granted them full voting rights and the right to hold public office. A small number of extremely wealthy Jews were granted (or sold) titles of nobility.[7] Their aristocratic allies also protected the Hungarian Jews from the sporadic outbreaks of anti-Semitism that were common in nineteenth-century Europe. In general, the Hungarian ruling elite before World War I did not tolerate expressions of popular anti-Semitism. Thus, for example, Prime Minister Coloman Tisza declared a radical populist anti-Semitic party that appeared in Hungary during the 1880s, like those organized in western Europe during the same period, to be "shameful, barbaric and injurious to the national honor," and it was summarily suppressed by the government.[8]

Between the two world wars, however, the Magyar elite's relationship with the Jews was assaulted ferociously by radical populists within Hungary as well as by Hungary's German allies. Hungarian fascists charged that the old elite had betrayed the nation to the Jews and demanded removal of the Jews, and those associated with them, from positions of influence. To save itself, the Magyar aristocracy agreed to restrict the political, economic, and civil rights of its former partners and to purge Jews from the government, the universities, and other important positions they had once occupied. Many Jews fled the country, but a large number of Hungarian Jews perished at the hands of the Germans and their Hungarian partners, members of the Arrow Cross Party, which came to power in Hungary in 1944.

Similarly, in seventeenth-century Ukraine, Jews were allied with the Polish nobility, whom they served as estate managers, tax collectors, administrators, and operators of such enterprises as mills and breweries. When in 1648, however, the Ukrainian peasantry led by Bogdan Chmielnicki revolted against the Poles and the Jews, the Poles tried to save themselves by handing the Jews over to the Ukrainians in exchange for their own lives. When denied access to or evicted from the fortified Polish towns where they had sought refuge, thousands of Jews perished.[9]

Even the most powerful of allies cannot always offer the Jews a guarantee of security. In twelfth-century England, Jewish financiers supplied the funds that supported the Crown's efforts to expand its authority vis-à-vis the aristocracy. As a result, when the barons moved to restrict the powers of the Crown during the thirteenth century, the Jews were among their chief targets. In the Magna Carta of 1215, the barons compelled King John to accept limits on the capacity of the Jews to recover debt from the landed gentry and on his own ability to acquire and recover debts that members of the gentry owed to the Jews. The acquisition of such debts had been a significant instrument through which the Crown enhanced its power over the nobility. Subsequently, the Crown sought to reduce its political exposure by distancing itself from the

Jews, first imposing severe restrictions on them and later expelling them from England, after expropriating as much of their capital as possible.[10]

The case of Nazi Germany exemplifies the third possibility: the overthrow of the entire elite stratum with which Jews are affiliated. Before World War I, Jews constituted barely 1 percent of the German populace. But, in a pattern not dissimilar to that of the contemporary United States, Jews were integrated into the urban bourgeoisie and played important roles in the financial, cultural, and political institutions controlled by them—banks, universities, the media, and so forth—while having little or no presence in other sectors or areas of Germany.

After World War I and the collapse of the Hohenzollern monarchy, the urban bourgeoisie became Germany's new ruling stratum and, along with gentile members of their social class, Jews came to occupy positions of leadership in the liberal Weimar Republic. Indeed, a Jewish socialist, Hugo Preuss, drafted the Weimar constitution, while Jewish businessmen, journalists, and politicians were among the most dedicated Weimar supporters.[11]

The Weimar Republic's various foes looked to discredit the government by pointing to the prominence of Jews among the regime's supporters. Rightists declared that the Jews and their puppets dominated the regime, working against the true interests of the German people, and derisively called Weimar a *Judenrepublik*. Germany's complete economic collapse in the 1920s undermined the power of traditional elites and opened the way to power for the Nazis, a political party led by radical and violent lower-middle-class elements, normally consigned to the outer fringes of the political process, the German equivalent of paramilitary training camps in Idaho. Yet, against the backdrop of economic chaos, the Nazi campaign of racism and violence made Hitler and his followers the most vital political force in Germany.

The Nazi accession to power meant a defeat not only for the Jews but for the liberal bourgeoisie in general. Overthrown, the entire social stratum that Jews were a part of and through whom Jews had risen to positions of prominence collapsed. Once the Nazis had taken control of the government, they used this stratum's association with Jews to cow the liberal bourgeoisie into utter submission. In particular, the Nazi system of racial laws and classifications made hundreds of thousands of non-Jewish members of the German bourgeoisie directly vulnerable to the Nazi regime's rewards and punishments. Germans and Jews had intermarried for generations. An enormous number of middle- and upper-middle-class Germans had sufficient Jewish ancestry and therefore were disqualified from desirable positions in the government and private sector; or they were considered *Mischlinge*, racially mixed persons, and therefore subject to several restrictions.[12]

The eagerness of such Germans to upgrade their status led to the creation of a new occupation, that of *Sippenforscher*, or genealogical researcher specializing in helping individuals prove their Aryan descent. The fortunate might have been able to secure reclassifications, or "liberations," enhancing their career opportunities while diminishing the possibility that the government might one day decide to consider them Jews. Millions of middle-class Germans, moreover, with no discernible Jewish ancestry had past or present social, business, professional, or romantic relationships with Jews that could bring them to the attention of the authorities. Their enemies, hostile neighbors, or business rivals could denounce them to the Gestapo for these associations. In this way, a once powerful, yet easily subdued, social stratum lost its nerve, with its Jewish allies expelled from German society and later murdered.

So Too in America

Two of the foregoing patterns of rise and fall have also manifested themselves to Jews in America. In alliance with other groups and forces, Jews have gained influence only to find themselves later pushed from power along with the entire stratum to which they belonged or abandoned by allies who decided that an association with Jews was damaging to their interests. A case of a ruling coalition collapse, which included Jews, was the antebellum South, while an alliance with Gilded Age industrialists was a case of Jewish exclusion by their erstwhile allies in response to an external attack.

The Rise and Fall of the Southern Jews

The antebellum South was mostly hospitable to Jews, allowing a small number to approach, if not to reach, its topmost rungs. A small group of Sephardic Jewish families from the Iberian Peninsula had settled in the South in the late seventeenth and early eighteenth centuries. By the nineteenth century, members of these families had become intellectuals, professionals, and important merchants. Though the total number of Jews in the antebellum South was small, so was the South's merchant and professional class. Hence Jews figured prominently within this stratum and achieved a measure of acceptance within southern society. Though the Jews were outsiders and subject to social restrictions, they were white. In a society that linked status and skin color, the Jews' Caucasian features granted them a privileged status that could never be available even to free people of color.

As is typical of highly stratified landlord-peasant societies (eighteenth-century Ukraine is another example), the antebellum South was a region in which technical, commercial, and intellectual skills were in short supply. Popular education had mostly been neglected in the region, so outside the planter class and the small business and professional stratum that served it, illiteracy was the norm. Private tutors, academies, and colleges educated the sons of planter-class members. Yet most members of this class regarded education more as a form of preparation for membership in polite society than as a source of training. As a result, secondary education in the South was extremely weak, and, with the partial exception of the University of Virginia, colleges had nowhere near the quality of their northern counterparts.

Given the lack of intellectual resources and training in the surrounding gentile society, the tiny Jewish community, which, as usual, insisted on educating its children, comprised a significant and visible fraction of the doctors, traders (including slave traders like the Davis family of Richmond, which was singled out for censure by Harriet Beecher Stowe in her *Uncle Tom's Cabin*), newspaper editors, shopkeepers, businesspeople, lawyers, and so forth. To a substantial extent, the South's professional stratum served the monied and propertied classes in this highly stratified society. Like other business and professional people, Jews depended on the patronage and favor of the southern landowners who dominated government, politics, and the economy. Landowners controlled access to politics, were the source of most legal business, and were the chief market for services and goods, including slaves, in the South.

In recent years, some radical blacks have charged that Jews controlled the slave trade in the antebellum South.[13] This charge is unfounded. Like other small businessmen of the period, Jewish merchants did deal in slaves. Because they had little capital to invest, Jewish merchants often became auctioneers, commodities brokers, and consignment sellers—fields in which little start-up capital was needed. Unfortunately, slaves were such an important part of the routine commerce of the South during this period that such merchants routinely bought and sold human beings. In cities throughout the South, Jewish auctioneers and brokers were visible participants in this aspect of the slave trade. However, small commodities brokers controlled only a tiny fraction of the traffic in human beings. The great bulk of the slave trade was organized and controlled by a few large firms that specialized in this form of commerce, including a small number of Jewish firms. The Davis family, as mentioned, was one such family; so too were the Cohens of Atlanta, the Goldsmiths of Mobile, the Mordecais of Charleston, and the Moseses of Lumpkin, Georgia. However, most of the large slave-trading companies were non-Jewish. Such firms as Franklin and Armfield, the largest slave-trading enterprise in the entire South—a firm that sold more slaves than all the Jewish firms combined—did not employ Jews. Like other southerners, Jews certainly owned slaves. According to some scholars, though, the number was small; free blacks owned more slaves than did Jews in the Old South.[14]

Though they were not prominent in the slave trade, Jews did serve the slaveholders. In the antebellum period, several Jews became important political and intellectual spokesmen for the planter stratum. Because education and intellectual skills were scarce among native-stock southern whites compared to their northern counterparts, Jews often had more opportunity for advancement in the South than in the North. As was true in other times and places, members of the southern elite often found Jews to be the most reliable agents and spokesmen because Jewish subordinates were more fully dependent on their patrons. Jewish politicians, editors, and lawyers usually had no independent base of support and were no threat to their patrons' interests.

This backdrop helps explain why America's first two Jewish senators were southerners rather than northerners. Judah P. Benjamin of Louisiana and David Yulee of Florida were Jewish politicians (Yulee, whose name had been Levy, converted to Christianity) who became important spokesmen for planter interests in the US Senate in the 1850s. Similarly, David Kaufman of Texas and Philip Phillips of Alabama spoke for the interests of southern planters in the US House of Representatives, defending states' rights and the expansion of slavery into the territories. Phillips in fact crafted Stephen A. Douglas's Kansas-Nebraska Act of 1854, creating the new territories of Kansas and Nebraska. The act effectively repealed the Missouri Compromise of 1820, which had prohibited slavery in the western territories above the 36°30' parallel. The Kansas-Nebraska Act provided for "popular sovereignty" when it came to slavery in the territories, authorizing each new territory's settlers to decide for themselves whether their territory should be slave or free. The South hailed the Kansas-Nebraska Act, but it led to protracted guerrilla warfare between pro- and antislavery forces in what came to be known as "bleeding" Kansas.

In the business world, Jews played a key role in those areas involving technical ability or technological innovation. In prewar South Carolina, for example, Jewish businessmen were at the forefront of efforts to modernize and industrialize the state's agrarian economy. Moses Mordecai was a pioneer in the commercial use of the steamship and won the government contract for the transport of mail between New York and Charleston. Solomon Solomons, an engineer, directed the construction of the North Eastern railroad. Michael Lazarus was another pioneer in the development of commercial steam transport and opened navigation by steam on the Savannah River. Joshua Lazarus founded the Charleston Gas Light Company and illuminated the city's streets.

Before the Civil War, Jews' talents had made them important political and intellectual spokesmen for the southern cause. Though the Jewish community was small, its intellectual skills were important in a region where technical ability was in short supply. For similar reasons, during the Civil War itself, a substantial number of Jews served as prominent Confederate government officials and high-ranking officers in the Confederate Army.[15] Jews were especially important in those roles requiring substantial technical or intellectual competence. Edwin DeLeon was an important Confederate propagandist and diplomat in Europe, serving as special envoy to the court of Napoleon III. David DeLeon served as Confederate surgeon general. Isaac Baruch was assistant surgeon general. Lionel Levy was Confederate judge advocate. Abraham Myers was Confederate quartermaster general. L. C. Harby of South Carolina served as a commodore in the Confederate Navy, commanding a fleet of river gunboats. J. Randolph Mordecai served as assistant adjutant general. Raphael Moses was the chief commissary officer for General James Longstreet's corps. All told, twenty-four Jews served as senior officers in the Confederate Army, while only sixteen served in comparable positions in the much larger Union Army—this at a time when the Jewish population of the North was some three times as large as that of the South. The highest-ranking Jewish Confederate was, of course, Senator Judah P. Benjamin, who served successively as the Confederate attorney general, secretary of war, and secretary of state.

Thus, before the war, Jews enjoyed greater acceptance and had more political opportunity in the South than in the North. After the war, however, the position of the Jews changed. Though Jews served and had been patronized by the southern elite, the common white populace of the region never accepted them. Many southerners questioned whether Jews were members of the white race or the black race or constituted a separate racial category.[16] This distaste for Jews became clear when the hardships of the war weakened the Jews' planter patrons and emboldened the normally quiescent white populace to speak its mind. Toward the end of the war, a wave of agrarian radicalism swept the South. One observer in South Carolina noted that as the war drew to its conclusion, many of "our citizens who have been accustomed to all the luxuries, have been compelled to live on government rations," while, at the same time, the common white country people showed increased "assertiveness" and stood ready to "terrorize" their enemies. In South Carolina, common folk expressed resentment when they heard about Charleston's active social scene and, on several occasions, accused the rich of dragging the state into a war for their own benefit and going as far as attacking members of the Secession Convention on the street.[17]

Yet, despite the potential for class conflict in the region and occasional flare-ups, the common whites of the South were extraordinarily loyal to the Confederacy and proved themselves willing to endure great hardship and privation as the war continued. This was despite the absence of any direct material stake in a war fought to preserve slavery and the power of the slave-holding planter elite. For example, in North Carolina before the war more than 70 percent of the populace owned no slaves at all. Yet large numbers of North Carolinians served in the Confederate Army and more than forty thousand gave their lives for the Confederate cause. The presence of millions of black slaves at the bottom of Southern society encouraged poor Southern whites to regard themselves as members of the white ruling class. So, unlike the Ukrainian peasantry, which it superficially resembled, the Southern white lower class had little animosity toward the region's landlords. Indeed, the poor willingly followed the rich into battle.

Nevertheless, as the war dragged on, price inflation and shortages of goods produced popular resentment with planters, who stood accused of hoarding, speculating, evading military service, and even trading with the enemy. In many parts of the South, popular resistance began to develop to conscription and military requisition of food and supplies. In certain areas, this resistance was expressed in the unmistakable language of class warfare.

In several of the Southern states, armed bands of poor whites resisting conscription and impressments fought Confederate authorities and attacked plantations. Even the newspapers that staunchly supported the war effort declared that impressment of provisions had led to "gross abuses, oppressing the people, and menacing the towns and villages of the state with starvation."[18] Some poor whites began to believe that a Northern victory would help them. A Confederate colonel sent to suppress bands of armed draft resisters in the Appalachian Mountains reported that some of his prisoners believed that the Union Army would come to help them, and when it did, "the property of Southern men was to be confiscated and divided amongst those who would take up arms for Lincoln." In South Carolina, as Sherman's forces approached the capital, Columbia, Colonel A. R. Taylor issued orders for the 23rd South Carolina militia to muster at the courthouse. Militiamen refused to report for duty and responded instead with death threats against the colonel.[19]

As the South began to collapse militarily, civil authority weakened as well, and state and local governments were no longer able to offer much protection to the property or privileges of the Southern elite. In 1864, a Georgia planter said, "The whole country is in a lawless condition," with mobs "availing themselves of the distracted state of the country, committing all depredations of plundering and murdering." By 1865, lawlessness had reached the point that "there is not a day or night passes but what someone is robbed of all the parties can carry away." In some regions, the military and civil authorities needed to look to the "better class" among the armed bands of resisters and deserters to supply security against the others.

One element of this agrarian radicalism was an attack on the planters' Jewish allies and agents. On several occasions in the later stages of the war, Confederate troops refused to serve under Jewish officers. For example, when a Texas regiment assigned a Jewish colonel to its ranks, the enlisted men rebelled. Soldiers made derisive comments and engaged in such forms of harassment as cutting off the tail of the officer's horse. When the colonel was reassigned, his departure sparked troop celebrations.[20]

Denunciation of the Jews as war profiteers spread across the South. Several members of the Confederate House of Representatives, including Foote of Tennessee, Chilton of Alabama, Miles of South Carolina, and Hilton of Florida, voiced such sentiments. Foote charged from the floor of Congress that Jews had taken over 90 percent of the business activity of the South and were engaged in illegal trade with the Union. The end of the war, said Foote, would find "nearly all the property of the Confederacy in the hands of Jewish Shylocks."[21]

Chilton, for his part, blamed wartime shortages and inflated prices directly on the Jews, who, in his view, hoarded goods and drove up costs. Chilton offered an example of a foiled Jewish scheme. A vessel looking to run the Union blockade had run aground on a desolate part of the Florida coast and its cargo had been confiscated by the authorities. Jews somehow learned the location of the confiscated cargo and "at least one hundred flocked there, led even to this remote point by the scent of gain, and they had to be driven back actually at the point of the bayonet."[22]

In newspapers, private correspondence, and diaries throughout the South, this theme of Jewish profiteering echoed. The well-known wartime diaries of John Beauchamps Jones, a clerk in the Confederate War Department, have many complaints against Jewish merchants. Instead of contributing to the war effort, the Jews, reported Jones, "are busy speculating on the street corners." Indeed, mused Jones, "they have injured the cause more than the armies of Lincoln. If we gain our independence, instead of being the vassals of the Yankees, we shall find all our wealth in the hands of the Jews." He also wrote, "They care not which side gains the day, so they gain the profits."[23]

Not only were Jews accused of profiteering; they were charged with shirking military service too. One writer charged that "the Israelites laid in stocks [of merchandise] which, in almost every instance, were retailed at rates from five hundred to one thousand per cent above ordinary prices." Moreover, "having husbanded their goods for one or two years and converted them into coin, if they did not decamp from the Confederacy altogether, they found a thousand and one excuses for not bearing arms."[24]

In several instances, such sentiments led to direct action against the Jews. One Southern community, Thomasville, Georgia, held a public meeting to discuss the conduct of Jewish merchants, who were accused of being unpatriotic for charging unreasonable prices for their goods. The town meeting adopted a series of resolutions denouncing Jews, prohibiting them from visiting the town, and ordering all those presently living there to leave. In another Georgia community, Talbotton, a grand jury denounced Jewish merchants for "evil and unpatriotic conduct." In still another Georgia village, a group of women, including the wives of soldiers, raided Jewish stores and seized merchandise at gunpoint, accusing the Jews of enriching themselves while the women's men were at war.[25]

Frequently, also, the charge was that Jews showed too much sympathy for and willingness to deal with blacks. Unlike certain other accusations, there was some truth in this one. Jewish traders usually occupied the lowest rungs of the southern commercial ladder and were inclined to sell used clothes and other articles to free blacks and slaves. Tightly regulated, commercial dealings between whites and slaves involved certain risks to a white merchant. Only the most marginal merchants, often Jews, risked becoming involved in this trade.

A special target for anti-Semitic rhetoric was Judah P. Benjamin, the former US senator from Louisiana, who served first as Confederate secretary of war and then secretary of state and was (arguably) the most able public official in the Confederate government. Nevertheless, every misfortune that befell the Confederacy became his fault. Vilified as "Judas Iscariot Benjamin," he was accused by Southerners of undermining their military effort, sabotaging Confederate diplomacy, and protecting Jewish speculators, who were charged with ruining the South's economy. Some, indeed, went as far as to suggest that because of the elevated position held by a Jew in its government, God was reluctant to listen to the prayers of Confederate citizens.[26]

The North, to be sure, was hardly free of anti-Semitic rhetoric during the Civil War era. Newspapers often charged that Jews shirked military service or, indeed, actively supported the rebellion. As in the South, Jewish merchants and speculators were blamed often for soaring prices and shortages. As much as Southerners maligned Benjamin, the Northern press was even more vicious toward that "little Jew" who showed the same mercy toward the Union "that his ancestors had shown toward Jesus Christ." In 1862, of course, General Ulysses S. Grant issued the famous order that expelled Jews from his Tennessee military district, on the grounds that they were engaged in trade with the enemy. Lincoln rescinded the order; Grant, himself, saw nothing anti-Semitic about his order. To this uncouth westerner, who later counted the Seligmans among his chief political backers, *Jew* was merely a synonym for "peddler."

Yet, even if anti-Semitic sentiment could be heard in the North as well as in the South during the war, it came as more of a surprise to southern Jews precisely because anti-Semitic rhetoric had been far less common in the antebellum South than in the North. Attacks on Catholics, foreigners, and Jews were a staple of northern journalism in the period before the Civil War. In the South, by contrast, Jews had been mostly spared criticism.

The Jews had thought southern society accepted them and were therefore shocked to discover what their neighbors really thought of them as the decline and the fall of the Confederacy unleashed a wave of popular anti-Semitism. During this period, some Jewish families, for example, the Straus family that founded Macy's, left the South to escape the anti-Jewish sentiments of their neighbors.[27] The Straus family had owned a store in Talbotton, one of the towns where Jews had come under attack. In the Old South, Jews had become allies of the planter aristocracy and through planter patronage had become governors, senators, members of Congress, judges, and state legislators. Jews would soon find themselves locked out of these positions and others in the post-Reconstruction South. During the 140 or so years between Reconstruction and 2008, the states of the former Confederacy produced one Jewish senator, no Jewish governors, and, outside the Florida coastal enclaves populated by Jewish retirees, only five members of Congress. The defeat of the southern planter aristocracy was good for the nation but not so good for southern Jews.

Jews in the Gilded Age

Confederate Jews went down to defeat with their slave-owning allies. Anti-Semitism and a loss of patronage had gone with defeat. The post–Civil War

North, however, proved equally inhospitable to Jews as northern Jews were abandoned by their rich northern allies due to a heated anti-Semitic campaign. The period following the Civil War was one of great industrial and commercial growth in the United States. Americans made huge fortunes in banking, railroad construction, and manufacturing. Under the influence of the business wing of the Republican Party, the government strongly supported economic and industrial expansion through railroad land grants and monetary and credit policies. In alliance with their gentile colleagues, German Jewish bankers, financiers, industrialists, and merchants achieved a great deal of economic success and political influence during this period. As we have seen, prominent Jewish entrepreneurs included the Warburgs, the Lewisohns, the Guggenheims, Joseph Seligman, Solomon Loeb, and Jacob Schiff—names synonymous with Gilded Age wealth.

The prominence of these and other Jews among the Gilded Age's captains of industry gave a weapon to two major political forces opposed to the late nineteenth-century economic transformations. The first of these forces consisted of western and southern radical agrarians organized in the Populist Movement. The second included old-stock New England patricians, some associated with the nominally Republican but independent Mugwumps, whose own economic and political importance had waned compared to the new post–Civil War class of industrialists and financiers. Both groups had reason to attack the industrialist regime, and both portrayed the entire ruling stratum of the new industrial order as controlled by Jews.

Populist intellectuals and politicians engaged in an extensive anti-Semitic discourse. For example, William Hope Harvey, a leading Populist intellectual, wrote two of the best-selling books of the late nineteenth century. The thesis of the first, *Coin's Financial School*, was that demonetization of silver—the Populist equivalent of original sin—was part of a plot by the Rothschilds and other Jews to dominate the entire world by obtaining a financial stranglehold. Harvey's second best seller, the novel *A Tale of Two Nations*, concerns a plot by nefarious Jewish financiers to bring about the financial ruin of the United States. A similar theme was developed by *Caesar's Column*, a best seller penned by the Populist intellectual Ignatius Donnelly, author of the preamble to the 1892 national Populist platform. The novel is set in a mythical future in which the United States has fallen into the hands of a small group of greedy and fabulously wealthy financiers, most of whom are Jews. The world, according to the novel's protagonist, has become "semitized."

And it was not only Populist intellectuals who castigated Jews. "One of the most striking things about the Populist convention in St. Louis," wrote an Associated Press reporter, "is the extraordinary hatred of the Jewish race. It is not possible to go into any hotel in the city without hearing the most bitter denunciation of the Jews." Democratic and Populist presidential candidate William Jennings Bryan told Jewish Democrats that the anti-Semitic rhetoric employed by some Populists did not mean an attack on Jews as a race. Jews were, he said, attacked only because they symbolized greed and avarice.[28] This was twisted logic at best, for by attacking Jews, Populists were indicting the entire industrialist order and affirming that their political foes were little better than the Jews with whom they associated.

The second major group to disparage the economic and political transformation of the late nineteenth century consisted of members of the old-stock New England gentry. This American quasi-aristocracy found that its own economic and political fortunes had declined compared to those of the new stratum of industrialists and financiers. For the New England Brahmins, the Jew served as a symbol of the greed and corruption of the new order. By assailing Jews, they attacked the industrialists, financiers, and railroad barons who were displacing them in the nation's economic and political life. This fear found expression in a stream of anti-Semitic writings and speeches on the part of New England's leading public figures and intellectuals during the late nineteenth century.

One of the foremost examples is Henry Adams, grandson of President John Quincy Adams. Adams blamed the failure of his plans to pursue a career of leadership and public service on the thoroughly Jewish character of the new materialistic political order. "In the [present] society of Jews and brokers," he observed in 1893, "I have no place."[29] Henry Adams's brother, Brooks, echoed these same themes. In his 1896 work, *The Law of Civilization and Decay*, Adams sought to show that Jews used their money and financial acumen as instruments of exploitation, domination, and oppression. In the United States, with the help of the Jews, productive industrial capitalism was replaced by parasitic finance capitalism, symbolized by the Jewish usurer.[30]

This became a common theme in the literary and scholarly works of the New England patricians and other upper-class intellectuals.

Like the populists, the patricians made the term *Jew* a synonym for the greed, corruption, and materialism of the new order. And by attacking the Jews, the patricians were also indicting gentile captains of industry who associated with Jews and were, from the patrician perspective, little better than Jews. Jews lacked values and culture and cared only for money, and those who associated with Jews came to think and act like them. For the patricians, the term *Jew* symbolized greed, materialism, and avarice, and *Jew* was interchangeable with the nouveau riche businessman or capitalist.[31]

In response to these efforts by populists and patricians to tarnish them with their Jewish connections, the gentile business classes rid themselves of their erstwhile Jewish associates and instead formed an alliance with the patricians. This feat was done through the creation or reconstitution of social institutions that effectively linked the interests of the old, privileged strata with those of the new moneyed classes. These institutions were *judenrein* in design and served as the basis for a united Anglo-Saxon ruling class. Members of the nation's old-stock patrician stratum had charged that the newly rich businessmen and financiers were greedy, unprincipled, uncouth, and indeed little better than the Jews with whom they associated. The business class responded by offering the patricians a share of their wealth and a renewed sense of importance in exchange for patricians granting them social acceptance and status.

So, by crafting or rebranding certain institutions, patricians and industrialists were brought together. These institutions included private boarding schools, college preparatory schools, summer resorts, country clubs, college fraternities, and private clubs. The new business stratum financed these institutions while the old elite ran them. This period saw the expansion of such New England boarding schools as Exeter and Andover and the founding of Groton, Hotchkiss, Choate, and several others. These schools enrolled and mixed the sons of the new and old rich, teaching them a common set of values and helping create a national ruling class.

While the industrialists found social acceptance, the Jews found rampant anti-Semitism instead, abandoned by their old allies. Subjected to discrimination, Jews were excluded from, or only admitted in sparse numbers to, the best schools and other places. Exclusion of their old Jewish allies was part of the price the new moneyed classes were willing to pay for an alliance with the patricians. Between the 1880s and the first two decades of the twentieth century, Jews were excluded from the resorts, clubs, schools, and universities that became the institutional bases of the new elite coalition. Universities became especially restrictive. Many elite universities closed their doors to Jews until the 1960s, while other elite institutions opened them up only slowly afterward.

This history is relevant to an understanding of contemporary events, and we will return to it in the book's epilogue.

6

Why Are the Jews Still Democrats?

RECENTLY I WAS was a guest on a radio "call-in" program based in Dallas, Texas. One listener called to tell me that having given the matter considerable thought, he had finally come to understand why most Jews were Democrats. "You vote for the Democrats," he declared, "to show the rest of us that you are not as smart as we think you are."

The listener's comments might have offended me, but as he spoke, I remembered a not dissimilar observation, albeit set in a different time and place, made by Hannah Arendt. In the early twentieth century, Arendt wrote that the Jews of Europe, in particular German Jews, were politically naïve and confused. They desperately clung to a particular political party, the *Staatspartei*, showing it "loyalty at any price" as political circumstances rapidly changed and their partisan attachment became irrelevant at best, dangerous at worst.

Though they are among America's wealthiest groups, Jews are also among its most politically liberal and, along with African Americans, are the nation's most reliably Democratic voters. Since 1932, Jews have unfailingly given a plurality of their votes to Democratic presidential candidates. In fact, on only one occasion have Jews delivered just a plurality, rather than an outright majority, of their votes to the Democrats: Jimmy Carter's unsuccessful bid for reelection in 1980. On seven occasions, Democratic presidential candidates received more than 80 percent of the Jewish vote.

Jewish liberalism and the Jews' attachment to the Democratic Party are ascribed by some commentators to the humanistic character of Judaism's religious values and traditions, and by other commentators to a species of political inertia, namely, once Democrats, always Democrats.[1] These explanations, however, are unconvincing. America's Jews have not always been Democrats. Many Jews were Republicans until the 1930s. And, as I have shown elsewhere, Jewish political perspectives and affiliations vary with the times. In some political settings, Jews have managed to overcome their humanistic scruples enough to organize and run such ruthless agencies of coercion and terror as the Soviet-era NKVD.[2] And, though its religious traditions are barely distinguishable from those of America's Jews, Israel's Jewish community, viewing the world through its own geopolitical concerns, would most certainly choose Republican presidents if it could vote in American elections. According to Israeli surveys, majorities of Israelis have rooted for the Republicans in American elections since 2000. In 2012, Israelis favored Republican Mitt Romney over Democrat Barack Obama by a two-to-one margin.[3] Like many Americans, Israelis initially expressed hesitance about Donald Trump, though by 2019 close to three in four Israeli Jews gave Trump a favorable rating, perceiving him to be staunchly pro-Israel.[4]

Kenneth Wald has offered an alternative explanation for Jewish loyalty to the Democrats. Wald argues that Jews will more than likely support the political party that favors separating citizenship and religion.[5] For some Jews this is, to be sure, a critical factor, but it is worth noting that the Democratic Party began to champion separation of church and state only during the 1960s. Jews began supporting the Democrats in overwhelming numbers in the 1930s.

To arrive at a better explanation of Jewish loyalty to the Democratic Party, let us consider the history of the relationship. The current political identification of America's Jewish community dates only from Franklin D. Roosevelt's New Deal. Before Roosevelt, many middle-class Jews, along with such communal leaders as Louis Marshall and Felix Warburg, identified with the Republican Party. Poor and working-class Jews, for their part, were often socialists. Comparatively few Jews supported the Democrats, a political party whose base was in the rural West and the South. Many Jews associated the Democrats with Christian fundamentalism and populism, a political movement whose leaders included, as we know, prominent nativists and anti-Semites. But, whatever their partisan affiliations, during the early years of the twentieth century, America's Jews were in general weak and victims of considerable discrimination in housing, public and private employment, college admissions, and access to hotels, restaurants, and resorts.

During the New Deal era, government policies and the Jewish community's talent to promote them was the starting point for the Jews' climb toward political influence and social acceptance. Impoverished by the Great Depression, millions of Jews had ample reason to support FDR's liberal social and economic agenda. However, over the ensuing decades, even as the Jewish community's influence and affluence increased, the Jews' special concerns and the unique character of the Jewish community's influence in American political life led them to continue supporting liberal causes and the Democratic Party.

The New Deal

When Roosevelt came to power in 1933, much of the nation's established Protestant elite, typically Republican and economically conservative, opposed him. Compelled to seek out alternative sources of talent, the administration turned to Jewish intellectuals and professionals to develop and administer its ambitious agenda of domestic programs. FDR, personally, had mixed feelings about Jews and was rumored to be fond of anti-Semitic humor. However, Jewish attorneys, economists, statisticians, and other talented professionals became critical sources of leadership and talent for the Roosevelt administration. Jewish labor leaders, most notably Sidney Hillman, president of the Amalgamated Clothing Workers of America, played an important role in Roosevelt's political campaigns.[6] More than 15 percent of Roosevelt's top-level appointees were Jews, at a time when Jews constituted barely 3 percent of the nation's populace and were the targets of considerable popular antipathy.[7] Most Jewish appointees were given positions in the new agencies created by the White House to administer New Deal programs. In these agencies, Jews came to constitute a large and highly visible group.

One of Roosevelt's top Jewish advisers was the Harvard law professor and (later) Supreme Court Justice Felix Frankfurter, who played a key role in formulating New Deal programs and in recruiting large numbers of Jewish professionals, known as Frankfurter's "Happy Hot Dogs," to staff New Deal agencies. Among Frankfurter's protégés was Benjamin Cohen, who wrote many important pieces of New Deal legislation. These included the 1933 Securities Act, the Federal Communications Act, the Wagner Act, and the

Minimum Wage Act, all of which remain cornerstones of American public policy. Other Jews who became prominent figures in the Roosevelt administration were Supreme Court Justice Louis Brandeis, who recommended ways of securing the Court's approval for these legislative enactments; Treasury Secretary Henry Morgenthau Jr.; and Securities and Exchange Commission Chairman Jerome Frank. And one of Roosevelt's Jewish senior advisers, Samuel Rosenman, coined the term *New Deal* itself.[8]

Such was the importance of Jews in FDR's camp that his opponents sometimes denounced the New Deal as the *Jew Deal* and claimed, falsely, that Roosevelt himself must be of Jewish descent. Service with New Deal agencies gave Jewish professionals a considerable measure of political influence and provided them with experience and contacts that were invaluable in the private sector. Corporations and firms that had engaged in discriminatory hiring practices before the New Deal began to open their doors, albeit slowly, to Jewish attorneys and other professionals, thus beginning the fuller integration of Jews into American society. Roosevelt, for his part, was happy to take full advantage of this pool of underemployed talent to develop ideas and programs and to staff his agencies. By the end of FDR's first term in office most of America's Jews had given the president and his party their full allegiance.

Anti-Semitism and the "Jew Deal"

Their importance to the New Deal and to the Democratic Party made Jews the targets of severe anti-Semitic attacks during the 1930s. In the 1930s, the economic hardships and social dislocations occasioned by the Great Depression were conducive to the rise of nativism, while New Deal social and economic programs enraged segments of the business community. Enemies of the regime saw anti-Semitism as a useful instrument through which to unite FDR's various opponents. Foes of the New Deal looked to discredit the administration by variously claiming that Roosevelt was a tool of Jewish Communists, Jewish bankers, or, curiously, both.

In upper-class circles, anti-Semitic rhetoric was commonplace. Frank Buxton, editor of the *Boston Herald*, wrote in 1934: "Substantial men sympathized with the anti-Semitism. I was amazed at the intensity with which highly intelligent men argued that the Jews were controlling the president."[9] This view was echoed the following year by the editors of *Fortune*, who averred that "Jew-baiting hysteria in anti-New Deal circles was common."[10] More than a hundred anti-Semitic organizations were formed between 1933 and 1941, and according to a 1936 *Fortune* survey, approximately a half million Americans at least occasionally attended anti-Semitic rallies or meetings.[11] Upper-class opponents of the Roosevelt administration were unwilling to be publicly associated with unseemly anti-Semitic rabble-rousing and preferred to make quiet contributions to groups like the Liberty League that, in turn, supported anti-Semitic agitators like Edward Edmondson, the radical populist radio priest Father Charles Coughlin, and William Pelley. Pelley, leader of the "Silver Shirts," ranted to his followers that Roosevelt and his top aides were Jews who had now taken over the country.

At the same time, isolationist and pro-German groups used anti-Semitic appeals to discredit the administration's efforts to pursue a more activist and pro-British foreign policy and to enhance American military preparedness. These included the America First Committee and such prominent Americans as Charles Lindbergh. Decades later, Donald Trump's use of the slogan "America First" raised eyebrows, but if Trump was even aware of the slogan's history, he had an agenda different from that of the original committee. As for Lindbergh, the famous aviator was an ardent admirer of Nazi Germany. Lindbergh warned in a 1940 speech, "Instead of agitating for war the Jewish groups in this country should be opposing it in every way, for they will be among the first to feel its consequences ... . A few farsighted Jewish people realize this and stand opposed to intervention. But the majority still do not. The greatest danger to this country lies in their large ownership and influence in our motion pictures, our press, our radio and our government."[12] In a later speech Lindbergh declared, "The three most important groups who have been pressing this country to war are the British, the Jewish and the Roosevelt administration."[13] Among other prominent anti-Semites of this era were isolationist senators Burton Wheeler and Gerald Nye and, of course, Ambassador Joseph P. Kennedy, who warned Jewish filmmakers to stop producing anti-Nazi films lest they offend their non-Jewish neighbors.[14] Wheeler declared that Roosevelt's Lend-Lease program for Britain had been promoted by "international bankers."

The virulence of anti-Semitism in the 1930s made American Jews feel even more dependent on and supportive of the Roosevelt White House. For his part, though, the president was leery of being identified too closely with Jews. FDR asked his Jewish advisers to keep a low profile, while keeping a careful distance himself from specifically Jewish causes, such as German persecution of the Jews under Nazi rule. In fact, Roosevelt had shown little interest in intervening against the persecution of European Jews in the 1930s, fearing that many might seek to come to the US.[15]

America's Jews, however, discovered that they had another set of allies. A large segment of the American upper class, particularly the northeastern Protestant establishment from which the president himself came, was strongly Anglophile, based on social and economic ties. As the German threat to Britain increased during the late 1930s, members of the eastern establishment found in the Jewish community the only consistent and reliable American ally for the British cause. Indeed, Jews and upper-class northeastern Protestants (along with Poles after 1939) were the two groups in American society that most vehemently opposed Germany and supported England at a time when large segments of the American public, including Americans of German, Italian, Irish, and Scandinavian descent, either supported Germany, opposed England, or were determinedly neutral.

So out of necessity, the eastern Protestant establishment, which had little true love for Jews and had, in fact, created the "exclusive" institutions at the turn of the century to exclude all but a handful of Jews from polite society, allied itself with them to work on behalf of Britain and against Germany. In the late 1930s, Jews and members of the eastern establishment formed the Century Group to work vigorously to promote American intervention against Nazi Germany. Jewish members of the group included the financier James Warburg, the film producer Walter Wanger, and the publisher Harold Guinzburg. Emblematic of the eastern establishment were the journalist Joseph Alsop, the diplomat Frank Polk, and the prominent attorneys and public servants Dean Acheson and Allen W. Dulles. Joining them later were other eastern establishment pillars, Grenville Clark, Sinclair Weeks, and the Episcopal bishop Henry Hobson. Subsequently, the same alliance produced the Fight for Freedom Committee, which worked to mobilize public opinion against Germany and to discredit isolationist, pro-German, and anti-Semitic groups.[16]

The Japanese attack on Pearl Harbor and America's entry into World War II discredited for a time anti-Semitic activity, which became associated with the enemy, Nazi Germany. The Roosevelt administration was freed therefore to take decisive action against anti-Semitic and pro-German groups in the United States through indictments, arrests, prison sentences, and deportations. Conscious of widespread anti-Semitism in the nation, Roosevelt was still careful not to appear too closely tied to Jews, refusing, for example, to bomb the rail lines leading to Auschwitz. Nevertheless, during the war years and in the war's immediate aftermath, even with Roosevelt's death, Jews continued to play important roles in the Democratic Party and the national government.

The Postwar Period

If America's Jewish community thought that anti-Semitism had ended with the defeat of Nazi Germany, they made a mistake. Not long after America's victory over Germany and Japan, a struggle for control of the Democratic Party led to the reemergence of an anti-Semitic discourse in the national political arena. Southern and conservative Democrats saw Roosevelt's death as an opportunity to reassert their own power within the Democratic Party at the expense of the labor leaders and liberal intellectuals who had become important political figures in the Roosevelt administration. Conservative and Southern Democrats were able to seize control of the House Un-American Activities Committee (HUAC), originally set up to investigate Nazis, and used it to investigate and smear their foes in the liberal and labor union wings of the Democratic Party by associating them with Communism.

Many of those accused of Communist sympathies were Jews. Soviet espionage in the US was, to be sure, a major problem before and during the war and in the postwar period. Some of the Jews investigated by HUAC, including the famous "Hollywood Ten," had been Communist Party members. Many other Jewish actors, writers, and intellectuals were simply victims of the fact that HUAC investigators knew that the gentile public would be ready to believe charges of Communism leveled at Jews. Often HUAC hearings seemed designed to embarrass prominent Jews, especially those who had anglicized their names or otherwise disguised their ethnic identities. For example, during

HUAC's probe of alleged Communist infiltration of the motion picture industry, Mississippi congressman John Rankin seemed to take great delight in revealing that several of the Hollywood stars with American-sounding names, who had signed a petition attacking HUAC, were Jews. One signature on the petition was June Havoc. "We found out," said Rankin, "that her real name is June Hovick." "There is one who calls himself Edward G. Robinson. His real name is Emmanuel Goldenberg." HUAC investigators declared Jewish writers and producers who had cooperated with the Roosevelt administration's anti-Nazi films in the late 1930s to have been "prematurely anti-Fascist" and hence possibly Communists.[17]

Jews responded to these attacks by distancing themselves from Communists or anyone with leftist sympathies and disciplining leftists in their own ranks. Jewish film producers, for example, fired and blacklisted writers, actors, and producers known to have leftist views. A variety of Jewish organizations such as the American Jewish Committee (AJC) and organizations in which Jews were influential, such as the American Civil Liberties Union (ACLU), cooperated vigorously with government investigators to prove the Jewish community's loyalty to America and aversion to Communism. Throughout the late 1940s and early 1950s, the ACLU took great pains to assert that no free-speech issues were at stake in the conviction of individuals for teaching or advocating Communism, and the AJC mounted a major public relations campaign to show that Jews were 100 percent American.

A renewal of the prewar alliance between Jews and the northeastern Protestant establishment also bolstered the Jewish community efforts to combat postwar anti-Semitism. As they had in the 1930s, Jews and northeastern Protestants found themselves facing a common set of enemies. Like the Jews, segments of the anti-Nazi Protestant establishment were under attack in the postwar period nominally for having been too tolerant of the Communist threat to America's security. The name most associated with this attack is that of Senator Joseph McCarthy, and, indeed, the term *McCarthyism* has become a synonym for political inquisition or witch hunt. In general, the McCarthyites represented midwestern Republicans and so-called national capital—that is, small business as well as domestic manufacturing industries whose orientation was the American rather than the world market. This GOP wing, led by Senator Robert Taft of Ohio, directed its animus toward its eastern establishment rivals within the Republican Party—rivals who, in Taft's view, had betrayed Republicanism by cooperating with the New Deal.

Because the upper-class, high-church Episcopalian foes of the midwesterners were unidentified culturally with Jews and had anti-Semitic traditions themselves, the McCarthyites found no particular use for anti-Semitism as a political weapon. Indeed, several of McCarthy's most important aides, such as Roy Cohn and David Schine, were Jews. McCarthy's targets mostly consisted of such pillars of the Protestant establishment as the British American secretary of state Dean Acheson. McCarthy characterized the secretary as the leader of the treasonous "Acheson gang," which had sheltered a spy, Alger Hiss, and had sold out American interests to the Soviet Union at the February 1945 Yalta Conference.

After Senator Taft's defeat in the 1952 Republican convention and Dwight D. Eisenhower's victory in the general election, the eastern establishment closed ranks against McCarthy and other right-wing opponents and, seeking allies, linked itself once again with the Jewish community, which was also eager to bring an end to the anticommunist campaign. Using the institutions in which one or both groups were influential—the media, the foundations, the universities, the courts, and public-interest groups—Protestant and Jewish opponents of the various anticommunist crusaders joined forces to charge them with violating civil liberties and "chilling" free speech.

Major news organizations such as CBS, a corporation owned by Jews and staffed by distinguished-looking Protestants like Edward R. Murrow, whose March 1954 episode of the *See It Now* series was instrumental in discrediting McCarthy, played a vital role. The ACLU, whose executive board was a Jewish-Protestant alliance, began vigorously to defend the victims of HUAC and the Hollywood blacklists as well as individuals prosecuted for refusing to take loyalty oaths. The Ford Foundation, an establishment bastion, sponsored books and articles defending civil liberties and presented awards to individuals who had fought against the anticommunist crusaders.[18]

The Jewish-Protestant alliance also used its influence over the national media to deprive its opponents, including anti-Semites, of access to print pages and airtime while securing and publicizing information that eventually sent several anticommunist crusaders, including onetime HUAC chairman J. Parnell Thomas (R-NJ), to prison for financial and other misdeeds. Together, Jews and eastern establishment Protestants were sufficiently powerful to declare that anti-Semitic commentary and charges of Communist ties "smacked of McCarthyism" and automatically considered beyond the pale of the politically permissible. From the late 1950s on, conservatives who sought to keep respectability avoided the least hint of anti-Semitism in their literature and broadcasts. The late William F. Buckley Jr. is an example of a prominent conservative author and pundit who warned his colleagues on the political Right to eschew anti-Semitic commentary.

Civil Rights, the New Frontier, and the Great Society

Beginning with the New Deal, Jews were assailed by anti–New Deal, pro-German, and isolationist forces and attacked politically. In the 1960s, though, in alliance with northeastern Protestants, Jews were able to take the offensive against their foes. The political instruments through which Jews looked to turn the tables on their adversaries were the civil rights movement, John F. Kennedy's New Frontier, and Lyndon Johnson's Great Society.

The administrations of Kennedy and Johnson solidified the loyalty of Jews to the Democratic Party, while traditionally GOP northeastern Protestants also migrated to the Democratic camp. Despite Eisenhower's 1952 victory over Taft, by 1960 the GOP had again come under the control of its midwestern wing, which represented small business and national capital. Now, led by politicians like Senator Barry Goldwater of Arizona, the GOP sought a return to a pre–New Deal era of small government and limited international engagement. The northeastern establishment, on the other hand, had accepted the New Deal and was internationalist in outlook and economic interest. The northeastern establishment's financial interests lay in such realms as international trade and financial services, and as a result it favored a party that would actively manage the domestic economy and vigorously promote America's postwar economic and political interests around the world. Because these goals overlapped with those of the Jewish community, the two groups had ample reason to make common cause within the Democratic Party under the rubric of an ideology of government activism and liberal internationalism.

The two groups reached accommodations in other areas as well. The Jews accepted the leadership of establishment Protestant politicians and provided them with financial and other support. The establishment Protestants, for their part, helped Jews bring an end to compulsory school prayer and other forms of public-supported religious expression that Jews found objectionable. Establishment Protestants also helped excluded Jews gain access to the universities and other institutions. At Yale, for example, President Whitney Griswold, together with Provost (later President) Kingman Brewster Jr. and Chaplain William Sloane Coffin, worked to open the admissions process and positions on the faculty and in the senior administrative ranks to talented Jews in the early 1960s.

Liberal Protestants in the academic world also gained from this relationship. Their alliance with Jews helped liberal Protestants free universities from subservience to their business-dominated boards and gave them access to the financial support of the federal government and foundations in the expanding grants economy, where Jews had considerable influence. Subsequently, Jews and liberal Protestants worked together to open elite universities to African Americans. Jewish leaders were even prepared to support quota systems (which Jews had historically opposed), such as affirmative action for black students, on the theory that Jews would have no difficulty winning more than their proportionate share of the remaining slots. Jews believed that by guaranteeing admission to blacks, they were also ensuring that they would not be excluded again either.

So, working together in the 1960s, Jews and the newly reformed liberal Protestants, along with a smaller number of liberal Catholics, gave their support to the civil rights movement and to the New Frontier and Great Society programs of the Kennedy and Johnson years. For Jews and northeastern liberal Protestants, support for civil rights was not only a moral commitment but also an important political tactic. By allying themselves with African Americans, enfranchising black voters, and delegitimating southern white state and local governments, Jews and other liberals hoped to undermine the power of the same forces that had accused them of disloyalty and subjected them to anticommunist witch hunts in the decades just after World War II. For Jews, gains achieved on behalf of blacks certainly promised to serve their own interest in ending discrimination. But there was another long-standing reason: Jews had been suspicious of conservative southerners at least since the 1913 Leo Frank case and were happy to reduce their influence in American politics.

As mentioned in the previous chapter, Jews served as major financiers and strategists for the civil rights movement, working closely with civil rights leaders in their struggle for voting rights, for the desegregation of public facilities and accommodations, and against employment discrimination. Jewish contributors targeted a large share of the funding for such civil rights groups as the National Association for the Advancement of Colored People (NAACP) and Congress of Racial Equality (CORE). Jewish attorneys were also in the forefront and on the front lines of the legal offensive against the American apartheid system. Jews, along with liberal Protestants, took part in civil rights marches and protests in the South throughout the 1960s, risking their lives.

In the mid-1960s, as the civil rights movement expanded its campaign to the North, liberals seized the opportunity to attack and weaken their opponents north of the Mason-Dixon line as well. Jews and liberal Protestants charged the northern Democratic Party's coalition of machine politicians and labor leaders with racism, worked to deny them representation at Democratic National Conventions, and looked to cut off their access to federal patronage. In this way, Jews and other liberals used the civil rights movement to enhance their influence over the Democratic Party in the North in addition to eroding the power of southern conservatives.

Similar considerations also underlay liberal support for the domestic social programs of the Kennedy and Johnson periods. In design, many of these programs undercut local political arrangements and expanded the power of federal agencies over local governments. This would weaken the power of local politicians and labor leaders while strengthening the federal government, where liberals exercised more influence. The presidential task forces that typically drafted New Frontier and Great Society programs notably averred that local governments did not command the resources, talent, or initiative to solve the so-called urban crisis, and those local bureaucracies were especially insensitive and unresponsive to the black community. The answer to the problem, some said, was an expansion of the federal government's efforts.

Jews played a leading role in this process. Though John F. Kennedy was a Catholic, his background, aspirations, and friendships led him to look mostly toward the eastern Protestant establishment for administrators and advisers. Thus his cabinet included individuals like Douglas Dillon and other pillars of the financial community. Kennedy, however, also saw himself as a reformer who would bring innovative programs and policies—indeed, a "New Frontier"—to America. For this purpose, the eastern establishment, rich and dedicated to the status quo, was not notably innovative. To further innovative programs, ideas, and policies, Kennedy turned to the Jews, a talented pool of proven administrators and reformers not part of the establishment.

Jews figured prominently among Kennedy's staffers, speechwriters, and "idea men." Thus, for example, right after his election, Kennedy created several task forces to develop innovative ideas and initiatives in domestic and foreign policy. Several Jews, including Paul Samuelson, E. M. Bernstein, and Robert Nathan, played important roles in these groups. Milton Semer and Morton Schussheim were significant housing policy advocates. Later, Arthur Goldberg served as secretary of labor before his appointment to the Supreme Court. Wilbur Cohen and Abraham Ribicoff both served as secretaries of the (then called) Health, Education, and Welfare department (HEW). Richard Goodwin and Meyer Feldman served as White House special assistants. Goodwin had been a law clerk for Felix Frankfurter and had responsibility for Kennedy's Alliance for Progress speech, which launched the Peace Corps. Walt Rostow served as a major foreign policy adviser. Adam Walinsky became Robert Kennedy's closest adviser, and Adam Yarmolinsky became Sargent Shriver's chief aide.

Jews continued to play major roles in the Johnson administration after Kennedy's assassination. Abe Fortas was Johnson's closest adviser and continued in that role even after his appointment to the Supreme Court. Rostow was Johnson's national security assistant. Johnson was eager to innovate and to make his mark too, and Jews were the idea men for LBJ as they had been for Kennedy. Yarmolinsky, for example, was a chief architect of Johnson's Great Society programs, particularly Legal Services and the Job Corps. Cohen was among the designers of the Elementary and Secondary Education Act of 1965. Large numbers of Jewish academics and intellectuals served on the task forces and study commissions that developed other Great Society programs.

Both Kennedy and Johnson believed that the established government agencies and federal civil service employees were often too rigid and inefficient to implement innovative programs. Hence both administrations greatly expanded the practice of contracting out government services to private entities, a practice that had begun after World War II.[19] Some of the same idea men who served the administration in official capacities moved into what became a rapidly expanding quasi-governmental sector where they built new foundations, think tanks, institutes, study commissions, and a host of agencies that sought government grants and contracts to study problems and provide government services. Today, of course, tens of billions of dollars in government contracts support a workforce of federal contractors and grantees who hugely outnumber the members of the official federal workforce.

The Vietnam War and the New Politics Movement

By the late 1960s, however, Jews and other liberals had broken with President Johnson over the Vietnam War. Many liberals were genuinely outraged by what they saw as the senseless carnage of Vietnam. At the same time, the war's enormous cost, which relentlessly drained resources from domestic programs, angered them. From the perspective of Democratic liberals, the war was undermining the programs and institutions to which they were committed and that constituted their unique base of power.

Jews had a stake in domestic institutions, programs, and expenditures. They had risen to positions of power and prominence through their roles in the public and quasi-public institutions of the domestic state—social service agencies, universities, think tanks, federal agencies, and the growing constellation of government contractors. These institutions, in turn, depended on higher levels of domestic social spending, now threatened by the war. As a result, Jews were far more likely than members of other groups to oppose the war and become involved in the antiwar movement that forced Johnson from office and, later, compelled the Nixon administration to negotiate an end to the war, early in the president's second term.

While in the White House, President Richard Nixon appointed conservative Republicans to positions of power in domestic agencies and looked to reorganize government agencies in ways that would reduce liberals' influence over them, controversially impounding, for example, funds that congressional liberals appropriated for domestic social purposes. The administration also looked to attack the quasi-public components of the domestic state through such means as using the Internal Revenue Service to investigate the tax-exempt status of liberal foundations. These actions set the stage for the great struggle that led to Nixon's ouster from office.

With their special stake in domestic programs and spending, several Jews played important roles in mobilizing opposition against the Nixon administration. Indeed, the testimony of White House counsel John Dean during the congressional Watergate hearings revealed that Jews constituted more than one-third of the administration's major critics on Nixon's infamous "enemies list."[20] The White House was so aware of the prominence of Jews and Jewish organizations among its opponents that it was suspicious even of GOP Jews.

Opponents of the Nixon administration were able to rely on the support of an important institution in which Jews played key roles: the news media. During the 1960s, the national television networks, which Jewish entrepreneurs had created, became increasingly important in American journalism. Mostly for commercial reasons, the networks had expanded their news and public affairs coverage and increasingly played a leading role in American politics.

In the 1930s and 1940s, and even as recently as the 1950s, the national news media were considered a conservative force in American politics. During the Vietnam War, however, the networks, along with elite newspapers, upon which Jews also had considerable influence—most significantly at the *New York Times* and the *Washington Post*—discovered there was a substantial middle- and upper-middle-class audience for investigative reporting and critical coverage of government policies. These segments of the media were able to enhance their own power, status, and autonomy in American politics by abandoning their traditionally respectful coverage of the White House and turning to a posture of criticism and opposition. Television and print journalists could count on their liberal audience to come to their defense when they came under presidential attack.[21] This alliance between segments of the media and liberal forces, of course, played a key role in the struggle that eventually drove Nixon from office.

Therefore, during the 1960s and 1970s, because of a convergence of interests, the elite media became linked to the liberal political camp. Subsequently, these media gave their support to a new set of institutions and organizations, calling themselves "public-interest" groups, organized by liberal political forces. The alliance between the media and the public-interest movement became an important force in American politics during the 1970s and is still important today. The influence of Jews in both the media and the public-interest movement significantly enhanced the importance of Jews in the Democratic Party and the American government in general.

The Public-Interest Movement

In the wake of Nixon's resignation, Jews along with liberal Protestants were prominent among the political activists who worked to solidify liberal control over the Democratic Party as well as to strengthen and expand the domestic state to which liberal Democrats were associated. The mechanism through which these goals were achieved had been through the activities of a host of public-interest groups created to promote the goals of what was then called the "new politics"—environmentalism, consumerism, feminism, and the like. During the first phase of the public-interest movement in the 1970s, some two hundred public-interest groups were created, and more than one hundred public-interest law firms organized to protect them. In addition, major liberal funding agencies, such as the Ford Foundation, provided these groups with tens of millions of dollars in support. The elite media, for their part, mostly supported such groups and seldom questioned their claim to speak for the "public interest."

The public-interest movement served a mix of purposes. On the one hand, liberals strongly supported such goals as affirmative action, equal rights for women, protection for the environment, consumer safety, and, later, gay rights. At the same time, through the public-interest movement, liberal forces worked to win control of the Democratic Party (and through it the government), to reorder national priorities to increase the flow of funds into agencies and programs they controlled that served their constituents, and to expand the federal government's penetration of society. To this end, liberals developed a domestic agenda consisting of political reform, affirmative action, diminution of military spending, and expansion of the government's regulatory efforts.

Jews played a key role in all these endeavors; they served as leaders of the public-interest movement and, through it, enhanced their political influence significantly. Beginning in the 1970s, Jews led or were influential in the new politics and related activities. Jews continue to play important roles in a diverse group of liberal political and public-interest organizations such as

Common Cause, People for the American Way, the Children's Defense Fund, the Women's Legal Defense and Education Fund, and hundreds of others.

The importance of liberal activist groups within the Democratic coalition waxed as the strength of other Democratic entities waned. Economic change undermined the power of organized labor, for decades an important force within the party. By the 1970s, moreover, old-fashioned political party "machines" had all but disappeared in the United States. Candidates for office now relied on ad hoc regiments of volunteers rather than the old-time phalanxes of party workers to staff their campaigns. Increasingly, the public-interest movement became the spearhead of the Democratic Party's political army, supplying the activists and workers needed for campaign efforts. As the most active of liberal activists, and a key element in the leadership cadre of the public-interest movement, Jews became increasingly important in Democratic Party politics.

The political weight of these activist groups had been enhanced further by the various political reforms they themselves helped bring about during the 1970s. Changes in the presidential nominating process, starting with the so-called McGovern-Fraser reforms that took effect in 1972, gave issue-oriented activists an important voice in the presidential selection process. Citizen lawsuit provisions, included in hundreds of federal regulatory statutes enacted since the 1970s, allowed activist groups to use the courts to press their agendas in such areas as environmental protection, consumer affairs, and civil rights.

Crucial was a series of changes in campaign finance rules, which made activist groups important conduits for campaign funds, particularly for Democratic Party candidates who were not as able as their Republican rivals to depend on the largesse of America's business corporations. The most recent reform of campaign finance laws, the 2002 Bipartisan Campaign Reform Act (BCRA), outlawed the so-called soft-money contributions to political parties that had been a major vehicle for funneling corporate money into political campaigns. But while BCRA prohibited soft-money contributions, the law and several Supreme Court decisions allow nonprofit groups and independent "Super PACs" considerable latitude to spend money on political campaigns. A nonprofit organized under Section 501(c)(4) of the tax code may spend up to 50 percent of its budget on political activities without showing any information on the sources of its funds or naming the recipients. Political advocacy groups may also form Super PACs under Section 527 of the tax code, which gives them the ability to raise and spend unlimited amounts of money for political drives—though 527s must report the sources and recipients.

These provisions were quite helpful to liberal activist groups, which quickly formed 527 committees that soon directed tens of millions of dollars into Democratic political efforts. Wealthy Jewish liberals have long been among the most important contributors to the Democratic Party's efforts, supplying a significant share of the money spent by Democrats in national elections, and Jewish political activists quickly assumed leadership roles in many of the groups, such as Priorities USA, which raised and spent hundreds of millions of dollars in support of Democratic candidates in recent national, state, and local elections. In 2016, Priorities USA, whose chief donors are wealthy Jewish entrepreneurs, spent close to $200 million on behalf of Democratic candidates and in 2020 spent as much as twice that amount—more than any other political committee—to defeat Donald Trump and elect Democrats to a variety of national and state offices. Jews, of course, also donate money to the Republicans—indeed, the GOP's single largest donor is a Jew—but even a casual glance through the list of major political contributors in 2020 shows the continuing loyalty of Jews to the Democratic Party.

As Jews became more important within the Democratic Party, they increasingly looked for and won both elections and appointments to high national office under Democratic auspices. Before the New Deal, only six Jews had ever served in the US Senate and only one had ever been a member of a presidential cabinet: Oscar Straus, who served as Theodore Roosevelt's commerce secretary. Today, Jews commonly hold high national office nearly always as Democrats. In the 117th Congress (2021–23), for example, nine Jews served in the US Senate. Eight of the nine were Democrats, and one other, Bernie Sanders, was an independent who caucused with the Democrats. During the same Congress, twenty-five Jews held seats in the US House of Representatives. Only two were Republicans. Also, in 2020, two Jews sat on the Supreme Court, both appointed by Democratic presidents. In a similar vein, no Jews served as cabinet secretaries in the Republican administrations of George H. W. Bush or Ronald Reagan, though two served in George W. Bush's cabinet. Indeed, since the GOP's founding, only six Jews have ever been members of Republican cabinets. In addition to Oscar Straus, they were

Eisenhower's commerce secretary, Lewis Strauss; Nixon's secretary of state, Henry Kissinger; Gerald Ford's attorney general, Edward Levi; and George W. Bush's attorney general, Michael Mukasey, and his homeland security secretary, Michael Chertoff. The only Jew appointed to Donald Trump's cabinet was Treasury Secretary Steven Mnuchin.

By contrast, Democrat Jimmy Carter appointed four Jewish cabinet secretaries, and Bill Clinton appointed five. The Carter appointees were Treasury Secretary W. Michael Blumenthal, Defense Secretary Harold Brown, Transportation Secretary Neil Goldschmidt, and Commerce Secretary Philip Klutznick. Clinton named Labor Secretary Robert Reich, Treasury Secretaries Robert Rubin and Lawrence Summers, Agriculture Secretary Dan Glickman, and Commerce Secretary Mickey Kantor. In addition, Clinton's national security adviser was Samuel Berger, and his most important diplomat was Richard Holbrooke. Even two of the nominal gentiles in Clinton's cabinet, Defense Secretary William Cohen and Secretary of State Madeleine Albright, were Jews, or half Jewish in Cohen's case. Barack Obama named two Jews to his cabinet, Commerce Secretary Penny Pritzker and Treasury Secretary Jack Lew. Obama also appointed many Jews to senior White House positions. Mary Schapiro chaired the SEC; Janet Yellin headed the Fed (replacing Ben Bernanke); David Axelrod became senior adviser to the president; Rahm Emanuel became Obama's chief of staff; Lawrence Summers became director of the National Economic Council; Peter Orszag became director of the Office of Management and Budget; and Elena Kagan became solicitor general of the United States (and then associate justice of the Supreme Court). The list continues today. Joe Biden nominated several prominent Jews to key positions. These included Anthony Blinken (secretary of state), Janet Yellin (secretary of the treasury), Alejandro Mayorkas (secretary of homeland security), and Merrick Garland (attorney general). Biden also named Ronald Klain as his chief of staff.

This pattern of presidential appointments reflects the importance of Jews in the Democratic coalition rather than any recent presidents' personal feelings about them. Thus Carter, who was not especially friendly to the state of Israel and did not have good relations with the American Jewish community, appointed many Jews to his cabinet, while Ronald Reagan and George W. Bush, staunch supporters of Israel and friends of the American Jewish community, appointed none. Donald Trump, for his part, appointed only one Jew to his cabinet (Mnuchin), though several of his senior advisers were Jewish, including his daughter and son-in-law.

Thus, since the New Deal launched the Jewish community on the path of political influence, Jews have risen to positions of considerable political prominence. That they have done so under Democratic Party auspices helps explain the continuing loyalty of the Jewish community to the Democrats. Most Jews believe that to abandon the Democratic Party would be to abandon the institution that continues to provide American Jews with access to political power and position.

Power and Policy

While there are many areas of disagreement within the Jewish community, Jews have made use of their positions of influence to promote policies to end racial and ethnic discrimination, strengthen the separation of church and state, expand domestic social programs, and bolster American support for the state of Israel. During the 1930s and 1940s, when Jews first won access to policy-making institutions, the chief goal of Jewish political leaders was to bring an end to discriminatory practices toward Jews. To this end, in 1944, several major Jewish organizations, including the American Jewish Committee, the American Jewish Congress, and the Anti-Defamation League, joined together to form the National Jewish Community Relations Advisory Council (CRC) to combat discrimination against Jews in employment, education, and housing. The CRC succeeded in persuading several state legislatures to enact laws prohibiting housing and employment discrimination and, in 1965, convinced President Lyndon Johnson to issue an executive order prohibiting firms holding federal contracts from discrimination based on religion or race. Johnson later expanded the scope of his order to include banks holding federal funds and insurance companies serving as Medicare carriers.

Jews were also at the forefront of the effort to reinforce America's constitutional separation of church and state. As a religious minority, Jews felt threatened by government-sponsored prayer in the public schools and the display of religious symbols in public places. So Jewish organizations backed a campaign of litigation aimed at ending both practices. Often Jewish groups worked from behind the scenes for fear of provoking anti-Semitism. For example, the heavily Jewish ACLU found non-Jewish plaintiffs and attorneys for its eventually successful effort in the case of *Zorach v. Clauson* to have the courts strike down a New York state law providing for released time from school for religious instruction.

Jewish organizations made an especially concerted effort to ban ethnic discrimination in the realm of education. After World War I, major American colleges and universities had imposed strict quotas on the admission of Jews to their undergraduate and professional programs. As a result, the proportion of Jewish students at such prestigious institutions as the Harvard Medical School and Columbia's College of Physicians and Surgeons fell from more than one-third of the class to barely 5 percent of each school's student body. Similarly, major institutions refused to hire Jewish faculty and administrators. Jewish organizations used their growing influence to launch two federal investigations of discriminatory practices by universities. These investigations, coupled with a series of lawsuits, forced colleges and universities to dismantle their quota systems in the early 1960s.

Jews' political alliances also help explain another major focus of Jewish political efforts: the expansion of domestic social programs. During the 1930s, many Jews were poor and supported the New Deal agenda of social programs as a matter of necessity. As Jews have become increasingly affluent, they have nevertheless continued to back government-sponsored housing, employment, pension, and healthcare programs. Part of the reason that one of the nation's most affluent communities supports programs designed to help the poor is that the Democratic political coalition in which the Jews play such a prominent role includes large numbers of minority and poor Americans. For the Jews, preserving the organizational coherence and power of the Democratic Party is an important end, and domestic social programs are an important means to that end.

Finally, Jews have used their influence in American politics to sustain American support for the security of the state of Israel. In the post–World War II period, the Jewish community was able to induce President Harry S. Truman to support the creation of a Jewish state despite the opposition of the State Department and America's most important ally, Great Britain. Over the ensuing decades, the efforts of such Jewish groups as the American Israel Public Affairs Committee (AIPAC) have helped keep a steady flow of

American military and economic aid for Israel, even as reluctance to offend Arab oil producers and their own Arab residents impelled other Western nations to distance themselves from the Jewish state.

Always Liberal?

This historical background and the ongoing relationship between Jews and the national government help explain the continuing adherence of the Jewish community to liberalism and the Democratic Party. Beginning in the 1930s, Jews became members of a political coalition organized by the Democrats around a liberal social and economic agenda.

This coalition expanded significantly the American domestic state, providing the Jews with opportunities not fully available to them in the private sector. Jews gained access to prominent positions in the public or quasi-public government sector, helping professions, private foundations, think tanks, and universities. These institutional affiliations gave Jews a stake in the liberal ideologies that, among other things, offer a justification for the power of such institutions. These institutional affiliations also strengthened the Jewish community's attachment to the Democrats—the party that defends the interests of the public and quasi-public sectors.

Over the past several decades, of course, private-sector opportunities have become more available to Jews than in the past, and many more Jews find employment and opportunity throughout the private economy. Indeed, unlike the situation in the middle of the twentieth century, jobs in federal or state agencies, or in local school systems, attract few Jews today. The shift of Jews from the public to the private sector, however, has not been sufficient to undermine Jewish support for an active and expansive domestic state and hence has not dramatically reduced Jews' commitment to the Democrats. Many Jews who entered the private sector did so with considerable personal or family experience in the public or quasi-public sector or found jobs because of their experience and contacts in government. For such individuals, a large and active domestic state was a useful instrument worth cultivating, not a fearful threat kept at bay.

More important, many of the private industries in which Jews are particularly prominent are precisely those that rely heavily on the protection and intervention of the federal government. Two important examples are the national media and the financial services industry. The media rely on the national government's protection from the private tort system and from state and local regulation and rely on the government to safeguard their intellectual property, both nationally and internationally, while the financial services industry is enveloped in a web of federal policies governing interest rates, lending practices, the money supply, and the like. It is so dependent on an active and expansive economic policy and the government's guarantees to depositors and investors that financial services are a quasi-private rather than a truly private-sector industry. Their involvement in these "private"-sector industries is hardly likely to persuade the Jews that their longtime commitment to economic and international liberalism is no longer relevant.

The benefits Jews derive from membership in the liberal Democratic coalition help explain why Jews, particularly the leaders and most influential spokespersons of the Jewish community, continue to support liberalism and the Democrats. Jews stay liberal Democrats because liberal democracy has protected them from their enemies and serves as the source of their power and place in American society.

Many Jews, moreover, have internalized these attachments to the point that identification with the Democratic Party is reflexive and not affected too much by the political events of the day. For these Jews, loyalty to the Democrats outweighs the anti-Zionism and sometimes more overt anti-Semitism of the liberal Left and some African Americans. Indeed, identification with the Democrats shapes political beliefs. Thus, when several quite pro-Palestinian placards appeared at the 2016 Democratic National Convention, Jewish Democrats averted their eyes. At the same time, many Jews professed to see in Republican candidate Donald Trump's populist campaign an echo of Nazism, despite the absence of any evidence that the GOP standard bearer had any shred of animus against Jews. As a result, many American Jews are Democrats first and Jewish second.[22]

Change and Continuity

While most American Jews are liberal Democrats, Orthodox Jews are the exception. The Orthodox, about 10 percent of the American Jewish community, are politically more conservative than other Jews and far more staunchly pro-Israel. Among Orthodox voters, Hillary Clinton won 56 percent of the Jewish vote in 2016, less than the 71 percent who supported Clinton in other segments of the Jewish community, but still a majority.[23] In 2020, according to some analysts, Orthodox Jews supported Trump by a wide margin over Joe Biden.

In 2020, many Jews viewed with natural satisfaction that two prominent, albeit unsuccessful, contenders for the Democratic presidential nomination, Bernie Sanders and Michael Bloomberg, were Jewish. Nevertheless, in recent years some cracks have developed in this bedrock of Jewish political involvement. One source of stress has been a fraying of the once close relationship between Jews and another loyal Democratic constituency, African Americans. Naturally, Jews have taken offense to anti-Semitic remarks attributed to several prominent African American politicians, including Jesse Jackson and Al Sharpton. Blacks, for their part, have expressed resentment at what they regard as Jewish efforts to intrude in the affairs of the African American community. In 2002, for example, Jewish organizations worked against black Democratic congresswoman Cynthia McKinney of Georgia, whom they viewed as anti-Semitic, by supporting another African American woman, Denise Majette. After McKinney's defeat, several other black politicians complained that she was singled out unfairly by a "special interest group."

Conflicts over the issue of Israel and the differing stances of Democratic and Republican leaders toward the Jewish state further shook Jewish allegiance to the Democratic Party. GOP presidents Ronald Reagan and George W. Bush, along with Republican candidates John McCain and Mitt Romney, were staunch supporters of Israel (though Jews found George H. W. Bush less than congenial). During the 2016 and 2020 campaigns, Donald Trump professed his staunch support for Israel and condemned the Democrats for wavering in their commitment to the Jewish state. As president, Trump recognized Jerusalem as Israel's capital and pursued an unswervingly pro-Israel policy in the Middle East.

Former Democratic president Barack Obama, on the other hand, raised Jewish concerns with his well-publicized fights with Israeli prime minister Benjamin Netanyahu. Matters came to a head when Netanyahu accepted an invitation from congressional Republicans in 2015 to address a joint session of Congress to express his opposition to the Iran nuclear agreement negotiated by Obama. From that time forward, the two leaders barely bothered to hide their contempt for one another. This split between the Obama administration and Israel was troublesome mostly to older Jewish Democrats. Millennials in general have a negative view of Netanyahu and were less likely troubled by Obama's contempt for the Israeli prime minister. At the end of Obama's term in office, the president declined to order an American veto of a UN Security Council resolution condemning Israel. Again, according to surveys, younger Democrats, who include many Jews, supported the president's position.[24]

Despite some misgivings, the bulk of the American Jewish community, exclusive of the Orthodox, stays firmly if not always happily within the Democratic camp, looking to balance affection for Israel with domestic liberalism. Membership in the Democratic coalition continues to allow Jews to exercise considerable political influence and has provided them with access to important political and social institutions. And then there is the matter of communal identification. Voting is an individual act, but voters take their cues from community notables and their friends and neighbors. Those notables, including publishers, rabbis, and the leaders of Jewish organizations, are very much aware of the fact that Jews in America exercise influence through the Democratic Party and urge ordinary Jewish voters to continue to support the Democrats. Jewish Republicans can be lonely folks, sneered at or even ostracized by their coreligionists. I recently attended a service at a large Washington, DC, congregation where the rabbi said with a condescending tone that he knew that none of his congregants supported the Republicans but urged members of the congregation to be tolerant and to try to understand why some Jews might stray into the GOP camp. Smiles and nods met his comments.

In the aftermath of the 2020 presidential election, few Jews saw the GOP as an attractive alternative to the Democrats, far more fearful of their enemies on the Right than their foes on the Left. The faint strength of white nationalism within the Republican camp is more threatening to most Jews than the real anti-Zionism voiced by a growing number of Democrats. It is noteworthy that the murder of Jewish worshippers in Pittsburgh perpetrated by a neo-Nazi received far more attention in the Jewish community than the ongoing violence perpetrated by African Americans against Jews in the New York area. For historical reasons, the former terrifies Jews. For political reasons, Jews choose to avert their eyes from the latter.

Three-quarters of a century ago, Franklin D. Roosevelt gave America's Jews a political home that they are not yet ready to leave, despite evidence of a chill in the relationship between the Jews and some of their longtime political allies. Of course, the decision about whether to leave or stay is not entirely up to the Jews. Jews have been compelled to leave many places where they would have preferred to stay.

7

New Alliances: Jews and the Christian Zionists

AS THE LAST chapter described, most American Jews continue to be liberal Democrats. They cling to a partisan affiliation dating back to the 1930s New Deal and a political perspective whose roots lie in the mid-nineteenth century, when liberalism promised social emancipation and political freedom. In the nineteenth and early twentieth centuries, Jews' most dangerous enemies were, indeed, concentrated on the political Right, so it was reasonable and prudent for Jews to seek allies on the political Left.

Jews more than anyone should know that even the most tolerant, open society can show an ugly face, however. In so many places and times—fifteenth-century Spain, the Ottoman Empire, Weimar Germany, postrevolutionary Russia, and now the Democratic Party—Jews achieved great power and felt an equally powerful sense of identification with the host nation only to see their situation rapidly deteriorate.

Rethinking alliances and tactics should be second nature to Jews by now. For what was once prudent can become a matter of "loyalty at any price" that is so dangerous for Jews. This can prevent them from accurately assessing current political realities and discovering that the nineteenth- and twentieth-century political paradigm they have internalized may be no longer helpful and indeed dangerous. For example, liberal Democratic loyalties allowed American Jews and large segments of the Jewish press to ignore, or not even see, the Palestinian flags prominently displayed both inside and outside the convention hall when the Democrats met, in a noisy pre-COVID-19 ceremony, to nominate their 2016 presidential candidate. The fact that the Democratic platform committee also included prominent foes of Israel like

Professor Cornel West received scant mention. When I pointed this out to Democratic friends and colleagues, many replied that these flags and individuals were associated with anti-Zionism, not anti-Semitism, and urged me to avoid conflating the two. Later, in December 2016, many liberal Jews supported Representative Keith Ellison's (D-MN) candidacy to chair the Democratic National Committee. Ellison, a Muslim member of Congress and former follower of Louis Farrakhan, had a long history of anti-Zionist commentary, but Jewish liberals said that Ellison had moderated his views in recent years and, besides, had never made explicitly anti-Semitic comments. Similarly, neither the mainstream media nor the Jewish press took much notice when sixteen of the seventeen members of Congress who voted against a 2019 resolution condemning boycott, divestment, and sanctions (BDS) happened to be Democrats.

Part of the problem for Jews in America is that they have little presence outside a small and privileged stratum in America. With the exception of recent immigrants, a negligible percentage of Jews are members of the working class or even the lower middle class, and Jews have hardly any involvement with the institutions associated with those strata. Few Jews live in working-class neighborhoods; few Jews attend community colleges or the lowest tier of four-year schools; and few Jews seek employment in industrial or service occupations.

When Jews were poor, they eagerly sought positions as teachers, clerks, and accountants or in the civil service, and despite rampant discrimination, some sought military careers like the rest of Middle America. Today, Jews are rarely in low-ranking government jobs, and, as is true of upper-middle-class Americans in general, almost none serve in the military. According to some estimates, America's 3 million men and women in uniform include only 15,000 Jews. Indeed, today, only a scattering of American Jews live outside upscale residential enclaves on the coasts, in a handful of large cities, or in Arizona's retirement communities. Moreover, residents of the West and South and the rural areas and small towns of America's heartland might never have a chance to know or meet a Jew.

Individuals who have seldom, if ever, had Jewish neighbors, classmates, or colleagues, and have no Jews in their social and family circles, have little or no reason to be concerned with the welfare of the Jews. Indeed, such persons have little reason to disbelieve assertions that Jews are too powerful, dishonest, disloyal, depraved, or otherwise undesirable. Having no firsthand knowledge, they sometimes accept the most outlandish stories about the Jews. A colleague tells me that when he was a child in the 1950s, customers often patted him on the head in his father's store in a small southern Indiana town where his was the only Jewish family. He had taken this to be a sign of his neighbors' affection until he learned that, apparently, many of the friendly "patters" were searching his scalp for the small horns they believed Jews had.

In fairness, those unacquainted with Jews personally are not automatically anti-Semites. Nevertheless, found among these mostly working- and lower-middle-class persons are many of the tens of millions of Americans who regularly express strongly anti-Semitic attitudes in response to surveys.[1] Today, this anti-Jewish sentiment on America's sociopolitical periphery is mostly a latent force, expressed most vehemently by those with the least political power. Indeed, for the past several decades Jews have been members in good standing of America's ruling class, which collectively determined some sixty years ago that overt expressions of anti-Semitism, including verbal attacks and public discrimination against Jews, were politically illegitimate, even criminal.

Yet this example of Jewish power also exemplifies Jewish weakness. Crucially, to mute expressions of anti-Semitism, the Jews depended on their connection to the ruling class, not their broader acceptance into American society. By contrast, the expression of hostility to, say, the Irish—common in the nineteenth and early twentieth centuries—did not become quasi-illegal. Discrimination against the Irish ended with the full integration of the Irish into American society.

America's Jews, to be sure, are not entirely unaware of this problem. Notice the Jewish community's concern about even the tiny hint of populist opposition to the nation's ruling elite represented by the Tea Party movement. Participants in the 2009–10 antitax Tea Parties were usually rural, socially conservative, opposed to what they termed "big government," and organized outside the control of the established political parties. Despite the occasional appearance of LaRoucheites and certain other marginal groups, the Tea Parties were not manifestly anti-Semitic. Yet, because they involved groups with little or no political or social connection to the Jewish community, some Jewish observers scanned the crowds for swastikas.[2]

Similarly, some Jews thought they saw anti-Semitic implications to Donald Trump's populism, even though Trump took pains to point with pride to his daughter's conversion to Orthodox Judaism. Of course, the fact that certain disparate white supremacists warmly supported Trump made Jewish fears worse, despite the fact that the president had Jewish grandchildren and was effectively in the same boat as they were.

Jews must address these old fears and change, and old allies who are promoting anti-Semitism must be jettisoned. For enemies on the Far Right may appear more dangerous and violent, but this is a wrong assessment moored in the past. Representative Ilhan Omar (D-MN), Black Lives Matter protestors, and their assorted allies may attack Jews only verbally, not with semiautomatic rifles, yet the anti-Semitism of the Left is a much greater threat to American Jews today.

First, there are no guarantees that the attacks from the Left will stay verbally abusive. They can escalate into violence. Black Lives Matter (BLM) protestors in the summer of 2020, while using anti-Semitic rhetoric, also engaged in looting and vandalism directed at Jewish-owned property. Yet, sadly, most Jews support liberal causes like BLM and dismiss anti-Semitism on the political Left as relatively insignificant. Some Jewish organizations go as far as to deny that left-wing anti-Semitism even exists. For example, after BLM protestors defaced and vandalized synagogues in a heavily Jewish neighborhood of Los Angeles in May 2020, the Anti-Defamation League (ADL) declared that "claims of targeted anti-Semitic violence [on the part of BLM demonstrators] have been exaggerated or misrepresented."[3] The venerable ADL has, in recent years, positioned itself as a politically progressive organization and endeavors to look the other way when its friends make rude comments about Jews. In Yiddish, one might say that the leaders of the ADL *machen sich nit wissendik* (prefer to look the other way). But we should not single out the ADL for criticism. In a reflexive spasm of virtue signaling, many synagogues also festooned their front lawns with BLM posters and banners.

Second, even if the anti-Semitism of the extreme Right stays a threat, the anti-Semitism of the broad Left should be a far greater concern to the place of Jews in the United States. As we know, the political and social standing of America's Jews is historically contingent on their alliances with gentiles. And for the past several decades, the substantial influence of Jews has been due to their alliance with the American gentile liberal and progressive bourgeoisie. Hence those progressives who continually engage in an anti-Semitic discourse, often camouflaged as anti-Zionism, represent a greater threat to America's Jews than the spasmodic violence of the Far Right. Neo-Nazi thugs the police can soon curb; the anti-Semitism of the liberal bourgeoisie is a far more insidious and enervating threat.

Third, the Right today is not the Old Right. William F. Buckley Jr., icon of the American Right after World War II, led the way in denouncing anti-Semitism among conservatives in the 1950s with lasting effect. Yet in 2016, many Jews still saw the right-wing Breitbart News Network as a hotbed of anti-Semitism, and the Jewish press joined the liberal media in castigating then president-elect Donald Trump for naming Breitbart chairman Stephen K. Bannon as a senior adviser. In its heyday, Breitbart was, to be sure, often read by members of right-wing fringe groups, but Jews missed something, which showed how the Right had changed. Breitbart's founder, the late Andrew Breitbart, was a Jewish conservative who built the service while living in Israel. Breitbart's goal was to supply a hawkish and pro-Israel slant on the news to combat anti-Semitism and anti-Zionism. Breitbart's successor, Larry Solov, along with two of the news service's most prominent editors and writers, Joel Pollack and David Horowitz, shared the company founder's ethnicity and political agenda. Many American Jews, however, viewing Breitbart through their liberal Democratic lenses, were convinced that the news service catered to anti-Semites.

While conservatives were shedding the vestiges of their pre–World War II anti-Semitism, events in the late 1960s and early 1970s had turned segments of the Left against Israel and its Jewish defenders, replacing the old anti-Semitism on the Right with a new anti-Semitism on the Left. Politically, this had the telling effect of increasing support for Israel and empathy for the Jews among politically conservative white evangelical Protestants, who had risen from their bastions in the South and Southwest, areas unfamiliar and menacing to many Jews, to become an important force in American politics and the GOP. Israel's new allies became known as "Christian Zionists" and have included such prominent evangelical ministers as the late Jerry Falwell, John Hagee, Richard Land, and the late Oral Roberts and Pat Robertson. Evangelicals are inclined to accept the literal truth of God's promise to Abraham in Genesis 12:3. During the 2014 Gaza War, for example, one prominent Christian Zionist, the Reverend Malcolm Hedding, declared:

> To stand with Israel now is not a difficult decision because the choice between good and evil is not a complex one. The God of the Bible also found this to be an easy decision because He states that while the nations rage at Israel He will, in the end, defend her and set up His King on His holy hill in Jerusalem. It would be good to choose what He has already chosen that it may go well with you on that day![4]

For his part, Israeli prime minister Netanyahu thanked the Christian Zionists for their "unwavering friendship" for Israel and said their support was critical to the defense of the Jewish state.[5]

Evangelicals also supported the Trump administration heavily, and two of its leading figures, Vice President Mike Pence and Secretary of State Michael Pompeo, strongly identified with the Evangelical movement and Christian Zionism. Both these men were staunch supporters of Israel and helped guide the Trump administration's strongly pro-Israel foreign policy. Through evangelicals and Christian Zionists, American Jews have an opportunity for the first time to connect outside their small and privileged stratum that they worked so hard to join but which is abandoning them through anti-Zionism.

A New Gentile Alliance

Before his death, the Reverend Jerry Falwell, politically influential leader of the Moral Majority, declared that God commanded Americans to support Israel, a command Americans must heed. "If this nation wants her fields to remain white with grain, her scientific achievements to remain notable, and her freedom to remain intact, America must continue to stand with Israel," Falwell said.[6] For just this reason, proclaimed John Hagee, founder of Christians United for Israel (CUFI), "fifty million Christians are standing up and applauding the State of Israel."[7] Pat Robertson, for his part, frequently fulminated against politicians who sought to compel Israel to relinquish even one square inch of the Arab territories captured in 1967. Robertson was even more vehement on this point than the Israelis themselves. In 2006, he famously declared Israeli prime minister Ariel Sharon's fatal stroke to have been God's punishment for Sharon's decision to abandon some Israeli settlements in Gaza and the West Bank.

Through years of Palestinian terrorism, two *intifadas*, wars in Lebanon, and major armed clashes in Gaza and the West Bank, Christian Zionists have stood with Israel. Evangelical leaders have raised money, organized rallies, and continually applied pressure on politicians on Israel's behalf. For example, when Israel bombed Iraq's Osirak nuclear reactor, the first call the late prime minister Menachem Begin made was (reportedly) to the Reverend Jerry Falwell to secure Falwell's support in justifying the attack to the Reagan administration and the American public.

In a similar vein, Falwell mobilized fifteen hundred evangelical ministers to come to Washington to show their support for Benjamin Netanyahu when President Bill Clinton summoned the Israeli prime minister to hector him over the expansion of West Bank settlements. The Reverend John Hagee led the assembled ministers in a chant of "Not one inch!" to express opposition to turning over land to the Arabs.[8] And during the 2006 Israeli battle with Hezbollah, Hagee called the Bible "God's foreign policy statement" and sent several thousand evangelicals to Capitol Hill to make certain that their representatives supported Israel. To show his solidarity with the Jews, the Reverend Pat Robertson went to Israel and broadcast his television program, *The 700 Club*, from the town of Metula while Hezbollah rockets fell nearby.[9]

Evangelicals say that their support for Israel is based directly on Holy Scripture, something they share with many Jews. They are also the only Christians today who hold that the Bible makes it clear that God gave the Holy Land to the Jews, a core principle of Zionism in general—that is, the God of Israel gave it to Abraham, Isaac, and Jacob, not to Ishmael, the biblical ancestor of the Arabs. According to a 2013 Pew survey, 82 percent of America's evangelicals believe that God gave the land of Israel to the Jewish people.[10] Christian Zionists also point to God's commitment to Abraham in the book of Genesis.[11]

This theological harmony, however, takes a twist with the 1948 founding of Israel. Certain Christian Zionists believe that the Jews returning to the Holy Land anticipates the Second Coming of Christ. To them, the 1940s creation of Israel and Israel's lightning victory over Egypt, Syria, and Jordan in 1967, resulting in the Israeli capture of Jerusalem, proved the truth of biblical prophecy. According to Jerry Falwell, these events were signs "indicating the imminent return of Jesus Christ."[12]

The fact that evangelicals are Bible-believing Christians is certainly important but does not entirely explain their total devotion to Israel. The same Bible that tells evangelicals to love Israel also has anti-Semitic passages that priests and preachers have cited for centuries to justify hatred for the Jews. Even today, while Christian Zionists find clear biblical sanction for championing Israel, other Christians continue to see compelling biblical justifications for opposing Israel and the Zionist agenda in general.[13] Some even say the Bible proves that Christians, not Jews, are God's Chosen People.[14]

Still, Christian Zionists love Israel despite the theological contradictions. Many American Jews have difficulty reciprocating their affection. As a religious minority in the United States, Jews are naturally suspicious of groups that try to introduce religious discourse into the political arena. And on issues such as abortion, gay marriage, LGBTQ+ rights, and the place of religion in public life, only the most orthodox Jews take positions like those espoused by conservative evangelicals.

Some Jews, moreover, still associate southern evangelicals with past anti-Semitism and find it awkward to be politically associated with the religious Right. For many, an alliance with Christian conservatives, who oppose, say, abortion and gay marriage and favor prayer in the schools, is out of the question, however much evangelicals support Israel. A marriage thus made in heaven can be difficult to consummate on earth, at least in America. Israel, of course, is a different matter. Israeli politicians have often found American conservatives to be reliable friends and are certainly accustomed to religious discourse in the public sphere. So Israelis have had little difficulty accepting the support of the Christian Zionists. American Jews should follow the Israeli lead.

Christian Zionists, moreover, accept the Jews as God's Chosen People, so they are uniquely philo-Semitic. Yet another twist, which is troubling to many American Jews, is the doctrine of premillennial dispensationalism, or dispensationalist theology, held by certain Christian Zionists. This theology, where Jews have a central eschatological role, started with a set of beliefs first popularized by the nineteenth-century British evangelist John Nelson Darby, who averred that his close reading of the Holy Scripture revealed that the return of the Jews to the Holy Land would set into motion a series of events leading to the Second Coming of Christ. Darby wrote and spoke extensively in England and America, where he built a following among pastors, Bible teachers, and revivalists.[15] Darby's ideas, particularly those relating to the importance of the Jews, have had a major impact on the views of generations of evangelical Protestants.[16] Today, a network of churches and institutes, and publications such as the Scofield Reference Bible, first published in 1909, promotes dispensationalism. Many aspects of dispensationalist doctrine, especially those relating to the importance of the Jews in "end times," have spread well beyond the core of adherents into the general evangelical community, including Pentecostals.

Dispensationalists notably divide the history of the world into seven epochs, called dispensations, beginning with the Garden of Eden. Most dispensationalists believe that we are currently living in the sixth epoch, the age of the Church, and will soon enter the seventh dispensation, the Millennial Kingdom or Millennium, a thousand-year reign of Christ on earth. Among dispensationalists, the details are open to dispute, but in general terms, sometime prior to the Millennium faithful Christians will ascend to the clouds in an event called the Rapture. While these true believers are safe with Jesus, the Antichrist will rule on earth for seven years. Apostates and unbelievers, including the Jews, left behind on earth will suffer terribly during this period of tribulation. At first, the Antichrist will present himself as a benevolent dictator and will allow the Jews to rebuild the Temple of Solomon. During the fourth year of his reign, however, the Antichrist will reveal himself, persecute the Jews, outlaw the Jewish religion, and demand to be worshipped as God. When the Jews refuse, he will lead armies against Israel, killing most of them, with a remnant finally accepting Christ. At this point, Christ and the raptured believers will return to earth and, in the battle of Armageddon near Jerusalem, defeat the Antichrist and his armies.

The Antichrist and his followers will then be thrown into a lake of fire, and Satan will be chained and tossed into a bottomless pit. God will gather the nations of the earth for judgment in the Valley of Jehoshaphat, where he will judge them on how they have treated his Chosen People, the Jews. After the destruction of the Antichrist and the judgment of the nations, Jesus will restore the throne of David and rule the world for a thousand years. At the end of this period, Satan will launch another rebellion, which God will suppress; this will be followed by the Day of Judgment, the resurrection of the dead, and the creation of a new heaven and a new earth.[17]

Dispensational doctrine is certainly one factor that makes Jews suspicious of evangelical backing. Many Jews believe that evangelicals support Israel only in the hope of bringing about the end of the world and the conversion of the Jews to Christianity. It is sometimes difficult to discern which of these events Jews fear more. For their part, Jewish secular intellectuals, a group that does not concern itself often with the Second Coming, find dispensationalist ideas strange and incomprehensible.

Dispensationalists are a minority of Israel's allies in the evangelical community. Only about 5 million evangelical Protestants in the United States call themselves dispensationalists, though millions of others are affected by dispensational ideas via popular books and films if not through their churches. But even outside the narrowly defined dispensational community, with its focus on the periods of human history, most white evangelical Protestants are premillennialists, believe that Israel has a critical role to play in end times, and accept the idea that Bible-believing Christians have a scripturally sanctioned obligation to support the state of Israel. Evangelicals in general accept God's promise to Abraham to bless those who bless the Jews and curse those who curse the Jews. Thus, while only 10 percent of evangelicals are full-fledged dispensationalists, more than 60 percent of evangelicals surveyed express a strong affinity for Israel.[18] Indeed, in a poll conducted prior to the 2004 presidential election, 31 percent of the evangelicals surveyed said that US support for Israel was their "primary consideration" in selecting a president, and another 64 percent cited it as "an important factor."[19]

Of course, certain evangelicals, including former president Jimmy Carter, as well as many mainline Christian churches, are quite critical of Israel and scornful of the Christian Zionists. Theology is a factor. Some of Israel's mainline Protestant critics are, by doctrine, covenantalists. This group avers that God's biblical promises to the Jews were fulfilled by the coming of Jesus, his death and resurrection, and the founding of the Christian church.[20] For these Christians, theology also has consequences for Israel. The presidency of Jimmy Carter was known to be unfriendly toward Israel, despite the Camp David

Accords. And in an added benefit to Israel, the dispensationalists, along with most other Southern Baptists and Pentecostals, dismiss these assertions as a form of replacement theology or "supersessionism," which ignores the plain language of the Bible. According to the dispensationalists, the covenantalists are guilty of implying that God's promises are untrustworthy, a grievous theological error.[21] It is not far-fetched to say that Jews should read their Christian theology carefully when choosing allies. For evangelical theology has political consequences too.

No doubt, biblical scholars can devote many hours, indeed many years, to the analysis of ambiguous biblical passages and to debates over their true meaning. For most individuals, however, even those who regard themselves as Bible believing, the appeal of a particular scriptural interpretation is likely to be complicated. For once chosen, a doctrine can have a powerful impact on its adherents' global view. Certain individuals, for example, are often drawn to biblical interpretations for religious *and* secular reasons. To take a well-known example, the rising European bourgeoisie of the seventeenth century found aspects of Calvinist religious doctrine attractive less because of its internal qualities than because many of its tenets seemed congruent with their own economic interests and political aspirations. The bourgeoisie did not accept Calvinism in its entirety, and the majority did not become Calvinists. Most tended, nevertheless, to internalize aspects of Calvinist doctrine that, in various and often changed forms, seemed consistent with their secular outlooks, interests, and values.[22]

In a similar vein, aspects of premillennial doctrine and eschatology, including the importance of the Jews in end times and the belief that support for Israel is biblically mandated, are vitally relevant to the secular interests and mundane perspectives of the evangelical community and to Jews. For evangelicals, the creation and continued existence of Israel is empirical proof of the truth and power of the Bible's literal word, Old and New Testaments. In this way, the success of the Jewish state furthers the worldly interests, ambitions, and message of the evangelical movement; evangelicals, like Jews, have a huge teleological stake in Israel's survival.

If this earthly interest is not enough to reinforce evangelicals' scriptural commitment to Israel, two other factors are also important. First, evangelicals are patriotic, and their patriotism tells them to respect a nation that does battle with America's foes. Second, unlike many other Christian groups to-day, evangelicals do just that: evangelize and, in this realm, come into sharp conflict with Israel's chief enemy: Muslims. This ongoing struggle, fought throughout the Middle East and Africa, gives evangelicals another reason to take pro-Israel positions.

Against this backdrop, the oft-expressed Jewish concern that Christian Zionism is some transient *narishkeit* that could disappear tomorrow is un-founded. Christian Zionism is firmly rooted not only in scriptural principles but in earthly concerns as well, which can also help the Jews, who have similar worldly and spiritual interests.

Christian Competition and Jewish Alliances

In the late years of the nineteenth century, a de facto schism developed among America's Protestant churches, which had proved important to Jews and their need for alliances. The mainline denominations of the Northeast, where many Jews lived, including the Methodists, Episcopalians, Presbyterians, and Congregationalists, came under the control of liberal theologians who tried to bring about a reconciliation between the Gospel and modern secular society, as in Reform Judaism. This reconciliation included acceptance of scientific theories such as evolution and a concern for lessening such social ills as poverty and inequality through the "social gospel," which called for the application of Christian principles to the problems and conflicts of industrial society. For liberal Protestants, the Bible was understood best, in most instances, meta-phorically, and salvation was not a final reward in the afterlife but a lifelong process of growth in love, service, and well-being.[23]

A quite different group of Protestants dominated the churches and Bible colleges of the South and Southwest, on the other hand, in areas where there were few Jews. These were the so-called fundamentalists, named for a series of pamphlets published by a group of conservative theologians early in the twentieth century titled "The Fundamentals: A Testimony of Truth." Dis-tributed and read widely in the South, the pamphlets defended traditional Christian views, called for a literal reading of the Bible, and attacked social gospel advocates for presuming that salvation was achieved through "works" rather than faith alone.

Before World War II, liberals and fundamentalists each dominated a discrete region of the country and ruled separate empires of churches, seminaries, and publishing houses. The two groups had serious spiritual disagreements but little direct contact. After the war, however, the liberals and fundamentalists fell into head-to-head competition in one another's territorial bastions. To begin with, during the war, large numbers of white southerners migrated from their home region to California and the upper Midwest to work in factories and defense plants. These transplanted southerners were uncomfortable in the Protestant churches—to say nothing of the secular culture—they found outside Dixie and welcomed visits from conservative ministers from their home states. These visits soon became large-scale revival meetings and crusades, where ministers of the old-time religion preached to the faithful and the curious. Southern California, which had been a focal point of immigration from the lower South, hosted several crusades in the 1940s and 1950s featuring such ministers as Billy Graham and "Fighting" Bob Shuler.[24] Graham and some of the other crusaders had already begun to call themselves evangelicals rather than fundamentalists to signal that their goal was to restore the primacy of the Gospel in a secular and sinful society. During the war, they founded the National Association of Evangelicals (NAE), which drew its membership from Pentecostals as well as fundamentalists.[25] These evangelicals built churches and religious organizations throughout the North and sought to broaden their membership base through evangelical outreach activities such as radio and television ministries, heavily publicized crusades and revivals, and organizations such as the Campus Crusade for Christ. Soon, evangelicals were locked in competition with the various liberal Protestant denominations on the latter's home turf.

On the heels of this southern conservative Protestant invasion of the North, northern liberal Protestantism invaded the South in an unusual way. The instruments of this counterinvasion were the federal courts, the civil rights movement, and the national media. As to the first of these, beginning in the late 1940s, the federal courts issued a series of decisions aimed at separating church and state, particularly where they intersected in the realm of public education and local morals ordinances. In its 1947 decision in *Everson v. Board of Education*, the US Supreme Court declared that the First Amendment's Free Exercise and Establishment Clauses applied to the states. This decision meant that traditional practices like school prayer and creationist teaching throughout the country, but especially in the Bible Belt, were potentially unconstitutional. When a series of cases and court decisions unfavorable to religious practices did happen, they were deeply offensive to evangelicals, especially in the South again, where religious leaders were accustomed to exercising what has been called "custodial" control over the local culture.[26] While such court challenges were initially spearheaded by civil liberties groups, they were endorsed by the mainline Protestant churches, whose increasingly ecumenical and secular orientation left them with little taste for imposing their religious practices on others. Evangelicals saw this endorsement as a betrayal of Christian principle and a direct attack on their own efforts to promote the Gospel. Liberal Protestants viewed evangelical efforts to defend creationist teaching and school prayer as embarrassing throwbacks to an earlier unenlightened era and soon gave their full support to efforts by the ACLU and other groups to bring these practices to an end.

A second instrument through which the northern churches invaded the South was the civil rights movement. The major civil rights organizations were in general led by black southern ministers, strongly supported by liberal Jews. Nevertheless, several prominent northern liberal ministers such as Eugene Carson Blake and William Sloane Coffin joined demonstrations and protest marches and castigated their southern counterparts for not raising their own voices against an unjust and un-Christian apartheid system.[27] The northern ministers' interference and accusations infuriated southern Protestants. The Reverend Jerry Falwell first achieved national prominence with a 1965 sermon titled "Marchers and Ministers," in which he attacked liberal Protestant ministers for intruding into southern society. The duty of the church, said Falwell, was to "preach the word," not to "reform the externals."[28]

Finally, liberal Protestants invaded the South through the mass media. Liberal Protestants had accepted, indeed embraced, the cultural revolution of the 1960s. The major liberal denominations, along with their umbrella group, the National Council of Churches (NCC), came to support abortion rights, an end to local moral codes, racial and gender equality, limits on religious displays and symbols in public places, and, broadly, the evolution of a more secular society. In many films, television series, and documentaries produced in the 1950s and 1960s, the ideas and sometimes the personalities of the liberal Protestants were presented in a favorable light—*A Man Called Peter*, for example, a biography and film of Peter Marshall, a wise and sensitive US Senate chaplain and the Washington, DC, New York Avenue Presbyterian Church pastor—while the fundamentalists and evangelicals were depicted as racist, Neanderthal "Bible thumpers," often venal, alcoholic, and committed to outmoded and discredited ideas. This genre includes such films as *Inherit the Wind*, a fictionalized account of the Scopes trial, and *Elmer Gantry*, the story of a drunken and dishonest Pentecostal preacher, patterned on the revivalist Billy Sunday.

If Hollywood needed encouragement to produce such films, the NCC was ready to provide it. Between World War II and the late 1960s, the NCC maintained the Protestant Film Commission in Hollywood, mostly to encourage the production of films that promoted Christian values. Expectedly, the commission encouraged the making of films that espoused the values of liberal Protestantism. For example, films that received awards from the commission in the 1960s were notably those that criticized segregation and promoted racial equality. Thus award winners included *A Patch of Blue*, the story of a love affair between a black man and a blind white woman, and *In the Heat of the Night*, a film in which a black northern police officer gradually wins the respect of a bigoted white southern sheriff.

Evangelicals responded vigorously to this northern assault on their social and religious institutions, making use of two weapons in particular: politics and doctrine. On the political front, between the 1960s and the 1980s, evangelical ministers and activists organized such groups as the Moral Majority, the Christian Coalition, Focus on the Family, and a host of others to battle on behalf of school prayer, against abortion, against the Equal Rights Amendment, against same-sex marriage, and, in general, to halt America's moral decline. Republican politicians, beginning with Ronald Reagan, viewed evangelicals as an important new GOP constituency and made major efforts to reach out to them through campaigns emphasizing "family values." Evangelical votes were critical to Reagan's election as well as the election of both George H. W. Bush and George W. Bush to the presidency. Since the 1980s, evangelicals have been an important force in the Republican Party.

In the beginning, Darby's premillennial dispensationalism was something of a fringe theology, popular among the tent-show revivalists who went from town to town in rural areas, primarily in the South and Southwest. These revivalists soon found that premillennialism was a crowd pleaser. The revivalists were early "masters of mass communication" and sought to appeal to people's "hopes, fears and resentments."[29] They saw in premillennialism a clear and powerful doctrine understandable to their audiences. While the rural folks attending a tent meeting might not catch all the subtleties of theological disputation, they could certainly understand the Rapture, the tribulation, the Second Coming, Armageddon, the fiery lake, and the other dramatic elements of the premillennialists' biblical story. As the historian Timothy Weber put it, revivalists preaching premillennialism "out-Bibled" the competition.[30] And as preachers saw the success of their colleagues making use of premillennialist doctrines, they followed suit. As one minister put it, "I do not mean to say that the apparent outstanding success of these godly men became conclusive … . But it did do this for me—it started me again to study my Bible."[31] Some preached dispensationalism, with its division of history into seven periods, while others preached related forms of premillennialism.

By World War II, premillennialism had moved from the fringes to the evangelical mainstream. Most evangelical pastors were now premillennialists and quite a few, full-fledged dispensationalists. As the evangelicals moved north and engaged in head-to-head competition with the mainline Protestant denominations, premillennialism proved as powerful a force as it had been fifty years earlier in the South and Southwest. Mainline Protestant ministers offered their congregants the thin gruel of a doctrine of personal growth and affirmation not so different from the ideas found in any secular self-help treatise. The evangelicals, on the other hand, offered fire and brimstone, rapture, and tribulation. And with the birth of Israel, they could point out that their truth was Bible centered.

The battle between premillennialism and the social gospel turned out to be an unequal contest. In the 1940s, most of America's Protestants belonged to the mainline liberal denominations. Today, the evangelicals outnumber their rivals by a two-to-one margin, though well-educated upper-income Protestants are still more likely to identify with the mainline denominations.

Nationalism

A second factor contributing to evangelical support for Israel is basic patriotism. White Protestant evangelicals are among the most nationalistic groups in America. Most believe that America has a special role to play in the world and that the nation has received special protection from God for much of its history.[32] In recent years, white Protestant evangelicals have been among the strongest supporters of the wars in Iraq and Afghanistan and generally have been staunch advocates of American military dominance in the world.[33] Many evangelicals believe they have a duty to send their sons and daughters to defend the nation. As one pastor said, "sacrificial patriotism" is a high value in the evangelical community.[34] Compare this view to that of the mainline Protestant churches. At the 2006 World Council of Churches Assembly, the American delegation, representing thirty-four mainline denominations, issued an apology to the world for America's misdeeds. They said that the United States was guilty of "entering into imperial projects that seek to dominate and control for the sake of our own national interests." They accused the United States of "raining down terror" and sowing "violence, degradation and poverty." In a slap at the evangelicals, the US delegation declared, "Nations have been demonized and God has been enlisted in national agendas that are nothing short of idolatrous."[35] Sacrificial patriotism was not on the agenda.

Since World War II, evangelical churches have been set up throughout America. The greatest concentration of Protestant evangelicals, though, is still in the South and Southwest, including Southern California, where southern migrants fueled the growth of the evangelical movement in the 1950s. The presence of tens of millions of evangelicals has helped make the entire region a bastion of support and major source of recruits for America's military services. The promilitary views of the region are, of course, strongly reinforced by the presence in the South of large numbers of military installations and military industries, often leading wags to characterize America's Sun Belt as its "Gun Belt."

Intense evangelical patriotism is a comparatively recent phenomenon, dating from World War II. Members of the evangelical community had mostly been unenthusiastic supporters of American involvement in World War I. Inspired, however, by the preaching of such ministers as Louis Bauman, many evangelicals came to see World War II as the beginning phase of the apocalyptic struggle that would lead to the Second Coming. Bauman, a dispensationalist, was able to interpret the events leading up to the conflict through the lens of the Bible and, forging a close link between religious belief and patriotism, to persuade evangelicals of their religious duty to go to war. Bauman linked Japan, Germany, and Italy with various aspects of biblical prophecy and, at one point, declared that Mussolini was the Antichrist. According to the historian Matthew Avery Sutton, the war made evangelicals "America's most patriotic (and xenophobic) citizens."[36] And, with the aid of biblical interpretation, patriotism had a continuing effect on the ways in which evangelicals read and understood the holy text.

With the defeat of the Axis powers and the start of the Cold War, evangelicals quickly became staunchly anticommunist and supportive of a strong military defense.[37] Dispensationalists, in particular, had no difficulty identifying the Soviet Union with the Gog and Magog, who in Ezekiel 38–39 lead an attack against the land of Israel.[38] Many dispensationalists believed that the book of Revelation foretold that a nuclear war midway through the period of tribulation would result in the destruction of one-third of the human race.[39] Despite this rather dire view of the future, dispensationalists were by no means averse to the expansion of America's military might. In this and other matters, they favored "giving the Devil all the trouble we can till Jesus comes."[40]

For their part, evangelicals with a more optimistic outlook had no difficulty recognizing that the United States was engaged in a struggle against godless Communism. Some evangelical leaders also saw the military as a fertile recruiting ground and made the armed services a major mission field.[41] During the Vietnam War, evangelical leaders supported the military, which, in turn, gave its support to evangelical chaplains in preference to those sent by the mainline denominations. Later, President Ronald Reagan elated evangelicals in a 1983 speech before the National Association of Evangelicals when he called on them to struggle against "the aggressive impulses of an evil empire."

For evangelicals, post–World War II events in the Middle East had both religious and patriotic significance. In the dispensationalist community, the founding of the state of Israel in 1948 caused enormous excitement, as it seemed to fulfill biblical prophecy and to portend so much more. The editor of the *Weekly Evangel* declared, "We may well wonder whether we are awake or lost in sleep merely having a very exciting dream … . Beloved, it can't be long until our blessed Lord takes us home to be forever with Him … . Oh, joy unspeakable."[42] In the larger evangelical community, however, where premillennial views were not universally accepted, opinions were mixed, with some expressing concern about the injustices suffered by the Palestinian Arabs. Later events in the Middle East, however, expanded and solidified evangelical support for Israel by drawing the Jewish state into the American security orbit: first, in America's global struggle against Communism, and later, in America's global war against terrorism. Viewing Israel through the lens of their own patriotism, evangelicals could ignore Arab claims and focus on God's promises to the Jews.

The first of these events was the 1956 Suez crisis. The crisis began with a decision by the United States to withdraw its offer to finance the construction of Egypt's Aswan High Dam. Egyptian president Gamal Abdel Nasser turned to the Soviet Union for support and secured a Soviet promise to finance the dam. On the heels of a 1955 agreement to provide Egypt with significant quantities of new Soviet bloc arms, this arrangement showed the development of ever closer ties between Egypt and the USSR, a development that might have posed a threat to Western oil interests. This threat quickly materialized when Nasser announced that he was nationalizing the Suez Canal, which an Anglo-French consortium owned and which Britain and France depended on for a sizable percentage of their Middle Eastern oil shipments.

Britain and France developed a joint plan to seize the canal by force. Israel had its own reasons for attacking Egypt, which had blocked Israeli access to the Red Sea and served as a base for terrorist attacks against Israeli settlements. At the invitation of the French, who were at that time Israel's chief military patrons, Israel agreed to add its own forces to those of the British and French. Launched in October 1956, the attack was militarily successful. In response to threats and pressure from the Soviet Union, however, the United States compelled Britain, France, and Israel to accept a cease-fire and to withdraw their forces.

As it had been after the creation of Israel, these events divided the evangelical community. Some were concerned about the rights of the Arabs and feared that Israel's actions would lead the world into a devastating war. Thus

Oswald Allis of the Princeton Theological Seminary wrote that Jews had no right to take possession of large parts of Palestine and to force the Arabs from it. Moreover, he asked, "Should Christians be willing to plunge the nations into a third world conflict just to restore unbelieving Jews to … a land from which they were driven nearly two thousand years ago?"[43] Most evangelicals, however, sided with Israel. The Jews, said Wilbur Smith of Fuller Theological Seminary, had made the desert bloom, while the Arabs had been "a curse to the land."[44]

Some evangelicals, noting that Israel had been fighting against a foe armed by Soviet Russia, found it hard to understand why the United States had formally condemned the British-French-Israeli attack on Egypt. One dispensationalist writer concocted a complex theory where God intended America's condemnation of Israel's actions to pave the way for a Russian invasion of Palestine and the fulfillment of biblical prophecies.[45] Thus, despite some continuing divisions, the fact that Israel was fighting on the side of the West against the Communists and their allies was beginning to influence evangelical perspectives. This fact became even more important in the next round of fighting between Israel and its Arab neighbors.

In the years following the Suez crisis, Egypt moved firmly into the Soviet camp, becoming a major recipient of Russian economic aid and military hardware. In the late 1950s, Syria too became a Soviet client and briefly joined with Egypt to form the United Arab Republic (UAR). Though a military coup in Syria led that nation to abandon the UAR in 1961, Egypt and Syria remained allies, and Syria joined Egypt as a Soviet military client. Now Israel's two main enemies were both armed and supported by America's great rival, the Soviet Union. For evangelicals, the Bible and the American flag now clearly sent the same message of support for Israel.

In 1967, after several years of skirmishing between Israel and the Arab states, Egypt sent a large army into the Sinai Peninsula to confront Israel, ejected UN peacekeepers from the Israeli-Egyptian border, and closed the Straits of Tiran to Israeli vessels, cutting off Israel's access to the Red Sea. Nasser boasted that he would drive the Jews into the Mediterranean. Not waiting for an attack, in June 1967 Israel launched a preemptive strike and within two days had annihilated the Egyptian air force and had driven the Egyptian Army out of the Sinai Peninsula and across the Suez Canal, destroying most of its Soviet-built tanks and other heavy arms. Believing initial Egyptian claims of victory, however, Syria and Jordan had also entered the war against Israel. Once they defeated Egypt, Israeli forces turned on both these nations. Quickly routed, the Syrians relinquished the strategic Golan Heights on the Israeli-Syrian border. Israel drove Jordanian forces from the West Bank of the Jordan River, and, on the third day of the war, Israeli forces entered and occupied East Jerusalem, site of the Western Wall, from which Jordan had barred Jews for decades. In six days of fighting, Israel had defeated all its Arab neighbors; captured the Sinai Peninsula, Gaza Strip, West Bank, and Golan Heights; and reunified the city of Jerusalem—an astonishing victory.

To evangelicals, the outcome of the Six-Day War was nothing short of a miracle. Many had thought the badly outnumbered Israelis faced defeat and Jews a second Holocaust. Bible-believing evangelicals thought God must have fought on Israel's side. For the dispensationalists, Israel's victory was a clear affirmation of biblical prophecy and a sure sign that the Second Coming was near. They saw Israel's capture and reunification of Jerusalem as a fulfillment of the prophecy of Luke that "Jerusalem shall be trodden down of the Gentiles, until the times of the Gentiles shall be fulfilled." With the reunification of Jerusalem by the Jews, events leading up to the return of Jesus Christ would soon take place.[46]

Those less convinced of the immediacy of the Second Coming, nevertheless, saw Israel defeat large armies that the Soviet Union had trained and equipped. If Israel had not yet confronted the minions of the Antichrist, it had battled and beaten the surrogates of the Communists. And, significantly, the Six-Day War came at a time when America itself was engaged in a bitter and inconclusive struggle against Communist forces in Southeast Asia. Many members of the various liberal Christian denominations, along with liberal Jews, were engaged in protesting the war in Vietnam, which they viewed as an expression of American militarism and imperialism and a diversion of resources from vital civil rights and social welfare programs. Evangelicals, on the other hand, supported the war, which they saw as a necessary battle against Communism, if not Satan himself.

These competing views helped induce vastly different reactions to Israel's victory on the part of liberal Christians and evangelicals. Like the evangelicals, mainstream Christians were divided over Israel's founding, with some seeing biblical prophecy and others seeing an injustice to the Arabs. View-ing the Six-Day War through the lens of Vietnam protests, antimilitarism, anti-imperialism, and the growing influence of liberation theology, liberal Christian groups, such as the National and World Councils of Churches, became increasingly antagonistic toward the Jewish state.[47] Evangelicals, though, viewed Israel's victory through the lens of a nationalistic, promilitary, and anticommunist perspective and believed that Israel's military triumph served America's global interests as well as Israel's own goals. The 1967 war was a watershed in the relationship between Christians and Israel. The lib-eral Christian denominations began to see Israel as a white colonial power repressing people of color—a position that hardened during later years of Israeli occupation of the West Bank and never-ending war between Israel and the Arabs. Evangelicals, on the other hand, thought Israel could do nothing wrong apart from returning so much as one square inch of conquered terri-tory to the Arabs.

With the collapse of the Soviet Union, both the notion that the USSR had a role to play in bringing about the Second Coming and Israel's value as an anti-Soviet bastion in the Middle East lost their significance. Soon, however, George W. Bush replaced Reagan's evil empire with militant Islam's "evildo-ers," which filled the former Soviet Russia's place in evangelical eschatology and politics. Several dispensationalists rediscovered the importance of Islam in biblical prophecy.[48] At the same time, just as Israel had been on America's side in opposition to the USSR, Israel was the enemy of the radical Islamic regimes and shadowy terrorist networks that attacked and threatened the United States. To radical Islamists, America was the "great Satan" and Israel the "little Satan," working arm in arm against the Muslim world. To evan-gelicals, it might be radical Islam that served Satan, but Israel and the United States certainly worked arm in arm.

Some critics of Israel, of course, argue that the alliance between America and Israel is a product of the political efforts of American Jews and Christian Zionists rather than an expression of America's own economic and security interests. While many liberal Christians, and some Jews, have accepted this argument, the evangelical community mostly rejects the idea. One prominent evangelical politician, Gary Bauer, founder of the Family Research Council, called Jerusalem and Washington "two shining cities upon a hill."[49] After the 9/11 terrorist attacks, said Bauer, news footage showed Arabs celebrating, while "in Israel they were crying with us."[50] Thus, as it did during the Cold War, evangelicals' patriotism reinforced a biblical understanding calling for support for Israel.

Evangelism

While premillennialism and nationalism provide evangelicals with reasons to support Israel, a third factor, evangelism itself, leads to bitter enmities with Israel's Muslim foes. During the nineteenth century and the early decades of the twentieth century, the mainline Protestant churches conducted extensive missionary activities in the Middle East, Asia, and Africa. The Congregational Church and the Presbyterian Church were particularly active, and the Board of Foreign Missions of the Presbyterian Church was one of the largest missionary organizations in the world. Protestant missionaries preached the Gospel to non-Christians and to members of the indigenous Christian communities of the Middle East, such as Coptic, Nestorian, and Syriac Christians, whom devout American Protestants considered "nominal" Christians. In addition to preaching the Gospel, Protestant missionaries built hospitals, schools, and universities. Protestant missionaries during this era also founded the American University in Beirut and the American University in Cairo as well as several other institutions of higher education.[51]

Today, the mainline Protestant denominations sponsor several organizations that engage in humanitarian work aimed at promoting justice, offering healthcare, and alleviating hunger overseas. These include the Episcopal Public Policy Network and Global Ministries, affiliated with the Disciples of Christ and United Church of Christ. These organizations typically act in partnership with local and international religious bodies, such as Churches for Middle East Peace and the World Council of Churches. The mainline Protestant denominations do not try to proselytize. They take an ecumenical perspective, endeavor to keep good relations with local governments and other religious faiths, and take the position that there are many paths to salvation. Consistent with the service orientation of their mother churches, mainline Protestant missionaries are concerned more with saving bodies than souls.

Whatever their goals, the mainline churches account for fewer than 10 percent of the tens of thousands of American Protestant missionaries currently serving in Asia, Africa, the Middle East, and Latin America. Evangelical church organizations deploy more than 90 percent.[52] These include the International Mission Board of the Southern Baptist Convention and Samaritan's Purse, an international evangelical organization directed by Franklin Graham, son of the late Billy Graham. While the mainline Protestants do not proselytize, evangelical missionaries are eager to win converts to Christianity. Like their mainline counterparts, evangelical missions offer humanitarian aid, including food, medical care, toys for children, and so forth. Accompanying the evangelicals' humanitarian work, though, is always a Christian message.[53] Thus food boxes sent to Iraqi refugees carried a biblical quote translated into Arabic: "For the Law was given through Moses; grace and truth were realized through Jesus Christ." In Afghanistan, Samaritan's Purse reportedly organized Christmas celebrations for Muslim children and handed out Christian Bibles along with relief supplies.[54] And some evangelical missionaries dispatched to hostile environments, particularly in Muslim countries where evangelizing is generally outlawed, have adopted a practice known as "tentmaking" or "tunneling," which entails engaging in another type of work as a cover while preaching in secret to avoid detection by the local authorities.[55] The evangelical missionaries rescued by American special forces at the outset of the Afghan war were tentmaking before being taken prisoner by the Taliban.

Because they do not actively proselytize, mainline Protestant missionaries can live and work in certain Muslim nations. Indeed, by often espousing pro-Palestinian and anti-Israeli (and often anti-American) positions, liberal Protestant organizations like the World Council of Churches curry favor with authorities in Arab countries, thus protecting the security of their facilities and safety of their workers.[56] Evangelical missionaries, however, actively proselytize and so risk arrest, imprisonment, and even murder, particularly in the Muslim world. In recent years, Muslim authorities have jailed many evangelicals, with Muslim citizens themselves also murdering them. For example, Muslims murdered an American evangelical nurse working in a clinic in southern Lebanon, while Muslims also murdered three other evangelical missionaries working in a clinic in Yemen. Whereas liberal Protestants point to these deaths as evidence of the futility of proselytizing in Muslim countries, evangelicals assert that the victims were Christian martyrs who should inspire others to preach the Gospel.[57]

Not surprisingly, considering the violence directed against them, many evangelicals have developed a good deal of animus toward Muslims. The late Jerry Falwell called Muhammad a terrorist, while Franklin Graham declared that Islam was a very evil and wicked religion.[58] The late J. Don George, pastor emeritus of Calvary Church in Irving, Texas, said, "Our faith is in Jesus Christ, and the Muslim community does not accept Jesus and God, and therefore we're at odds with Muslims … any religion or ideology that refuses to acknowledge the lordship of Jesus Christ could be typified as [satanic]."[59]

Of course, Jews are another religious group that refuses to accept the lordship of Jesus Christ. Jews, however, do not kill Christian missionaries. Despite the annoyance sometimes expressed by Israel's government and religious authorities over evangelical missionary activities, evangelicals proselytize quite actively and without much interference in the Jewish state. Among the most visible is the Union of Messianic Jewish Congregations, which has made use of Israel's law of return to settle a few of its members in the Holy Land. Here they preach primarily to Jews from the former Soviet Union, whose minimal religious background and training may make them especially susceptible to Christian appeals.

Thus missionary activities generate little conflict between evangelicals and Jews. Indeed, Israeli Jews are the enemies of evangelicals' Muslim foes, and, in this world (though unlikely in the next), the enemy of my enemy is as close to a friend as one can get. If evangelicals have a bone to pick with the Jews in this area, it is with American Jews who sometimes criticize evangelical preachers for their anti-Muslim statements. On one such occasion, after Jewish groups objected to his intemperate remarks about Islam, Pat Robertson indignantly said, "If I say something that Islam is, you know, an erroneous religion, then I get criticized by the Anti-Defamation League. You just want to say: When are you going to open your eyes and see who your enemy is."[60]

Epilogue
Final Thoughts on Anti-Semitism Today: What's Good for the Jews

A NUMBER OF commentators have observed that American Jews seem blind to anti-Semitism on the political Left.[1] At the same time that anti-Zionism suffuses the progressive political universe, Muslim activists, Black Lives Matter protestors, LGBTQ+ demonstrators, and so on, all find common cause in anti-Zionism through the lodestone of intersectionality. For some, anti-Zionism is obviously a disguised form of anti-Semitism. The Palestinian American activist Linda Sarsour recently dismissed the importance of this fact, asserting that, unlike more important hatreds like antiblack racism and Islamophobia, anti-Semitism is "not systemic."[2] Saying that anti-Semitism is not systemic is an egregious form of denial and a lethal threat to Jews.

Worse, Jews who strongly sympathize with progressive causes pretend that anti-Zionism directed at them is not a concern. Even the Anti-Defamation League, which ought to know better, is prepared to respond to the least hint of an anti-Jewish comment on the political Right but avoids offending its progressive allies by asserting that anti-Semitic comments emanating from the Left either don't exist or, if they do, the First Amendment protects them. And some Jews, as we have seen, are so eager to curry favor with their fellow progressives that they often and loudly proclaim that they, too, are anti-Zionists. Given Jewish history, this will not end well.

Once again, the Jewish community is divided hopelessly on the source of the threat. Within the Democratic Party, support for Israel and its Jewish supporters has plummeted, anti-Semitic commentary from the Left goes unanswered and gets louder, and Jews—unwilling to accept overtures from mainstream conservatives, including Christian Zionists—are more politically isolated in the United States than at any time since the period before World War II. Unlike members of other white American ethnic groups, as I have noted, many Jews decline to assimilate fully into American society, which carries obvious risks. Jews instead form societal and political alliances with, but do not fully integrate with, gentiles. Political alliances are, however, inherently unstable. Most Jews currently find themselves on the outs with some of their longtime liberal friends and certain Democratic allies, but are reluctant to embrace their equally longtime conservative foes, where being pro-Israel—either as a Christian Zionist or as just part of the broader GOP base—is a political obligation today.

However successful and influential they might appear, Jews in the diaspora, including Jewish Americans, often view themselves in a quasi-dependent position, having to consider whether events, policies, politicians, and the like are "good for the Jews." Writers for American Jewish newspapers typically struggle to interpret stories through this lens. Such a writer once called me to ask whether the thunderstorms predicted for Election Day might depress voter turnout and, if so, how would this affect the Jews? I explained, tongue in cheek, that Jews were in general more resolute than other voters, so severe weather would increase the Jewish percentage of the electorate. Election Day storms, I asserted, might be good for the Jews! The newspaper gave this fanciful idea front-page coverage.

This story is another illustration of Jews' lack of full assimilation into American society. The Jews have lived in America for some four hundred years, longer than most Irish, Italians, Poles, and so many others. But unlike these other American ethnic groups, Jews keep an unshakable communal identity, as explained in an earlier chapter. The Irish, the Italians, and most of the older white ethnic groups long ago seized the opportunity to disappear into the American melting pot. The question "Is it good for the Irish?" has no meaning unless one is referring to Notre Dame's football team.

America has been exceptionally good for the Jews, giving them substantial freedom and opportunity and, if not exactly handing the Jews a ticket to success, opening a path that allowed them to succeed—at least since the removal of most anti-Semitic barriers shortly after World War II. For their part, the Jews have been incredibly good for America, playing a key role in propelling the United States to the positions of economic, scientific, and technological leadership it continues to enjoy. A match or, as Jews might say, a *shidduch* made in heaven and the fulfillment of Genesis 12:3.

And yet, as Jewish history amply shows, nothing is forever, and rise and fall are predictable. Despite their addiction to the dozens of Jewish success narratives published every year, Jews have good reasons to be aware of this fact. Though Jews may rise to a great height, it usually rests on an insecure foundation. The risks to Jews are obvious in America today, as they were in the past. During the elite consolidation of the late nineteenth century, Jews were expelled from their earlier positions of influence when America's leading patricians and industrialists joined forces to rule America. In other times and places in history, exclusion was the mildest ostracism Jews could face, but it also often signaled the worst was still to come.

In contemporary America, the established, mostly Protestant, elites who control major foundations, important sectors of the media, elite universities, and government bureaucracies have sought a rapprochement with what Michael Lind calls America's "overclass" of fabulously wealthy tycoons, rentiers, and corporate managers.[3] As in the nineteenth century, this entails a marriage of money and social prestige with a new woke dialect, first heard in the elite universities, serving as a virtue marker. Those uncertain about how to use such terms as *microinvalidation* or *nonbinary* were less likely to receive a wedding invitation to this marriage of money and prestige.[4]

Both money and prestige also favor programs of higher levels of public spending for social stability and liberal internationalism. The overclass notably favors a world with porous borders in which the corporations they control can engage in tax, labor, and regulatory arbitrage, choosing the most favorable nations and regimes in which to pay taxes and recruit workers while escaping burdensome regulations. For both groups, support for African American claims and certain causes, such as Black Lives Matter, is important both as a form of virtue signaling and to justify higher levels of public spending.

Where do Jews fit into this ongoing elite consolidation? Jews are certainly in both elites of money and prestige, yet, as in the past, they are not fully welcome in either group. Jews can be useful political allies, but they can also be "pushy"—that is, they are not content to be followers but seek to compete for leadership positions in the universities and foundations and in corporate boardrooms.[5] This is an echo of the complaint that Joseph Sobran once voiced about Jewish neoconservatives. He said that once welcomed into the church choir, the neocons wanted to supplant the minister.

Through an anti-Semitic or anti-Zionist discourse, some members of the liberal gentile bourgeoisie look to subordinate their Jewish allies while continuing to harness Jewish wealth and activism on behalf of progressive causes. Jews willing to pay the price of admission might have to prove they are fully woke, and not crypto-Zios. This form of inquisition can already be found on university campuses where professors suspected of pro-Israel deviationism are attacked as racists, and within the elite media where, for example, the liberal *New York Times* editor Bari Weiss was hounded from the press room for her alleged Zionist sympathies, which made her insufficiently antiracist.[6] The Jewish founders of some Silicon Valley firms, moreover, are currently denounced from the Left as "Zionist capitalists."

Jews' allies also doubt the sincerity of Jewish wokeness and humiliate them. Sometimes, indeed, their allies require Jews to abandon all reality as the ticket of admission to woke elite America. For example, gay Jews must pretend that Muslim Middle Eastern states are friendlier to the LGBTQ+ community than Israel or risk the accusation of "pink-washing." In such a political climate, Jews can never feel secure even when they try to present themselves as being, in the apt German phrase, *päpstlicher als den Papst* (more papal than the Pope). But this is the point: insecurity equals weakness, subordination, and a return to the politically enfeebled Jewish condition of previous centuries. Unfortunately, this is one plausible Jewish future in America.

Consider what the growth of anti-Semitism in general means for American Jews who will have fewer American allies to protect them—that is, abandonment of the Jews by the Left and Jewish rejection of an alliance with the Right, including Christian Zionists. It is obvious that no Jew can ever afford to ignore the far-right threat. Yet without an alliance with the Left, which is deteriorating in America and Europe, Jews are more vulnerable than they have been in close to a century to right-wing extremists, especially if the Far Right joins forces with the Far Left and Muslim extremists, which has been happening in alarming ways. While my parents escaped to the Soviet Union to avoid certain death at Nazi hands, that "alliance," too, proved short-lived, for Soviet Communism turned on the Jews, tapping into traditional Russian anti-Semitism, even though (or because) certain Jews had been leading Bolsheviks.

So we can add to the growing, no longer benign, anti-Semitism on the Left today, a growing, traditionally violent, lunatic fringe of skinheads, Ku Klux Klansmen, and neo-Nazis. Estimates put their numbers at twenty thousand, though at any point in time many are in prison, where they form "Aryan" prison gangs and do battle with black and Hispanic gangs. Those interested in getting the flavor of these groups might read Christian Picciolini's illuminating memoir, *Romantic Violence: Memoirs of an American Skinhead.*[7]

In addition to these violent but inarticulate anti-Semites, there exists an even smaller cadre of middle-class, mostly college-educated white nationalists, once grouped by the media under the banner alt-right (alternative Right), a term coined by an ultraconservative Jewish professor, Paul Gottfried, though his onetime student Richard Spencer also claims credit. There is no single alt-right organization, and the hodgepodge of groups loosely associated with the term espouses a variety of ideologies. Most are nationalist and nativist, "masculinist," and some are anti-Semitic, blaming the Jews for America's social ills. Anti-Semitism for some alt-right groups seems to be more a tactic of provocation designed to generate media attention than a reflection of deeply held beliefs.[8] For others, however, anti-Semitism is the central focus. These are the so-called 1488ers. The number 1488 has special significance to neo-Nazis. The number 14 refers to a fourteen-word neo-Nazi slogan, "We must secure the existence of our people and a future for white children." The number 88 underscores the eighth letter of the alphabet, *H*. Thus 88 is code for HH, which is, in turn, code for "Heil Hitler."

So, in certain instances, intellectual anti-Semites should seem more frightening than the skinheads and Ku Klux Klanners, whom the police can control, for the latter are capable of only isolated, scattered acts of violence, while the former scheme and plan to attack Jewish influence, which has the greater potential for violence and other hostile measures. Yet the vital point about them is that while the intellectuals see themselves as the leaders of a movement, until recently, at least, they had no followers, unlike on the Left or within the Democratic Party today, which have certain allies and a greater potential for more. They spend their time chatting with one another in obscure corners of the internet; they speak in code about the "JQ" (Jewish Question) and other topics that only insiders, privy to the lingo, can follow; and they use a double set of closed parentheses ((())) around a name to show a

Jew and a double set of open parentheses))((around a name to show a fellow Aryan. Pretty sophisticated, huh? The intellectual anti-Semites seem engaged in an elaborate, if sinister, game more than an exercise in *Realpolitik*, if I may use a German term in this context.

A mass base of support for anti-Semitic movements did exist in the United States during the 1930s, but World War II pulled it up by the roots. Worryingly, tens of millions of unemployed workers, like their counterparts in Europe, were willing to listen to the claims of Father Coughlin, the German American Bund, the "Silver Shirts," and a host of other organizations blaming the Jews for their plight. The anti-Semitism of the 1930s, however, was discredited by its association with America's German enemy. And during and after the war, workers found good jobs, enrolled in labor unions, and were mobilized by the Democratic Party. The working class became part of the bourgeoisie, raised families, even joined bowling leagues, and had no further interest in radical politics. Millions even attended evangelical churches where they learned to support Israel and the Jews, leading to the growth of Christian Zionism and philo-Semitism.

Yet consider the status of the white working class today. Millions of blue-collar jobs have left the country as employers have sought cheaper labor in China, Southeast Asia, and Mexico—an exodus encouraged by free trade policies that reduced or ended tariffs on the repatriation of the finished products. In addition, as many as 1 million jobs may have been lost during the past several years simply because of increased federal regulation affecting heavy industry, railroads, mining, and other elements of America's industrial core.[9] Even before the COVID-19 pandemic shattered the economy, between 20 million and 30 million blue-collar workers joined the ranks of the unemployed or underemployed. Many have been jobless since the Great Recession of 2008.[10] Once-thriving industrial cities like Scranton, Pennsylvania; Middletown, Ohio; Flint, Michigan; Charleston, West Virginia; Youngstown, Ohio; Buffalo, New York; and, of course, Detroit, Michigan, have become the capitals of America's Rust Belt. These capitals and their deindustrialized hinterlands are home to shuttered factories and damaged lives. Older unemployed workers look forward to Social Security. Lacking the stabilizing force of steady employment, younger members of the once working class, particularly those with low levels of educational attainment, have turned in dismaying numbers to petty crime and the abuse of opioids, heroin, and alcohol. Within this group, divorce and suicide rates are high; church attendance is low; and ties to families and social networks are frayed.[11]

As to labor unions and political parties, once important institutions in the working-class world, both have abandoned workers. Industrial unions in the United States have lost much of their former vitality.[12] Contemporary unions focus more on public employees than the shrinking base of blue-collar workers. The two parties, for their part, follow agendas irrelevant to, when not actually hostile to, working-class interests. The Democrats, while purporting to create jobs through rebuilding America's infrastructure, pursue a regulatory agenda that threatens to kill jobs in mining and heavy industry and an immigration policy that can only increase competition for the remaining jobs while offering empty promises of job retraining for technical positions beyond the reach of those accustomed to muscular work. The Republicans, at least before Donald Trump, pursued free trade policies that may have been good for investors and consumers but were harmful to the interests of industrial workers.

These developments pose a danger to social stability in general and to the Jews in particular. Unemployed white workers are not inherently anti-Semitic. Many have never met a Jew, and surveys do not point to them as a hotbed of anti-Semitic sentiment. Yet young, alienated, uneducated, and rootless workers have often been the foundation for violent and nihilistic political movements. Indeed, the social historian Jefferson Cowie noted the rise of "racial tribalism."[13] With the right guidance, can it be more than a half step from racial tribalism to the JQ yet again? And, indeed, white nationalism and such fantasies as QAnon appeal to certain of these individuals. Jews know their history, whether in Germany, the Soviet Union, Spain, or ancient Persia.

This is where the ideas advanced by Trump and his evangelical, including Christian Zionist, allies entered the picture, and Jews, stuck in the past politically, missed an opportunity and larger trend. In 2022, many American Jews were offended when Trump chastised them for being insufficiently supportive of Israel—though Trump was not altogether incorrect. Most Jews blame Trump—and anyone else who supports him, even other Jews—for promoting white nationalism. However, there is a better, less destructive, way for Jews to understand Trump's significance or the need for a broader alliance with evangelicals. In 2016, Trump focused his campaign on three promises to working-class voters. First, Trump promised to bring an end to free trade policies to keep jobs in America. Second, Trump promised to curtail job-killing environmental and industrial regulatory programs. Third, Trump promised to end immigration programs that, among other things, increased competition for blue-collar jobs. Primarily because of these promises, non-college-educated whites swung to the GOP by a fifteen-point margin in 2016 relative to 2012 and increased their support for the GOP in 2020. More than any other factor in 2016, Trump won because of this enormous jump in Republican support among white working-class voters.[14] These same voters nearly carried him to victory in swing states in 2020.

Jews are currently among the millions of upper-middle-class liberal Democrats who cheered Trump's defeat. While conceding Trump's many defects, let me suggest this is wrongheaded. A successful Republican administration of two terms, even more than inclement weather on Election Day, could have been good for the Jews. The question has become this: Can President Joe Biden successfully address the ongoing depopulation and desertification of an area that includes his own hometown of Scranton, Pennsylvania, before the locals move on from QAnon to develop an interest in the meaning of 1488? Is it inevitable? No. Is it highly possible? Yes, given the growing anti-Semitism around the world.

Given these certain facts, let us consider the worst-case scenario, since Jewish history is chock-full of worst-case, inevitable scenarios. Let us imagine for a moment that in a perfect storm the plight of the white working class is unaddressed and deteriorates further. Let us imagine that the 1488ers and their ilk, realizing the possibilities, stop engaging in titillating conversations with one another on the internet and bring the JQ to a larger audience and join forces with other anti-Zionists, as a few are already doing today. How would the now-divided and politically isolated Jewish community confront such a threat? More important, could Jews look to the anti-Zionist Left for support? No, of course not. Worse, too many Jews have rejected an alliance with Christian Zionists and other evangelicals, distrusting their biblical exegesis and political support for Trump. If they are attacked by a collection of anti-Semites on the Left and the Right, yet reject the natural support of philo-Semitic Christians, what will happen? We know from history not so long ago.

In the nineteenth century, a politically isolated liberal Jewish community, assailed from the Left and Right, excluded from mainstream American society, faced harsh, anti-Semitic restrictions and relegation to the economic and political margins until the 1930s, and, for some Jews, even longer. How many Jews can say this will not happen again? They know Jewish history. Jewish angst is rational. I might add, given Jewish history, anti-Zionist Jews who loudly renounce their "right of return" to Israel might want to give the decision deeper thought.

Appendix

THOUGH IT HAD less impact upon America, the "brain gain" and "brain drain" associated with the rise and fall of the Jews also played a role in other areas of the world. These include medieval England, the Ottoman Empire, and, most important, Spain. It is worth briefly reviewing the events that took place in these regions, though a full account is beyond the scope of this volume.

During the eighth century, from their base in the Carolingian Empire, Jewish merchants became a powerful force in Mediterranean commerce. They exported slaves, furs, and silk to Italy, Spain, and the Middle East and imported luxury goods, including spices, dates, and precious metals. This trade generated significant tax revenue for the Crown and became so important to the imperial economy that Charlemagne's successor, Louis the Pious, was willing to forgo some taxes to encourage the Jews to settle in his realm. Louis accorded Jewish merchants a number of privileges, including exemptions from some taxes and duties as well as royal protection for their property.[1] In a similar vein, Holy Roman Emperor Henry IV found that Jewish traders were so important to the economic health of his realm that he gave the Jewish merchants of Speyer special privileges, declaring that they "should have the freedom to trade their goods in just exchange with any persons, and that they may freely and peacefully travel within the confines of Our kingdom, exercise their commerce and trade, buy and sell and no one shall exact from them any toll or impost, public or private."[2] Both Louis and Henry were motivated by the fact that other rulers frequently sought to lure prominent Jewish merchants away to their own lands in order to bolster their economies.

A second field in which Jews came to play a significant role during the Middle Ages was moneylending and banking. Jews became a dominant force in these endeavors for several reasons, including the matter of religious belief and custom. Both Christian and Muslim religious authorities forbade lending money at interest, while the Talmud limited Jews only from charging excessive rates of interest. Moreover, by declaring debt to be impersonal and providing for its transfer, Talmudic law eased the granting of credit and the pooling of money by creditors—in effect, bank creation—to supply larger loans than any individual could undertake.

No large-scale economy can function without banking and credit, and certainly until at least the early modern period, Jews dominated these endeavors, particularly in Europe. As Max Dimont has described it, the feudal man went to the Jews when he needed money because his harvest failed, or his cattle died, or he needed money to pay his taxes. It was to the Jews that members of the nobility went when they needed money to build new castles. And it was to the Jews that even the cardinals and bishops of the Church went to finance new cathedrals and monasteries.[3]

In several instances, states and principalities issued special invitations to Jewish moneylenders and bankers to set up shop within their borders to ensure an adequate supply of credit to sustain their economies. For example, during the thirteenth and fourteenth centuries, several Italian republics invited Jews to settle there "to provide credit to the needy population."[4] Often, these invitations to Jewish bankers included a variety of guarantees and privileges. The city of Reggio went as far as to assure Jewish moneylenders formally that the city government would fully indemnify them if they ever sustained losses from a popular riot.[5]

Because of the Jews' acumen in trade and banking, states that gave the Jews an opportunity to engage freely in these endeavors profited in two ways. Their overall economies gained, while their treasuries received healthy tax payments from Jewish merchants and bankers. When, as occasionally happened, such states expropriated or expelled their Jewish residents, the economic and fiscal consequences could be disastrous. Take the case of medieval England, for example. During the thirty-five-year reign of Henry II (1154–89), Jews received royal privileges and protection in exchange for the useful commercial and fiscal services they provided to the Crown.[6]

During this period, Jewish merchants, a tiny fraction of England's population, paid approximately one-seventh of all the taxes collected in the kingdom. At the same time, Jewish financiers, most notably Aaron of Lincoln, as well as consortia headed by Moses of Bristol, Brun of London, and others, were essential to the Crown's finances. These financiers earned money through the loans they made to members of the nobility and others needing cash. They then advanced funds to the Crown for its day-to-day expenditures and received, in turn, royal notes secured by expected tax revenues. Thus they performed functions like those undertaken by commercial banks and such institutions as the US Treasury today. Without the Jewish financiers, the Crown would soon have found itself in financial difficulties. With the help of the Jews, England under Henry was quite prosperous.

Henry's successors continued to depend on the Jews for taxes and to fund the Crown's debt. Indeed, during the reign of Richard I, the Crown created an institution that came to be known as the "Exchequer of the Jews" to govern transactions between the Crown and Jewish financiers and to safeguard the king's interests. While the Jews faced considerable popular and clerical anti-Semitism, made worse by their identification with the unpopular, however necessary, occupation of moneylending as well as the continued growth of a crusading spirit in the realm, their value to the Crown meant that the Jews could normally count on the king's protection.

King John, who followed Richard on the throne, seems to have been unaware of the idea that one should not kill the goose that lays the golden egg. Desperate for revenues, John instituted a series of heavy new taxes and assessments against the Jews; held Jews in prison, demanding ransom from their coreligionists; and confiscated a good deal of Jewish property. These policies made it difficult for the Jews to pay their customary taxes or to support the royal debt on a regular basis.

To make matters worse, the outbreak of a civil war between the king and several of his barons created great hardships for the Jews who came under attack from both sides, but particularly from the king's foes. The barons saw the Jews as instruments of the Crown both because of the king's dependence on Jewish financiers and the king's practice of accumulating debts that members of the nobility owed to the Jews. Indeed, in the Magna Carta of 1215, the barons compelled King John to accept limits on the ability of the Jews to recover debts from the landed gentry. The barons also forced the king to agree to accept restrictions on his own power to acquire and recover debts that members of the gentry originally owed to the Jews. The acquisition of such debts had been a significant and hated mechanism through which the Crown extracted resources and enhanced its power over the nobility.

The hardships of the civil war coupled with harsh royal fiscal policies led most of England's Jews to flee the country toward the end of John's reign. In the absence of the Jews, the finances of the kingdom suffered, and with the death of John and the succession of the child-king Henry III in 1216, William Marshal and Hubert de Burgh, successive regents, set about repairing the realm's financial system. To this end, they appealed to the Jews to return, and, to reassure Jewish returnees of their welcome, the regents released Jews being held in prison, promised to protect the Jews from anti-Semitic violence, restored some of the property that had been confiscated, and even went so far as to strike the clauses referring to the Jews when the Magna Carta was reconfirmed after John's death.[7] Many Jews did return, and the old fiscal regime was reestablished.

Unfortunately, however, when Henry III reached majority and began to rule on his own, the Crown's revenue needs for foreign campaigns, for participation in crusades, and for expensive construction projects led the king to reintroduce the harsh policies of his late father, wanting as much short-term revenue from the Jews as possible without considering the long-term fiscal consequences. Thus Henry introduced a variety of confiscatory taxes. If a Jew was unable to pay, the Crown might order his arrest, the imprisonment of his entire family, and the confiscation of his property. Henry's successor, Edward I, continued his policies, extorting money from the Jewish community by imprisoning large numbers of Jews and demanding a ransom from their coreligionists. Jews who could, fled England again, and as a last act, in 1290 Edward expelled England's handful of remaining Jews and confiscated their property.

Fiscal problems for the Crown and capital shortages followed the expulsion of the Jews from England. As a matter of course, however, England began to develop a banking system and to rely on Florentine financiers to provide the Crown with credit. Jews are obviously not the only source of human or financial capital, and England survived their exodus. Interestingly, however, more than four centuries later during the rule of Oliver Cromwell, some argued that the expulsion of the Jews had been a mistake that had weakened England's economy compared to its rivals. The Puritans, of course, also had a more benign attitude toward Jews than others of their time, believing, like today's Christian Zionists, that the Jews had a significant role to play in bringing about the Second Coming.

Cromwell himself was more concerned with practical matters and had noted that the growth and prosperity of cities like Amsterdam, Hamburg, and Leghorn (Livorno) were due to the Jews. Cromwell believed that, if invited to return to England, Jews might contribute to London's prosperity as well. Cromwell saw the Jews as a source of capital, commercial ability, and worldwide commercial connections.[8] Accordingly, Cromwell proposed the readmission of the Jews, a step that King Charles II later authorized in 1664.

Over the ensuing two centuries, Jews began to resettle in England. Though their numbers were small—Jews never amounted to even 1 percent of the English population—they helped make London a center of commerce and banking as Cromwell had foreseen. Jewish immigrants, mostly from Holland and Portugal, founded many of the investment firms and banking houses that even today are major forces in international commerce. These include the Westminster Bank, the Hambros Bank, the Wagg Banking firm (today known as J. Henry Schroder Wagg & Co.), and Mocatta & Goldsmid, a major bullion broker today. The de Costas, the de Medinas, the Montefiores, and the Ricardos started investment firms. Taken together, these immigrant Jews were a powerful brain (and financial) gain for England.

Most of the Jews forced to leave England in the thirteenth century migrated to France and a smaller number to several of the German principalities. Jews, as we saw earlier, had played a key role in French commerce since the days of the Carolingian Empire. Their economic importance, in turn, led successive rulers to grant the Jews several privileges and royal protection. During the twelfth and thirteenth centuries, however, particularly in association with the reigns of Philip Augustus (Philip II) and Louis IX, royal avarice and fiscal ineptitude led to the adoption of confiscatory policies like those of King John and his successors in England. In 1182, faced with an empty royal treasury, Philip Augustus confiscated all Jewish property and expelled the Jews from his kingdom. Within a few years, however, Philip found to his chagrin that the cumulative revenues lost from the termination of Jewish taxes and loans were greater than the onetime gain he had derived from expropriating the Jews.[9] Thus in 1198, Philip invited the Jews to return to the kingdom and resume their economic and fiscal place.

During the reign of Louis IX (Saint Louis), who ruled from 1226 to 1270, the Crown adopted a variety of harsh policies toward the Jews, including the compulsory wearing of distinctive badges, residential limitations, and severe taxation. Given the crusading spirit that prevailed in France during this period, these policies were quite popular. Louis wisely contented himself with continually imposing new taxes on the Jews while allowing them the opportunity to earn the funds with which to pay the taxes. His grandson, Philip IV (known as Philip the Fair), however, emulated the policies of Louis IX. Facing a fiscal crisis, Philip confiscated all Jewish property and expelled the Jews from his kingdom, a step favored by members of the nobility who owed debts to Jewish creditors. Within a few years, however, Philip learned the same lesson forced on his predecessor, Louis IX. The longer-term loss from confiscating Jewish property far exceeded the short-term gain from having no Jews. So Philip invited the Jews to return. This pattern of confiscation, exile, and return continued for close to a century until the Jews were able to find havens in Germany and farther east. In the several French provinces, Provence for example, which resisted royal authority in the fourteenth and fifteenth centuries, the Jewish communities went unmolested because provincial noblemen found that Jewish merchants and moneylenders bolstered the local economy and fattened their own coffers.[10] Unlike their nominal sovereigns, these noblemen eschewed policies that would produce a brain drain.

Spain

The center of Jewish civilization in the Middle Ages was Spain, and it was here that the expulsion of the Jews produced a substantial brain drain with a concomitant brain gain elsewhere in Europe. Medieval Spain consisted of several independent kingdoms, having large numbers of Muslims as well as more than three hundred thousand Jews in a total population of about 5 million. Jews were integrated into Spanish society far more than had ever been the case in England or France. Throughout Spain, Jews were active in the crafts, trade, scholarship, and the learned professions, especially medicine. Jews were so prominent in the economies of the Spanish kingdoms that their tax payments were major factors in royal treasuries, sometimes accounting for half of all royal revenues.[11]

In sharp contrast to England and France, where clerical orders played an important part in the royal administration, the Spanish church and clerical orders, militarized during the centuries-long war against the Moors, had come to be intricately linked with the territorial nobility more so than the Crown. As a result, kings had little alternative but to draw heavily on the talents of Jews as administrators.[12] Spanish kings also depended on Jews as tax collectors and financiers, particularly in Castile, the most powerful and populous of the Christian realms where, as John Crow has noted, royal power in essence was sustained by Jewish money, industry, and intelligence.[13] Jews played a particularly important role in the efforts of Alfonso X (1252–84), Pedro the Cruel (1350–69), Juan II (1406–54), and Henry IV (1454–74) to centralize royal authority at the expense of the nobility as well as in the efforts of these monarchs to expand the boundaries of the Castilian state.[14]

To be sure, Jews were ineligible to serve in the very highest offices. The number of literate and educated Christians in medieval Spain, however, was small. Consequently, to secure administrators with the requisite talents, Spanish kings often found it necessary to appoint Jews who had nominally converted to Christianity—the so-called conversos or new Christians—to high administrative positions. At the end of the fifteenth century, for instance, the occupants of the five highest administrative offices in Aragon were all conversos.[15] Indeed, even the Spanish Church was heavily dependent on this source of administrative talent. A particularly notable example is the career of Solomon Halevi. Though he served as chief rabbi of Burgos, Halevi converted to Christianity in 1390, adopting the name Pablo de Santa María. Soon thereafter, as Henry Kamen reports, Halevi took holy orders and became in turn bishop of Cartagena, bishop of Burgos, tutor to the son of Henry II, and papal legate. One of his sons, Gonzalo, became bishop successively of Astorga, Plasencia, and Sigüenza. Another son, Alonso de Cartagena, succeeded him as bishop of Burgos.[16]

There had been little anti-Semitism in Spain before the fourteenth century. In fourteenth-century Castile, however, efforts by the Crown to expand its own power and revenue base sparked bitter struggles with the nobility.[17] Jews were intricately linked to the Crown and served notably as its revenue agents. This tie between Jews and royal authority led the Castilian nobility to frame its opposition to the Crown and its fiscal demands in anti-Semitic terms. Where the nobility was able to escape increased taxation, the result was to shift the burden of new taxes to the lower ranks of Castilian society, who joined the attack on the Jews as a way of assailing the Crown and its demands for taxes. The Catholic Church encouraged the growth of anti-Jewish sentiment and hoped to increase its influence within the Castilian state by supplanting the Crown's Jewish advisers and administrators.

In 1369, dissident members of the nobility helped Henry II of Trastámara overthrow his half-brother Pedro I and ascend to the Castilian throne. Pedro was closely identified with the Jews and had been supported by them during the struggle with Henry. In the years following Pedro's defeat, Jews became the targets of demonstrations and pogroms. Indeed, anti-Jewish violence throughout Spain in the late fourteenth century led to tens of thousands of conversions, many forced. These conversions had an unanticipated consequence. Even if they had converted at the point of a sword, in their role as nominal Christians, converted Jews could hold royal offices forbidden to them earlier.

During the reign of Juan II of Castile (1406–54) and his successor Henry IV (1454–74), conversos came to occupy key roles in the Castilian government and even began to intermarry with segments of the Castilian nobility. Thus the ironic effect of fourteenth-century anti-Semitism was to enhance the role of converso Jews in the government of Castile during the fifteenth century. However, with the enlarged role of Castilian Jews, it became easier, too, for the regime's opponents to associate it with them and to make use of anti-Semitic appeals to foment resistance to taxation and the expansion of royal authority. This resulted in an upsurge of anti-Semitic activity during the reign of Henry IV and demands by his opponents that the king agree to the establishment of an inquisition, a special ecclesiastical process designed to root out heresy.[18]

Because conversos were nominally Christian, they were subject to the authority of the Church and liable to severe punishment if found guilty of any violation of ecclesiastical law. In this way, an inquisition could be useful to attack the conversos and the state with which they were associated. Forced to allow the creation of an inquisition, Henry was able to keep it under tight rein. After Henry's death, however, his half-sister Isabella assumed the throne of Castile. Isabella's husband, Ferdinand, succeeded to the throne of Aragon in 1479, uniting the two most important Christian kingdoms. Ferdinand and Isabella moved to make use of Henry's widespread unpopularity and, especially, the identification of his regime with the Jews to fortify and expand the power of the newly unified Spanish state.[19]

In 1480, Ferdinand and Isabella brought about the establishment of an inquisition to examine charges that many conversos secretly continued to practice Judaism, thereby violating the laws of the Catholic Church. By 1481, hundreds of conversos were found guilty of this charge and burned at the stake as heretics. Although the Inquisition was mostly an ecclesiastical institution, the Crown kept complete control over its activities and made use of the Inquisition to enhance royal power and national unity. Indeed, the Inquisition played a leading role in the construction of the Spanish state during the late fifteenth century and into the sixteenth century.

First, because the Crown confiscated the lands and property of suspected heretics, the Inquisition provided the royal treasury with a substantial part of the revenues needed to prosecute the war against the Muslims and complete the territorial unification of the Spanish kingdom. Second, the Inquisition played a key role in Spanish national unification. The public trials and the terrible spectacle of the auto-da-fé in which convicted heretics were burned publicly at the stake were designed to unite Spaniards against the enemies of God and the state while building public support for the regime by showing its power and majesty. Finally, as it uncovered plots and heresies among the conversos, the Inquisition functioned to intimidate the regime's opponents and to subordinate local and regional authorities to the authority of the Crown. An enormous number of Spaniards, especially among the nobility and upper classes, were vulnerable to the Inquisition. Over the previous centuries and especially during the previous fifty years, members of the upper classes had intermarried with Jews and conversos, and as a result, many had, or were accused of having, some Jewish ancestry. Their enemies could easily denounce them as secret Judaizers (that is, clandestine practitioners of the Jewish religion) and give them over to the inquisitors. Since the Inquisition's standards of proof were arbitrary, there was no guarantee that a charge could be disproved. The result was to place the upper classes and nobility at the mercy of the Crown.

In many areas, most notably Aragon, Catalonia, Cordoba, Saragossa, and Valencia, the nobility resisted the Inquisition. For example, virtually every noble family in Saragossa was involved in the plot that led to the murder of the chief inquisitor. Such resistance, however, could prove futile. With the help of the Inquisition, the Crown gradually expanded and centralized its power. Not surprisingly, through the mid-seventeenth century Spanish monarchs continued to view the Inquisition as an enormously important instrument for keeping the unity of the state and the power of the Crown.[20] Indeed, the Inquisition was so important an instrument of royal power that Jews who had refused to convert to Christianity—the one group legally not subject to its control—were expelled from Spain in 1492. The Crown saw the continued presence of unconverted Jews in Spain as a threat to national unity and to the state's authority, while the Church saw them as a threat to the religious loyalty of the conversos.

Between fifty thousand and a hundred thousand Jews left Spain in 1492 by force, while another fifty thousand accepted baptisms to remain in their homes. Of those who left, the largest number immigrated to the Ottoman Empire and were received warmly. Others immigrated to Holland and smaller numbers to parts of Germany, France, Italy, and, eventually, England. Some even came to the New World. There are descendants of conversos in Mexico and the US state of New Mexico. Several thousand Jewish refugees also crossed the Spanish border into Portugal, where the Portuguese initially welcomed but later forcibly baptized them. The conversos who remained in Spain were constantly threatened by Spanish officials with exposure as Judaizers and mostly barred from holding key offices by new requirements that reserved them and other prominent positions for individuals who could prove Christian ancestors for several generations.

The overall result of the expulsion and related measures was a massive transfer of talent and experience from Spain to other nations. The chief beneficiaries were the Ottomans. Jewish exiles from Spain, known as the Sephardim, from the Hebrew word for Spain, quickly became important merchants and traders in the Ottoman realm. Jews from Istanbul and Salonica, the main centers of Jewish settlement, developed trade routes through Greece to southeastern Europe and, via the Danube, to Hungary, Austria, central Europe, Poland, and Russia. During the course of the sixteenth century, Ottoman Jewish merchants developed trade with France and Germany and some even ventured into Spain itself, though disguised as Muslims.[21] Over time, Jewish traders created major markets for Ottoman products and raw materials throughout Europe and the Far East, exporting medicines, woolens, silk, dried fruits, rugs, cement, cotton, linens, and a host of other goods.[22] In this way, Jewish traders enriched the Ottoman realm and, through their taxes, the sultan's government. Such was the contribution of Jewish merchants and traders that Ottoman rulers would often settle several Jewish families in areas recently conquered by Ottoman forces to hasten their economic development.

Subsequently, Jews came to play a leading role in the fiscal affairs and administration of the Ottoman Empire. Jews were particularly useful to the Ottomans because they lacked ties to any of the subjected populations of the multiethnic empire and therefore could be entrusted with unpopular tasks such as tax collection. Jews dominated the imperial revenue system, serving as tax collectors, tax farmers, tax intendants, and tax inspectors. Jews also created and ran the imperial customs service. Indeed, so complete was Jewish control over this segment of the Ottoman state that Ottoman customs receipts were often written in Hebrew. Jews also went with provincial governors, or pashas, as financial advisers and fiscal administrators. In the latter days of the empire, when provincial governorships became hereditary or quasi-independent, local Jewish financiers continued in this role. For example, the Farhi family of Damascus directed the financial affairs of Syria from the eighteenth century through the termination of Ottoman rule after World War I.[23]

Several Jews also became important advisers and physicians to the Ottoman court. The most famous was Joseph Nasi, who was the principal counselor to two sultans and ennobled as the duke of Naxos. Nasi used his influence to secure the sultan's support for the reestablishment of a Jewish homeland in Palestine, then under Ottoman rule. With the sultan's help, a Jewish settlement began in Safed, in the upper Galilee, which became a center for rabbinic study. Unfortunately, not all Nasi's advice was sound. It was his plan that helped bring about the Turkish naval defeat in the Battle of Lepanto in 1571, and as a result, his influence at court declined.[24] Another major Ottoman state institution that relied on Jewish administrators was the imperial army—the janissary corps. Jews dominated the position of *ocak bazirgani*, or chief quartermaster, for the corps. This became the hereditary possession of a small group of Jewish families in Istanbul and Salonika. In addition, each provincial janissary garrison had its own quartermaster, virtually always a Jewish merchant.[25]

Those Jews who migrated from Spain to the various other nations of Europe did not fare so well as their compatriots in the Ottoman realm. Jewish and converso merchants nevertheless became important in the commerce of several European cities. According to Werner Sombart, Jewish refugees from Spain contributed hugely to the economic rise of the Italian city of Leghorn (Livorno) as well as the German cities of Hamburg and Frankfurt. And in France, Sombart credited the rise of Marseilles, Bordeaux, and Rouen to their willingness to admit Jewish émigrés.[26]

Several thousand Jewish refugees, followed by exiles from Portugal, settled in Holland, where they played a key role in enhancing Dutch economic and political power. Sephardic merchants in the Netherlands made that nation the center of a lucrative set of trade routes involving the shipment of goods to and from the Netherlands, Spain, and Portugal and the Spanish, Portuguese, and Dutch colonies in the New World.[27] In the late seventeenth century, Dutch Sephardim became active in finance and shipping and as commodities brokers. Sephardim organized one of the world's first stock and commodities exchanges, and in 1688 a Sephardic writer, Joseph Pensa de la Vega, wrote the earliest-known account of the operations of a stock exchange.[28] In the mid-seventeenth century, when a group of Dutch Sephardim petitioned Oliver Cromwell to admit Jews to England, the Dutch government became quite anxious, fearing that it would lose important merchants and financiers to the English. The Jews reassured the government that this was not their intention, but, when Jews were readmitted to England, Sephardim from Holland became some of London's leading bankers and financiers. It could be said that the Jews were able to avenge themselves on the English for the 1290 expulsion and reward the Dutch when the wealthy Sephardic financier Francisco Lopes Suasso supplied the financing for the Protestant Glorious Revolution, which allowed the Dutch stadtholder William of Orange to take possession of the English throne in 1688.[29] All in all, the nations that offered refuge to Sephardic exiles gained considerably.

As to Spain itself, the immediate effect of its expulsion of the Jews was a series of economic dislocations, including shortages of credit, the collapse of the important wool industry, and a decline in manufacturing. These were all realms in which the Jews had been important. In the early years of the sixteenth century, though, these seemed minor problems as a flood of gold from the New World helped make Spain the wealthiest and most powerful nation in Europe. As the century wore on, however, the absence of the Jews and subordination of the conversos came to play a role in the decline of Spain as a world power.

The causes of Spain's rapid decline after a dizzying rise to power are complex, but three factors stand out. First, compared to its foes, including the Dutch and French, seventeenth- and eighteenth-century Spain had almost no manufacturing base. In the sixteenth century, for example, only five military ordinance factories existed in Spain, and these were inadequate to supply the military needs of the Spanish armies. Two were usually out of service, and one was only able to work at half its nominal capacity.[30] These problems, in turn, reflected the larger problem of an absent Spanish industrious middle class able to manage such matters as manufacturing processes.[31] Second, the royal revenue system was a fiscal disaster. Despite the flow of gold from the Americas, successive Spanish governments were unable to devise a fiscal system that would meet the government's expenditures without the imposition of ruinous taxes on the kingdom.[32] Finally, there was the general matter of administrative leadership. Many members of the Spanish nobility, like their counterparts elsewhere in Europe, disdained administrative tasks usually relegated to the Jews. No less an authority than the Count-Duke of Olivares, (arguably) the most able Spanish minister, declared that the Spanish nobility lacked adequate leadership abilities. Olivares, in fact, made an unsuccessful attempt to sponsor the creation of a leadership school for young noblemen.[33]

Such mundane undertakings as manufacturing, fiscal matters, and government administration had previously been in the hands of a persecuted religious group, expelled from Spain at the end of the fifteenth century. Absent the Jews and conversos, Spain suffered from serious deficiencies in realms critical to the maintenance of its status as a great power. One reason, for example, that Spanish manufacturing fell behind its rivals is that the conversos, who were overall leaders in this realm after 1492, were anxious to deflect any lingering suspicion by leaving occupations formerly associated with Jews. Hence, rather than improve their business and manufacturing methods, according to the historian John Lynch, conversos sought to leave business, buy noble titles, and become landowners.[34]

Another example that helps make this point pertains to the events of the War of the Grand Alliance (1688–97), in which Spain allied with the Dutch against France. Because of Spain's customary fiscal muddle and administrative incompetence, the royal government was unable to provision or pay its army, which, in turn, threatened to mutiny. Only the intervention of Francisco Lopes Suasso (originally Abraham Israel Suasso), the son of a Sephardic refugee living in Holland, averted disaster (the same extraordinary man who helped finance the English Glorious Revolution, which defeated a Catholic king, James II). Lopes Suasso reorganized the Spanish army's finances and secured funds with which to pay the troops. Spanish authorities praised Lopes Suasso for his *galantería* (gallantry).[35] What a pity that this *galantería* went unrecognized when the Spanish Crown decided to expel some of its most talented subjects.

Notes

Introduction

1. Anti-Defamation League, newsletter, n.d., https://www.adl.org/disinformation
-exaggerated-claims-of-targeted-antisemitic-violence-in-los-angeles.
2. Shane Harris and Brittany Shammas, "Antisemitic Attacks on Rise in U.S. Cities," *Washington Post*, May 24, 2021, A7.

Chapter 1. Anti-Semitism Today: Three Questions to Ask Anti-Semites

Parts of this chapter appeared in the following publications and, with permission from the copyright holder, are reproduced with amendments: Benjamin Ginsberg, "American Jews in Political and Social Movements," in *Encyclopedia of American Jewish History,* ed. Stephen H. Norwood and Eunice G. Pollack (Santa Barbara, Calif.: ABC-CLIO Inc., 2008). © 2008 ABC-CLIO Inc.; Benjamin Ginsberg, *How the Jews Defeated Hitler* (Lanham, Md.: Rowman & Littlefield, 2013). © 2013 Benjamin Ginsberg; and Benjamin Ginsberg, "Christian Zionism: Is It Good for the Jews?" in *From Antisemitism to Anti-Zionism: The Past and Present of a Lethal Ideology,* ed. Eunice G. Pollack (Boston: Academic Studies Press, 2017). © 2017 Academic Studies Press.

1. Sarah Hall in The Guardian, Ap.12, 2022. https://www.theguardian.com/world/2002/apr/13/israel.booksnews.
2. Richard Landes, "The Wages of Moral Schadenfreude in the Press," in *From Antisemitism to Anti-Zionism*, ed. Eunice Pollack (Boston: Academic Studies Press, 2017), 194.
3. Rebecca Vilkomerson, "I'm Jewish, and I Want People to Boycott Israel," *Washington Post*, June 24, 2016, https://www.washingtonpost.com/posteverything/wp/2016/06/24/im-jewish-and-i-want-people-to-boycott-israel.
4. Deadly Exchange, https://deadlyexchange.org/.
5. J. J. Goldberg, *Jewish Power: Inside the Jewish Establishment* (New York: Basic Books, 1996), chap. 5. See also Yuri Slezkine, *The Jewish Century* (Princeton, NJ: Princeton University Press, 2004).
6. John J. Mearsheimer and Stephen M. Walt, *The Israel Lobby and U.S. Foreign Policy* (New York: Farrar, Straus and Giroux, 2007).

7. Mitchell Cohen, "Anti-Semitism and the Left That Doesn't Learn," *Dissent* (Winter 2008), https://www.dissentmagazine.org/article/anti-semitism-and-the-left-that-doesnt-learn-2.

8. "CNN Poll: Majority of Americans Side with Israel in Gaza Fighting," CNN/ORC Poll, July 21, 2014, http://politicalticker.blogs.cnn.com/2014/07/21/cnn-poll-americans-clearly-side-with-israel-in-gaza-fighting.

9. Cornel West, "There is a relationship between the ghetto of Gaza and the ghettos of America," Facebook, August 13, 2014, https://www.facebook.com/drcornelwest/posts/10154494189395111.

10. Ari Hart, "Black Lives Matter Lost Me with That Israel-Bashing Platform," *Forward*, August 4, 2016, http://forward.com/opinion/346865/black-lives-matter-lost-me-with-that-israel-bashing-platform.

11. Domenica Ghanem, "Why We Should Be Alarmed That Israeli Forces and U.S. Police Are Training Together: The Israeli Forces Mowing Down Unarmed Palestinian Protesters Also Train U.S. Police Forces That Brutalize Communities of Color," *Foreign Policy in Focus*, June 7, 2018, https://fpif.org/why-we-should-be-alarmed-that-israeli-forces-and-u-s-police-are-training-together/.

12. Bernard Harrison, *The Resurgence of Anti-Semitism: Jews, Israel, and Liberal Opinion* (Lanham, MD: Rowman & Littlefield, 2006).

13. See, for example, the 2009 Goldstone report: UN Human Rights Council, "Human Rights in Palestine and Other Occupied Arab Territories: Report of the United Nations Fact-Finding Mission on the Gaza Conflict," https://archive.org/details/TheGoldstoneReport-ReportOfTheUnitedNationsFactFindingMissionOnThe. For a critique of the Goldstone report, see Peter Berkowitz, "Blaming Israel First," *Weekly Standard*, January 18, 2010, 14–16.

14. David Shulman, *Dark Hope* (Chicago: University of Chicago Press, 2007).

15. Jacqueline Rose, *The Question of Zion* (Princeton, NJ: Princeton University Press, 2005).

16. Gabriel Schoenfeld, *The Return of Anti-Semitism* (New York: Encounter Books, 2004), chap. 3.

17. Alison Weir, "Israeli Organ Harvesting," *CounterPunch*, August 28, 2009, https://www.counterpunch.org/2009/08/28/israeli-organ-harvesting.

18. Israel Shamir, "Bloodcurdling Libel," *Writings of Israel Shamir*, n.d., http://www.israelshamir.net/English/blood.htm.

19. Adam Holland, "Alison Weir Continues to Promote Blood Libel," October 11, 2009, http://adamholland.blogspot.com/2009/10/alison-weir-continues-to-promote-blood.html.

Chapter 2. How Anti-Semitism Became a Progressive Ideology

Parts of this chapter appeared in the following publications and, with permission from the copyright holder, are reproduced with amendments: Benjamin Ginsberg, *The Fatal Embrace: Jews and the State* (Chicago: University of Chicago Press, 1993). © 1993 University of Chicago Press; Benjamin Ginsberg, "Why University Administrators Tolerate Antisemitism," in *Antisemitism on the Campus: Past and Present*, ed. Eunice G. Pollack (Boston: Academic Studies Press, 2011). © 2011 Academic Studies Press; and Benjamin Ginsberg, *How the Jews Defeated Hitler* (Lanham, Md.: Rowman & Littlefield, 2013). © 2013 Benjamin Ginsberg.

1. Izabella Tabarovsky, "Soviet Anti-Zionism and Contemporary Left Antisemitism," *Fathom*, May 2019, https://fathomjournal.org/soviet-anti-zionism-and-contemporary-left -antisemitism.

2. Harold Evans, "The View from Ground Zero," in *Those Who Forget the Past*, ed. Ron Rosenbaum (New York: Random House, 2004), 36–56.

3. Kevin Sack, "Transplant Brokers in Israel Lure Desperate Kidney Patients to Costa Rica," *New York Times*, August 17, 2014, 1.

4. Benjamin Ginsberg, *The Fatal Embrace: Jews and the State* (Chicago: University of Chicago Press, 1993), 8.

5. Christopher Caldwell, *Reflections on the Revolution in Europe: Immigration, Islam, and the West* (New York: Doubleday, 2009).

6. "Interview with Dore Gold: Why the UN Has Failed," George Washington University, History News Network, January 7, 2005, http://hnn.us/roundup/entries/9530 .html.

7. Malise Ruthven, "The Big Muslim Problem!," *New York Review of Books*, December 17, 2009, 62.

8. Jonathan Freedland, "As British Jews Come under Attack, the Liberal Left Must Not Remain Silent," *Guardian*, February 4, 2009, https://www.theguardian.com/ commentisfree/2009/feb/04/gaza-jewish-community.

9. "Palestine and the Left," *Jacobin*, April 21, 2013, https://www.jacobinmag.com /2013/04/palestine-and-the-left.

10. Lorenzo Vidino, "Along Came Sharia: Islam and European Secularism Clash," *National Review*, February 19, 2004, https://www.nationalreview.com/2004/02/along -came-sharia-lorenzo-vidino-erick-stakelbeck.

11. Alex Callinicos, "The European Radical Left Tested Electorally," International Viewpoint, December 9, 2004, https://www.internationalviewpoint.org/spip.php?article10.

12. Bret Stephens, "Islamosocialism," *Wall Street Journal*, March 18, 2007, https:// www.wsj.com/articles/SB117375197026135001.

13. Callinicos, "European Radical Left Tested Electorally."

14. Robert S. Wistrich, *Muslim Anti-Semitism* (New York: American Jewish Committee, 2002), 11.

15. Matthias Kuntzel, *Jihad and Jew Hatred* (New York: Telos, 2007), 136.

16. Kuntzel, *Jihad and Jew Hatred*, 151.

17. Wistrich, *Muslim Anti-Semitism*, 12.

18. Wistrich, *Muslim Anti-Semitism*, 14.

19. Wistrich, *Muslim Anti-Semitism*, 19.

20. Kuntzel, *Jihad and Jew Hatred*, 151.

21. Anti-Defamation League, *ADL Global 100: An Index of Anti-Semitism*, n.d., https:// www.scribd.com/document/223766774/ADL-Global-100-Executive-Summary.

22. *On the Record with Greta Van Susteren*, Fox News, June 24, 2002, http://www .danielpipes.org/426/how-central-is-muslim-anti-semitism.

23. Daniel Schwammenthal, "Europe Reimports Jew Hatred," *Wall Street Journal*, January 13, 2009, http://online.wsj.com/article/SB123180033807075069.html.

24. Gabriel Schoenfeld, *The Return of Anti-Semitism* (New York: Encounter Books, 2004), chap. 3.

25. Schoenfeld, *Return of Anti-Semitism*, 68–71.

26. Andrew Bostom, "The Islamization of European Anti-Semitism," *American Thinker*, September 7, 2006, http://www.americanthinker.com/articles/2006/09/the_islamization_of_european_a.html.

27. Anti-Defamation League, "ADL Survey in Ten European Countries Finds Anti-Semitism at Disturbingly High Levels," press release, March 12, 2012, https://www.adl.org/news/press-releases/adl-survey-in-ten-european-countries-finds-anti-semitism-at-disturbingly-high.

28. Gabriel Schoenfeld, "Israel and the Anti-Semites," in *Those Who Forget the Past*, ed. Ron Rosenbaum (New York: Random House, 2004), 104.

29. Schoenfeld, *Return of Anti-Semitism*, 34.

30. Bernard Harrison, *The Resurgence of Anti-Semitism: Jews, Israel, and Liberal Opinion* (Lanham, MD: Rowman & Littlefield, 2006), 106.

31. Schoenfeld, *Return of Anti-Semitism*, 98.

32. Robert Jan Van Pelt, "The Case for Auschwitz," in *Those Who Forget the Past*, ed. Ron Rosenbaum (New York: Random House, 2004), 396.

33. Mark Strauss, "Antiglobalism's Jewish Problem," in *Those Who Forget the Past*, ed. Ron Rosenbaum (New York: Random House, 2004), 276.

34. Strauss, "Antiglobalism's Jewish Problem," 281.

35. Schoenfeld, *Return of Anti-Semitism*, 74.

36. Seth Mydans, "Malaysian Premier Sees Jews behind Nation's Money Crisis," *New York Times*, October 16, 1997, https://www.nytimes.com/1997/10/16/world/malaysian-premier-sees-jews-behind-nation-s-money-crisis.html.

37. Jewish Telegraphic Agency, "Hamas: 'Jewish Lobby' Caused Financial Crisis," October 7, 2008, https://www.jta.org/2008/10/07/default/hamas-jewish-lobby-caused-financial-crisis.

38. Anti-Defamation League, "Iranian President Mahmoud Ahmadinejad in His Own Words" (excerpts from a speech titled "Holocaust, the Holy Lie of the West," at Sharif University in Tehran, September 23, 2008, https://www.adl.org/news/article/iranian-president-mahmoud-ahmadinejad-in-his-own-words).

39. David Patterson, "Denial, Evasion, and Antihistorical Antisemitism," in *Deciphering the New Antisemitism*, ed. Alvin H. Rosenfeld (Bloomington: Indiana University Press, 2015), 326–49.

40. Max Fisher, "Why Home-Grown Islamic Terrorism Isn't a Threat," *Atlantic*, November 11, 2009, https://www.theatlantic.com/politics/archive/2009/11/why-home-grown-islamic-terrorism-isnt-a-threat/29993.

41. Lisa Katz, "Muslim Views of Jews," Learn Religions, January 27, 2016, http://judaism.about.com/od/americanworldjewry/a/muslimviews.htm.

42. Ben Harris, "Israel Apartheid Week Kicks Off," Jewish Telegraphic Agency, March 2, 2009, https://www.jta.org/2009/03/02/news-opinion/the-telegraph/israel-apartheid-week-kicks-off.

43. Gustavo Arellano, "Amir Abdel Malik Ali, A UCI Muslim Student Union Fave," *OC Weekly*, May 16, 2009, https://www.ocweekly.com/news-amir-abdel-malik-ali-a-uci -muslim-student-union-fave-an-anti-semitic-homophobic-coward-6451105/.

44. "CAIRwatch: Keeping an Eye on Hate," profile of Affad Shaikh, n.d., Americans against Hate, http://www.americansagainsthate.org/cw/profiles_cw.php.

45. Leon Cohen, "Churchill Has Targeted Jews and Israel," *Wisconsin Jewish Chronicle*, March 31, 2008, https://www.jewishchronicle.org/2008/03/31/churchill-has-targeted -jews-and-israel/.

46. Alain Goldschlager, "The Canadian Campus Scene," in *Academics against Israel and the Jews*, ed. Manfred Gerstenfeld (Jerusalem: Jerusalem Center for Public Affairs, 2007), 157–58.

47. "U. Michigan Students Involved in BDS Motion: 'Jews Not a Nation,' Zionism a 'Dirty Ideology,'" The College Fix, November 25, 2017, https://www.thecollegefix.com/u -michigan-students-involved-bds-motion-jews-not-nation-zionism-dirty-ideology/.

48. Lawrence Summers, "Address at Morning Prayers, Memorial Church, Harvard University, September 17, 2002," in *Those Who Forget the Past*, ed. Ron Rosenbaum (New York: Random House, 2004), 59.

49. US Commission on Civil Rights, "Campus Anti-Semitism," Briefing Report, Washington, DC, July 2006, 14.

50. Hannah Elka Meyers, "The Flames of Anti-Semitism Are Growing Higher, Fueled by Both the Left and Right," Tablet, February 4, 2021, https://www.tabletmag.com/ sections/news/articles/anti-semitism-review-2020.

51. Mitchell Bard, "Jewish Students Must Learn How to Protest—and Fight Back," *Algemeiner*, June 5, 2017, http://www.algemeiner.com/2017/06/05/jewish-students-must -learn-how-to-protest-and-fight-back.

52. "Discrimination and Harassment of Jewish Students at UC Davis," AMCHA Initiative, November 19, 2012, https://amchainitiative.org/discrimination-and-harassment-of -jewish-students-at-uc-davis-on-november-19-2012/.

53. "Jewish Student Punched in Face and Called 'Kike' in Anti-Semitic Attack," The Yeshiva World, August 21, 2014, https://www.theyeshivaworld.com/news/headlines -breaking-stories/255325/temple-univ-jewish-student-punched-in-face-and-called-kike-in -anti-semitic-attack.html.

54. Bard, "Jewish Students Must Learn."

55. Kenneth Walzer, "From Intersectionality to the Exclusion of Jewish Students: BDS Makes a Worrying Turn on US Campuses," Fathom, July 2018, http://fathomjournal.org /from-intersectionality-to-the-exclusion-of-jewish-students-bds-makes-a-worrying-turn -on-us-campuses/.

56. Yair Rosenberg, "How Oberlin Has Repeatedly Failed to Confront Anti-Semitism on Campus," Tablet, May 24, 2016, https://www.tabletmag.com/scroll/203330/how -oberlin-has-repeatedly-failed-to-confront-anti-semitism-on-campus.

57. "A Portrait of Jewish Americans," Pew Research Center, October 1, 2013, https:// www.pewforum.org/2013/10/01/chapter-5-connection-with-and-attitudes-towards-israel.

58. Linda K. Wertheimer, "The Middle East Conflict on Campus," *New York Times Education Life*, August 7, 2016, 10.

59. John J. Mearsheimer and Stephen M. Walt, *The Israel Lobby and U.S. Foreign Policy* (New York: Farrar, Straus and Giroux, 2007).

60. Joshua Muravchik, *Making David into Goliath: How the World Turned against Israel* (New York: Encounter Books, 2014).

61. Schoenfeld, *Return of Anti-Semitism*, 90.

62. Steven Erlanger, "French Protest of Israeli Raid Reaches Wide Audience," *New York Times*, June 13, 2010.

63. Mearsheimer and Walt, *Israel Lobby and U.S. Foreign Policy*, vii, 6.

64. James Petras, *Rulers and Ruled in the U.S. Empire: Bankers, Zionists, Militants* (Atlanta, GA: Clarity Press, 2007), 103.

65. See Bob Woodward, *Bush at War* (New York: Simon & Schuster, 2003).

66. Gary Felton, *The Host and the Parasite: How Israel's Fifth Column Consumed America* (Tempe, AZ: Dandelion Books, 2007).

67. "Americans Closely Divided over Israel's Gaza Attacks," Rasmussen Reports, December 31, 2008, https://www.rasmussenreports.com/public_content/politics/current_events/israel_the_middle_east/americans_closely_divided_over_israel_s_gaza_attacks.

68. "Growing Majority of Americans Oppose Israel Building Settlements," World Public Opinion, April 29, 2009, http://worldpublicopinion.net/growing-majority-of-americans-oppose-israel-building-settlements.

69. "End the Occupation! Cynthia McKinney Preaches Hate and Silences Opposition at Binghamton," Vocal Minority, November 20, 2009, http://vocalminority.typepad.com/blog/2009/11/end-the-occupation-cynthia-mckinney-preaches-hate-and-silences-opposition-at-binghamton.html.

70. Adam Kredo, "Congressman: Jewish Settlers Are like Termites," *Washington Free Beacon*, July 25, 2016, http://freebeacon.com/politics/congressman-jewish-settlers-like-termites.

71. Ginsberg, *Fatal Embrace*, 146.

72. Dan Gilgoff, "Rev. Jeremiah Wright Says Jews Are Preventing Obama from Talking to Him," *U.S. News & World Report*, June 11, 2009, https://www.usnews.com/news/blogs/god-and-country/2009/06/11/rev-jeremiah-wright-says-jews-are-preventing-obama-from-talking-to-him.

73. Seth Lipsky, "Zero-Sum Politics," *Wall Street Journal*, August 23, 2000, https://www.opinionjournal.com/columnists/slipsky/?id=65000141.

74. Lipsky, "Zero-Sum Politics."

75. Ginsberg, *Fatal Embrace*, 167.

76. Daniel Pipes, "Cynthia McKinney's Arab and Islamist Donors," Daniel Pipes Middle East Forum, last updated October 25, 2007, https://www.danielpipes.org/blog/2004/07/cynthia-mckinneys-arab-and-islamist-donors.

77. Jinjirrie, "End Apartheid, Slavery, Caste & Racism—Support WCAR 2009," Kadaitcha, March 3, 2009, https://www.kadaitcha.com/2009/03/03/end-apartheid-slavery-caste-racism-support-wcar-2009-2.

78. Harold Cruse, *The Crisis of the Negro Intellectual* (New York: Quill, 1984), 147–70.

79. Alvin H. Rosenfeld, *Progressive Jewish Thought and the New Anti-Semitism* (New York: American Jewish Committee, 2006).

80. Otto Weininger, *Sex and Character* (New York: Putnam's, 1908; originally published as *Geschlecht und Charakter*, 1903), chap. 8.

81. David Aaronovitch, "The Ironies of Hating Oneself," *Jewish Chronicle*, August 6, 2009, https://www.thejc.com/the-ironies-of-hating-oneself-1.10713?.

82. "Fugitive 'Aryan' Making Life Miserable for His Parents—Again," Southern Poverty Law Center, October 19, 2006, https://www.splcenter.org/fighting-hate/intelligence -report/2006/fugitive-aryan-making-life-miserable-his-parents-again.

83. Ruth Wisse, *If I Am Not for Myself . . . The Liberal Betrayal of the Jews* (New York: Free Press, 1992).

84. Norman Podhoretz, *Why Are Jews Liberals?* (New York: Doubleday, 2009).

85. Edward Alexander, "Introduction," in *The Jewish Divide over Israel*, ed. Edward Alexander and Paul Bogdanor (New Brunswick, NJ: Transaction, 2006), xiv–xvi.

86. Alexander, "Introduction," xv.

87. Tony Judt, "Israel: The Alternative," *New York Review of Books*, October 23, 2003, https://www.nybooks.com/articles/2003/10/23/israel-the-alternative/.

88. Ilan Pappé, *The Ethnic Cleansing of Palestine* (Oxford: Oneworld Publications, 2006).

89. Noam Chomsky, *Fateful Triangle: The United States, Israel, and the Palestinians* (London: Pluto Press, 1999).

90. Michael Neumann, "What Is Anti-Semitism?," in *The Politics of Anti-Semitism*, ed. Alexander Cockburn and Jeffrey St. Clair (Oakland, CA: AK Press, 2003), 2–10.

91. Norman Finkelstein, *The Holocaust Industry*, 2nd ed. (London: Verso, 2003).

92. Doron Ben-Atar, "Historicizing the Transhistorical," in *Deciphering the New Anti- semitism*, ed. Alvin H. Rosenfeld (Bloomington: Indiana University Press, 2015), 134.

93. Judith Butler, "No, It's Not Anti-Semitic," *London Review of Books* 25, no. 16 (August 2003): 19–21, https://www.lrb.co.uk/v25/n16/judith-butler/no-its-not-anti-semitic.

94. Alexander, "Introduction," xxiv.

95. Jimmy Pasch, "LGBTQ Protests against Israel Are about Justice, Not Anti-Semitism," *In These Times*, January 19, 2016, http://inthesetimes.com/article/18809/creating -change-protest-lgbtq-anti-semitism-israel-palestine.

96. Justin Katz, "Protestors Link Justice for Black Americans to Palestinians," *Washington Jewish Week*, August 18, 2016, 4.

Chapter 3. Why the Jews Persist

1. For an excellent review of the debate between the optimists and the pessimists, see Chaim Waxman, "Is the Cup Half-Full or Half-Empty? Perspectives on the Future of the American Jewish Community," in *American Pluralism and the Jewish Community*, ed. Seymour Lipset (London: Routledge, 1989), 71–85. See also the essays in David M. Gordis and Yoav Ben-Horn, eds., *Jewish Identity in America* (Los Angeles: Wilstein Institute, 1991). For an excellent study that underlines the long-term strength and cohesiveness of the American Jewish community despite assimilationist pressures, see Calvin Goldscheider, *Jewish Continuity and Change* (Bloomington: Indiana University Press, 1986). See also Steven M. Cohen, *American Assimilation or Jewish Revival?* (Bloomington: Indiana

University Press, 1988). Cohen's analysis of the data also leads him to reject the notion that the American Jewish community is likely to disappear because of assimilation into the larger society.

2. Hannah Arendt, *The Origins of Totalitarianism*, rev. ed. (New York: Harcourt, 1967), chaps. 2 and 3.

3. Paul Johnson, *A History of the Jews* (New York: Harper & Row, 1987), pt. 2.

4. Ahad Ha-am, *Al Parashat Derakhim* (Tel Aviv, Israel: Dvir & Hotzaah Ivrit, 1964), 2:139.

5. Data from the 2008 yearbook; the current edition is Arnold Sashefsky and Ira M. Sheskin, eds., *American Jewish Year Book 2017* (New York: Springer, 2018).

6. Jonathan Woocher, *Sacred Survival: The Civil Religion of American Jews* (Bloomington: Indiana University Press, 1986).

7. Woocher, *Sacred Survival*, 75.

8. The classic work describing the processes through which the maintenance of an organization can become more important than an organization's nominal goals is Philip Selznick, *TVA and the Grass Roots: A Study in the Sociology of Formal Organization* (Berkeley: University of California Press, 1949).

9. Genesis 17:7–8. Unless otherwise indicated, the source for all biblical references is the Jewish Publication Society's 1985 English translation of the Tanakh, or Holy Scriptures (Philadelphia: Jewish Publication Society, 1985).

10. Exodus 19:4–6.

11. Deuteronomy 7:6.

12. Amos 3:2.

13. Abba Hillel Silver, *Where Judaism Differs* (New York: Macmillan, 1956), chap. 4.

14. Genesis 28:14.

15. Silver, *Where Judaism Differs*, 75.

16. Numbers 23:9.

17. Leviticus 20:26.

18. Jeremiah 11:16.

19. Ezekiel 20:32.

20. Silver, *Where Judaism Differs*. See also Emil L. Fackenheim, *What Is Judaism?* (New York: Summit, 1987), chap. 5.

21. Leviticus 18:3.

22. Jacob Neusner, trans., *The Mishnah* (New Haven, CT: Yale University Press, 1988), 4th division, Abodah Zarah 2:1.

23. Hayim Halevy Donin, *To Raise a Jewish Child* (New York: Basic Books, 1977), 123.

24. Shirley Newman, *An Introduction to Kings, Later Prophets, and Writings* (New York: Behrman House, 1981), chaps. 16 and 17.

25. 1 Kings 11–15.

26. Newman, *Introduction to Kings*, 76.

27. Newman, *Introduction to Kings*, 78.

28. Exodus 33:16.

29. Exodus 34:10–16.

30. See Ari Goldman, "Poll Shows Jews Both Assimilate and Keep Tradition," *New York Times*, June 7, 1991, A14.

Notes | 207

31. Abraham Regelson, ed., *The Passover Haggadah* (New York: Shulsinger Brothers, 1965), 32.

32. Regelson, *Passover Haggadah*, 12.

33. Regelson, *Passover Haggadah*, 53.

34. Esther 3:8.

35. Esther 3:13.

36. Esther 5:13.

37. Esther 8:12. The Jewish Publication Society's translation omits this passage. It can, however, be found in other translations such as the *New Jerusalem Bible* (New York: Doubleday, 1990).

38. Norman Stillman, *The Jews of Arab Lands* (Philadelphia: Jewish Publication Society, 1979), chap. 3. See also Walter Fischel, *Jews in the Economic and Political Life of Medieval Islam* (New York: KTAV Publishing, 1969), 68–89.

39. Deborah Pessin, *The Jewish People*, book II (New York: United Synagogue of America, 1952), 55.

40. See, for example, Hella Taubes, *The Bible Speaks*, vol. 3 (London: Soncino Press, 1971). This work devotes two chapters to the Maccabees.

41. 1 Maccabees 1:11–15. For the books of Maccabees, I have relied on the *New Jerusalem Bible* translation.

42. 1 Maccabees 2:24.

43. 1 Maccabees 6:23–27.

44. 1 Maccabees 4:15–16.

45. 2 Maccabees 4:37.

46. Cohen, *American Assimilation or Jewish Revival?*, chap. 6.

47. Rafael Medoff, *The Deafening Silence: American Jewish Leaders and the Holocaust* (New York: Carol Publishing Group, 1986), chaps. 8–10. See also Leon Weliczker Wells, *Who Speaks for the Vanquished? American Jewish Leaders and the Holocaust* (New York: Peter Lang, 1987), 268–89.

48. Arthur Hertzberg, *The Jews in America—Four Centuries of an Uneasy Encounter: A History* (New York: Columbia University Press, 1998), 342.

49. Hertzberg, *Jews in America*, 343.

50. See Wells, *Who Speaks for the Vanquished?*, 269.

51. Woocher, *Sacred Survival*, 64. See also Daniel Elazar, "Developments in Jewish Community Organization in the Second Postwar Generation," in *American Pluralism and the Jewish Community*, ed. Seymour Lipset (London: Routledge, 1989), 173–92; and Steven M. Cohen, *American Modernity and Jewish Identity* (New York: Tavistock Publications, 1983), chap. 8.

52. Peter Novick, *The Holocaust in American Life* (New York: Mariner Books, 2000).

53. Robert Shogan, *Prelude to Catastrophe: FDR's Jews and the Menace of Nazism* (Chicago: Ivan Dee, 2010).

54. Wells, *Who Speaks for the Vanquished?*, 154.

55. Medoff, *Deafening Silence*, chap. 7.

56. See Wells, *Who Speaks for the Vanquished?*, chap. 9.

57. Benjamin Ginsberg, *How the Jews Defeated Hitler* (Lanham, MD: Rowman & Littlefield, 2013), chap. 2.

58. Bea Stadtler, *The Holocaust: A History of Courage and Resistance* (New York: Behrman House, 1974), 30.

59. Stadtler, *Holocaust*, 70.

60. Ginsberg, *How the Jews Defeated Hitler*.

61. Wells, *Who Speaks for the Vanquished?*, chap. 7.

Chapter 4. The Benefits of Philo-Semitism and the Costs of Anti-Semitism: Genesis 12:3

Parts of this chapter appeared in the following publications and, with permission from the copyright holder, are reproduced with amendments: Benjamin Ginsberg, *The Fatal Embrace: Jews and the State* (Chicago: University of Chicago Press, 1993). © 1993 University of Chicago Press; Benjamin Ginsberg, *Moses of South Carolina: A Jewish Scalawag during Radical Reconstruction* (Baltimore: Johns Hopkins University Press, 2010). © 2010 Johns Hopkins University Press; and Benjamin Ginsberg, *How the Jews Defeated Hitler* (Lanham, Md.: Rowman & Littlefield, 2013). © 2013 Benjamin Ginsberg.

1. Genesis 12:3.

2. Stephen Spector, *Evangelicals and Israel* (New York: Oxford University Press, 2009), 24.

3. See Stephen Birmingham, *Our Crowd: The Great Jewish Families of New York* (New York: Harper, 1967).

4. Richard Franklin Bensel, *Yankee Leviathan: The Origin of Central State Authority in America, 1859–1877* (New York: Cambridge University Press, 1990), 252.

5. Barry E. Supple, "A Business Elite: German-Jewish Financiers in Nineteenth-Century New York," *Business History Review* 31, no. 2 (Summer 1957): 143–78.

6. E. Digby Baltzell, *The Protestant Establishment: Aristocracy and Caste in America* (New Haven, CT: Yale University Press, 1987), 106–7.

7. Marcia Graham Synott, *The Half-Opened Door: Discrimination and Admissions at Harvard, Yale, and Princeton, 1900–1970* (Westport, CT: Greenwood, 1979), 240.

8. Morton Rosenstock, *Louis Marshall: Defender of Jewish Rights* (Detroit: Wayne State University Press, 1965).

9. John Higham, *Send These to Me: Immigrants in Urban America*, rev. ed. (Baltimore: Johns Hopkins University Press, 1984), 139.

10. "Jews in Physics," JINFO.org, http://www.jinfo.org/Physics.html.

11. "Jews in Computer & Information Science," JINFO.org, http://www.jinfo.org /Computer_Info_Science.html.

12. "Jews in the Medical & Life Sciences," JINFO.org, http://www.jinfo.org/ Biomedical_Research.html.

13. Steven L. Pease, *The Golden Age of Jewish Achievement* (New York: Deucalion, 2019), chaps. 15 and 19.

14. Gordon Fraser, *The Quantum Exodus* (New York: Oxford University Press, 2012).

15. Benjamin Ginsberg, *The Fatal Embrace: Jews and the State* (Chicago: University of Chicago Press, 1993).

16. Charles Murray, "Jewish Genius," *Commentary*, April 1, 2007, https://www.commentarymagazine.com/articles/jewish-genius.

17. Hannah Arendt, *The Origins of Totalitarianism*, rev. ed. (New York: Harcourt, 1967).

18. Quoted in Robert McKenzie and Allan Silver, *Angels in Marble: Working Class Conservatives in Urban England* (Chicago: University of Chicago Press, 1968).

19. Jack Kugelmass, ed., *Jews, Sports, and the Rites of Citizenship* (Urbana: University of Illinois Press, 2007).

20. Simon Kuznets, "Economic Structure and the Life of the Jews," in *Jewish Economics*, vol. 1, ed. Simon Kuznets, Stephanie Lo, and E. Glen Weyl (New Brunswick, NJ: Transaction, 2012), 99.

21. Werner Sombart, *The Jews and Modern Capitalism* (Glencoe, IL: Free Press, 1951), chap. 7.

22. Steven Gimbel, *Einstein's Jewish Science: Physics at the Intersection of Politics and Religion* (Baltimore: Johns Hopkins University Press, 2012).

23. Fraser, *Quantum Exodus*, 74–76.

24. Many of Kevin MacDonald's ideas can be found in his book *The Culture of Critique* (New York: Praeger, 1998).

25. See Mancur Olson, *The Logic of Collective Action* (Cambridge, MA: Harvard University Press, 1971).

26. Paul Johnson, *A History of the Jews* (New York: Harper, 1987), 207.

27. David Biale, *Power and Powerlessness in Jewish History* (New York: Schocken, 1987), 105.

28. Arendt, *Origins of Totalitarianism*, 24.

29. Biale, *Power and Powerlessness*, 103.

30. Ginsberg, *Fatal Embrace*, 44–52.

31. Ginsberg, *Fatal Embrace*, chap. 4.

32. Max I. Dimont, *Jews, God and History* (New York: Penguin Books, 1962), 267.

33. Dimont, *Jews, God and History*, 266.

34. Sombart, *Jews and Modern Capitalism*, chap. 6. See also Jerry Z. Muller, *Capitalism and the Jews* (Princeton, NJ: Princeton University Press, 2010).

35. Dimont, *Jews, God and History*, 267.

36. Selma Stern, *The Court Jew* (New Brunswick, NJ: Transaction, 1985).

37. Johnson, *History of the Jews*, 254.

38. Johnson, *History of the Jews*, 254.

39. Johnson, *History of the Jews*, 255–57; and Stern, *Court Jew*, chaps. 1–3.

40. Richard Davis, *The English Rothschilds* (Chapel Hill: University of North Carolina Press, 1983).

41. Fritz Stern, *Gold and Iron: Bismarck, Bleichröder, and the Building of the German Empire* (New York: Knopf, 1977).

42. Sombart, *Jews and Modern Capitalism*, 38.

43. Stern, *Gold and Iron*.

44. Fritz K. Ringer, *The Decline of the German Mandarins: The German Academic Community, 1890–1933* (Cambridge, MA: Harvard University Press, 1969), chaps. 3 and 4.

45. Peter Pulzer, *The Rise of Political Anti-Semitism in Germany and Austria*, rev. ed. (Cambridge, MA: Harvard University Press, 1988), 13.

46. W. E. Mosse, *Jews in the German Economy* (Oxford: Clarendon Press, 1987), chap. 8. See also Donald Niewyk, *The Jews in Weimar Germany* (Baton Rouge: Louisiana State University Press, 1980), chap. 2.

47. Niewyk, *Jews in Weimar Germany*, chap. 2.

48. Hugo Munsterberg, *Unspoken Bequest: The Contribution of German Jews to German Culture* (New York: Saroff Publishing, 1995), chap. 4.

49. Niewyk, *Jews in Weimar Germany*, chap. 4.

50. Pulzer, *Rise of Political Anti-Semitism*, 326.

51. Pulzer, *Rise of Political Anti-Semitism*, 317–18.

52. Fraser, *Quantum Exodus*, 118.

53. Quoted in Fraser, *Quantum Exodus*, 111.

54. Fraser, *Quantum Exodus*, appendix.

55. Fraser, *Quantum Exodus*, 119.

56. Fraser, *Quantum Exodus*, 125.

57. Quoted in Richard Rhodes, *The Making of the Atomic Bomb* (New York: Simon & Schuster, 1986), 415.

58. Quoted in Rhodes, *Atomic Bomb*, 445.

59. Fraser, *Quantum Exodus*, 78–83.

60. Yuri Slezkine, *The Jewish Century* (Princeton, NJ: Princeton University Press, 2004), chap. 3.

61. Benjamin Pinkus, *The Jews of the Soviet Union* (Cambridge, UK: Cambridge University Press, 1988), chap. 1.

62. Louis Rapoport, *Stalin's War against the Jews* (New York: Free Press, 1990), chaps. 3 and 4.

63. Slezkine, *Jewish Century*, 222.

64. Rapoport, *Stalin's War against the Jews*, 54.

65. Pinkus, *Jews of the Soviet Union*, 145–209.

66. Pinkus, *Jews of the Soviet Union*, 140–41.

67. Benjamin Nathans, "The Wild Desire to Leave: On Soviet Jewry," *Nation*, November 10, 2010, https://www.thenation.com/article/156375/wild-desire-leave-soviet -jewry?page=0,1#.

68. Dan Senor and Saul Singer, *Start-Up Nation: The Story of Israel's Economic Miracle* (New York: Hachette, 2009).

69. Stanislav Simanovsky, Margarita Strepetova, and Yuriy Naido, *Brain Drain from Russia: Problems, Prospects, Ways of Regulation* (New York: Nova Science Publishers, 1996), 23.

70. Suzanne Possehl, "Russian Brain Drain Flows Directly into U.S. Science Talent Reservoir," *Los Angeles Times*, February 26, 1995.

71. Michael Banka, "Russian Science in a State of 'Decline,'" *Physics World*, January 26, 2010, http://physicsworld.com/cws/article/news/2010/jan/26/russian-science-in-a-state-of -decline.

72. Simanovsky, Strepetova, and Naido, *Brain Drain from Russia*, 27.

Chapter 5. The Myth of American Exceptionalism

Parts of this chapter appeared in the following publication and, with permission from the copyright holder, are reproduced with amendments: Benjamin Ginsberg, *The Fatal Em-*

brace: Jews and the State (Chicago: University of Chicago Press, 1993). © 1993 University of Chicago Press.

1. Benjamin Ginsberg, *The Fatal Embrace: Jews and the State* (Chicago: University of Chicago Press, 1993), 53–54.

2. C. A. Macartney, *The Habsburg Empire, 1790–1918* (New York: Macmillan, 1969), 710.

3. Andrew Janos, *The Politics of Backwardness in Hungary, 1825–1945* (Princeton, NJ: Princeton University Press, 1982), 114.

4. William McCagg, "Hungary's Feudalized Bourgeoisie," *Journal of Modern History* 44, no. 1 (March 1972): 65–78.

5. Janos, *Politics of Backwardness*, 116.

6. McCagg, "Hungary's Feudalized Bourgeoisie."

7. William McCagg, *Jewish Nobles and Geniuses in Modern Hungary* (New York: Columbia University Press, 1972).

8. Jacob Katz, *From Prejudice to Destruction* (Cambridge, MA: Harvard University Press, 1980), 230–44. See also Janos, *Politics of Backwardness*, 117; and Robert Kann, "Hungarian Jewry during Austro-Hungary's Constitutional Period (1867–1918)," *Jewish Social Studies* 3, no. 4 (October 1945): 357–86.

9. Hillel Levine, *Economic Origins of Anti-Semitism: Poland and Its Jews in the Early Modern Period* (New Haven, CT: Yale University Press, 1991).

10. Cecil Roth, *A History of the Jews in England* (New York: Oxford University Press, 1941), chaps. 3 and 4.

11. Ginsberg, *Fatal Embrace*, 26–27.

12. Detlev J. K. Peukert, *Inside Nazi Germany: Conformity, Opposition, and Racism in Everyday Life* (New Haven, CT: Yale University Press, 1987). See also Michael Geyer, "The Nazi State Reconsidered," in *Life in the Third Reich*, ed. Richard Bessel (Oxford: Oxford University Press, 1987), 57–68; and Bryan Mark Rigg, *Lives of Hitler's Jewish Soldiers* (Lawrence: University Press of Kansas, 2009).

13. The Historical Research Department of the Nation of Islam, *The Secret Relationship between Blacks and Jews* (Chicago: Latimer, 1991).

14. Robert Rosen, *The Jewish Confederates* (Columbia: University of South Carolina Press, 2000), 17.

15. Rosen, *Jewish Confederates*. See also Bertram W. Korn, *American Jewry and the Civil War* (Philadelphia: Jewish Publication Society, 1951).

16. Leonard Rogoff, "Is the Jew White? The Racial Place of the Southern Jew," *American Jewish History* 85, no. 3 (1997): 195–230.

17. Walter Edgar, *South Carolina: A History* (Columbia: University of South Carolina Press, 1998), 373.

18. Charles Cauthen, *South Carolina Goes to War, 1860–65* (Chapel Hill: University of North Carolina Press, 1950), 183–84.

19. Edgar, *South Carolina*, 372.

20. Korn, *American Jewry*, 210.

21. Korn, *American Jewry*, 133.

22. Korn, *American Jewry*, 212.

23. John B. Jones, *A Rebel War Clerk's Diary* (Philadelphia: Lippincott, 1866), 1:213.

24. Korn, *American Jewry*, 214.

25. Korn, *American Jewry*, 213.

26. Korn, *American Jewry*, 210.

27. Rosen, *Jewish Confederates*, 334.

28. Richard Hofstadter, *The Age of Reform* (New York: Knopf, 1955), 80.

29. Quoted in Louise Mayo, *The Ambivalent Image: Nineteenth Century America's Perception of the Jew* (Rutherford, NJ: Farleigh-Dickinson University Press, 1988), 58.

30. Brooks Adams, *The Law of Civilization and Decay* (New York: Macmillan, 1896).

31. Barbara Solomon, *Ancestors and Immigrants: A Changing New England Tradition*, rev. ed. (Boston: Northeastern University Press, 1989), 39.

Chapter 6. Why Are the Jews Still Democrats?

Parts of this chapter appeared in the following publications and, with permission from the copyright holder, are reproduced with amendments: Benjamin Ginsberg, *The Fatal Embrace: Jews and the State* (Chicago: University of Chicago Press, 1993). © 1993 University of Chicago Press; Benjamin Ginsberg, "American Jews in Political and Social Movements," in *Encyclopedia of American Jewish History*, ed. Stephen H. Norwood and Eunice G. Pollack (Santa Barbara, Calif.: ABC-CLIO Inc., 2008). © 2008 ABC-CLIO Inc.; and Benjamin Ginsberg, *How the Jews Defeated Hitler* (Lanham, Md.: Rowman & Littlefield, 2013). © 2013 Benjamin Ginsberg.

1. Norman Podhoretz, *Why Are Jews Liberals?* (New York: Doubleday, 2009).

2. Benjamin Ginsberg, *The Fatal Embrace: Jews and the State* (Chicago: University of Chicago Press, 1993).

3. Herb Keinon, "Poll: Romney Cares More Than Obama about Israel," *Jerusalem Post*, August 16, 2012, https://www.jpost.com/International/Poll-Romney-cares-more-than-Obama-about-Israel.

4. Richard Wike et al., "Trump Ratings Remain Low around Globe, While Views of U.S. Stay Mostly Favorable," Pew Research Center, January 8, 2020, https://www.pewresearch.org/global/2020/01/08/trump-ratings-remain-low-around-globe-while-views-of-u-s-stay-mostly-favorable/.

5. Kenneth Wald, "The Choosing People: The Puzzling Politics of American Jewry," *Politics and Religion* 8, no. 1 (March 2015): 4–35.

6. Steven Fraser, *Labor Will Rule: Sidney Hillman and the Rise of American Labor* (New York: Free Press, 1991).

7. Geoffrey C. Ward, *A First-Class Temperament: The Emergence of Franklin Roosevelt* (New York: Harper, 1989), 254.

8. Samuel Hand, *Counsel and Advise: A Political Biography of Samuel I. Rosenman* (New York: Garland, 1979).

9. Myron Schnolick, *The New Deal and Anti-Semitism in America* (New York: Garland, 1990), 66.

10. "Jews in America," *Fortune*, February 1, 1936.

11. "Jews in America."

12. Mark Lincoln Chadwin, *The Hawks of World War II* (Chapel Hill: University of North Carolina Press, 1968), 210.

13. Chadwin, *Hawks of World War II*, 210.

14. Neal Gabler, *An Empire of Their Own: How the Jews Invented Hollywood* (New York: Crown, 1988).

15. Rafael Medoff, *The Jews Should Keep Quiet: Franklin D. Roosevelt, Rabbi Stephen S. Wise, and the Holocaust* (Lincoln: University of Nebraska Press, 2019).

16. Chadwin, *Hawks of World War II*, chaps. 3 and 4.

17. Gabler, *Empire of Their Own*, chaps. 9 and 10.

18. Samuel Walker, *In Defense of Civil Liberties: A History of the ACLU* (New York: Oxford University Press, 1990), 212.

19. Harold Seidman, *Politics, Position, and Power* (New York: Oxford University Press, 1998).

20. R. W. Apple, *The Watergate Hearings: Break-in and Coverup* (New York: Bantam, 1973), 593–95.

21. Benjamin Ginsberg and Martin Shefter, *Politics by Other Means* (New York: Basic Books, 1990), chap. 1.

22. John Sides, "Why Most American Jews Vote for Democrats, Explained," *Washington Post*, March 24, 2015, https://www.washingtonpost.com/news/monkey-cage/wp/2015/03/24/why-most-american-jews-vote-for-democrats-explained/?utm_term=.01deaba7b61f.

23. Judy Maltz, "Clinton Won Overwhelming Majority of Jewish-American Vote, Polls Say," *Haaretz*, November 9, 2016, https://www.haaretz.com/world-news/u-s-election-2016/1.752212.

24. Shibley Telhami, "American Attitudes on the Israeli-Palestinian Conflict," Brookings, December 2, 2016, https://www.brookings.edu/research/american-attitudes-on-the-israeli-palestinian-conflict.

Chapter 7. New Alliances: Jews and the Christian Zionists

Parts of this chapter appeared in the following publication and, with permission from the copyright holder, are reproduced with amendments: Benjamin Ginsberg, "Christian Zionism: Is It Good for the Jews?" in *From Antisemitism to Anti-Zionism: The Past and Present of a Lethal Ideology*, ed. Eunice G. Pollack (Boston: Academic Studies Press, 2017). © 2017 Academic Studies Press.

1. Ben Sales, "The Stats of US Anti-Semitism: A New Survey Has Some Clear and Dismal Data," *The Times of Israel*, October 28, 2022, https://www.timesofisrael.com/the-stats-of-us-anti-semitism-a-new-survey-has-some-clear-and-dismal-data/.

2. See, for example, Richard Greenberg, "Tea Time for (Some) Jews: Unlikely Contingent Crashes the Party," *Washington Jewish Week*, February 25, 2010, 1.

3. "The Black Lives Matter Movement and Anti-Semitism," *Camera*, October 22, 2020, https://www.jns.org/the-black-lives-matter-movement-and-anti-semitism/.

4. Malcolm Hedding, "Denying the Truth and Supporting Wickedness," August 12, 2014, http://malcolmhedding.com/denying-the-truth-and-supporting-wickedness.

5. "Prime Minister Netanyahu Affirms Christian Zionists," *Jerusalem Connection Report*, March 11, 2010, http://thejerusalemconnection.us/blog/2010/03/11/prime-minister -netanyahu-affirms-christian-zionists.

6. Stephen Spector, *Evangelicals and Israel* (New York: Oxford University Press, 2009), 24.

7. John Hagee, *In Defense of Israel* (Lake Mary, FL: Frontline, 2007), 2.

8. Barton Gellman, "Strong Ties of '48 Have Yielded to Today's Ambiguity," *Washington Post*, April 29, 1998, https://www.washingtonpost.com/archive/politics/1998/04/29 /strong-ties-of-48-have-yielded-to-todays-ambiguity/3e940259-41f0-495e-8dd8- 97dbcfde0f39. See also Spector, *Evangelicals and Israel*, 149.

9. Zev Chafets, *Match Made in Heaven* (New York: Harper, 2007), 203.

10. Michael Lipka, "More White Evangelicals Than American Jews Say God Gave Israel to the Jewish People," Pew Research Center, October 3, 2013, https://www. pewresearch.org/fact-tank/2013/10/03/more-white-evangelicals-than-american-jews-say -god-gave-israel-to-the-jewish-people/. For a discussion of evangelical beliefs regarding Israel, see Rick Richman, "Christians Respond to the War on the Jewish State," *Tower*, September 2014, https://www.thetower.org/article/christians-respond-to-the-war-on-the -jewish-state.

11. Genesis 12:3.

12. Spector, *Evangelicals and Israel*, 28.

13. Stephen Sizer, *Zion's Christian Soldiers? The Bible, Israel and the Church* (Downers Grove, IL: InterVarsity Press, 2007).

14. Sizer, *Zion's Christian Soldiers?*, chap. 3.

15. Timothy P. Weber, *On the Road to Armageddon: How Evangelicals Became Israel's Best Friend* (Grand Rapids, MI: Baker, 2004), 26.

16. Spector, *Evangelicals and Israel*, 15.

17. Spector, *Evangelicals and Israel*, 14. Many of these prophecies were popularized in such best-selling books as Hal Lindsey's *The Late Great Planet Earth* and Tim LaHaye's Left Behind series, which has sold more than 60 million copies and served as the basis for film and television productions as well as tapes and assorted items of clothing, curios, and knickknacks. In LaHaye's stories, after the sudden rapture of millions of Bible-believing Christians, ordinary people are left behind to suffer through the seven years of tribulation. Some, albeit belatedly, repentant individuals, led by the hero, airline pilot Rayford Steele, form a "tribulation force" to resist the Antichrist, who turns out to be Nicolae Carpathia, the charismatic new Romanian secretary-general of the United Nations, a proabortion, one-world ecumenicist. Many battles are fought and treacheries, plagues, and disasters overcome. Eventually, Christ appears on a white horse, leading his raptured followers to defeat the forces of darkness.

18. Sizer, *Zion's Christian Soldiers?*, 11.

19. Victoria Clark, *Allies for Armageddon: The Rise of Christian Zionism* (New Haven, CT: Yale University Press, 2007), 238.

20. Sizer, *Zion's Christian Soldiers?*, 12.

21. Spector, *Evangelicals and Israel*, 21.

22. Terry Lovell, "Weber, Goldmann, and the Sociology of Beliefs," *Archives Européennes de Sociologie* 14, no. 2 (1973): 304–23, doi:10.1017/S0003975600002769.

23. Richard W. Fox, "Liberal Protestantism," in *A Companion to American Political Thought*, ed. Richard W. Fox and James T. Kloppenberg (Oxford: Blackwell, 1995), 394.

24. George M. Marsden, *Fundamentalism and American Culture* (New York: Oxford University Press, 2006), 239.

25. Sydney Ahlstrom, *A Religious History of the American People* (New Haven, CT: Yale University Press, 1972), 1099.

26. Grant Wacker, "Uneasy in Zion: Evangelicals in Postmodern Society," in *Evangelicalism and Modern America*, ed. George Marsden (Grand Rapids, MI: Eerdmans, 1984).

27. Michael B. Friedland, *Lift Up Your Voice Like a Trumpet: White Clergy and the Civil Rights and Antiwar Movements, 1954–73* (Chapel Hill: University of North Carolina Press, 1998).

28. Marsden, *Fundamentalism and American Culture*, 238.

29. Weber, *Armageddon*, 33.

30. Weber, *Armageddon*, 36.

31. Weber, *Armageddon*, 35.

32. Luis E. Lugo, "International Obligations and the Morality of War," *Society* 44, no. 6 (2007): 109–12.

33. Robert L. Williams and Colin C. Quillivan, "The Relationship of Political Evangelicalism to Critical Thinking and Selected Sociopolitical Values in 2007," *Journal of Religion and Society* 10 (2008), http://moses.creighton.edu/JRS/toc/2008.html.

34. James K. Wellman, *Evangelical vs. Liberal* (New York: Oxford University Press, 2008).

35. Chafets, *Match Made in Heaven*, 84.

36. Matthew A. Sutton, "Praise the Lord and Pass the Ammunition: World War II, the Apocalypse, and Fundamentalist Political Activism" (paper presented to the 124th annual meeting of the American Historical Association, San Diego, CA, January 8, 2010).

37. Angela Lahr, *Millennial Dreams and Apocalyptic Nightmares: The Cold War Origins of Political Evangelicalism* (New York: Oxford University Press, 2007).

38. Weber, *Armageddon*, 204.

39. Weber, *Armageddon*, 151.

40. Weber, *Armageddon*, 200.

41. Anne C. Loveland, *American Evangelicals and the U.S. Military: 1942–1993* (Baton Rouge: Louisiana State University Press, 1996).

42. Weber, *Armageddon*, 173.

43. Quoted in Weber, *Armageddon*, 178.

44. Weber, *Armageddon*, 178.

45. Weber, *Armageddon*, 177.

46. Weber, *Armageddon*, 185.

47. Paul Merkley, *Christian Attitudes towards the State of Israel* (Montreal: McGill-Queen's University Press, 2001).

48. Weber, *Armageddon*, 207.

49. Clark, *Allies for Armageddon*, 241.

50. Clark, *Allies for Armageddon*, 247.

51. Eleanor Doumato, "Protestantism and Protestant Missions," in *Encyclopedia of the Modern Middle East and North Africa*, 2nd rev. ed., ed. Philip Matter (New York: Macmillan, 2004).

52. Allen Hertzke, Laura Olson, and Kevin Den Dulk, *Religion and Politics in America*, 3rd ed. (Boulder, CO: Westview, 2004), 181.
53. Doumato, "Protestantism and Protestant Missions."
54. "Campaign against Operation Christmas Child," Innovative Minds, http://www.inminds.com/occ.html.
55. Joel C. Rosenberg, "Time Magazine Tackles 'Radical' Christian Evangelists in Muslim Nations," Newsmax, April 21, 2003, https://www.newsmax.com/Pre-2008/Time-Magazine-TacklesRadical-/2003/04/21/id/675157.
56. Chafets, *Match Made in Heaven*, 83.
57. Duomato, "Protestantism and Protestant Missions."
58. Lucky Severson, "Anti-Islam," PBS, *Religion & Ethics Newsweekly*, December 20, 2002, https://www.pbs.org/wnet/religionandethics/week616/cover.html.
59. B. A. Robinson, "Attacks on Muslims by Conservative Protestants: Graham, Hinn, Falwell, Robertson, Swaggart & Baldwin," Religious Tolerance, last updated May 13, 2003, http://www.religioustolerance.org/reac_ter18b.htm.
60. http://www.patrobertson.com/PressReleases/bushresponse2.asp.

Epilogue. Final Thoughts on Anti-Semitism Today: What's Good for the Jews

1. Jonathan A. Greenblatt, "It's Time to Admit It: The Left Has an Antisemitism Problem," *Newsweek*, July 9, 2021, https://www.newsweek.com/its-time-admit-it-left-has-antisemitism-problem-opinion-1608397.
2. James Kirchick, "On Linda Sarsour's Politics of Hate and the Pathos of Her Jewish Enablers," *Tablet*, June 2017, https://www.tabletmag.com/sections/news/articles/linda-sarsour-jewish-enablers.
3. Michael Lind, *The New Class War* (New York: Portfolio, 2020).
4. Michael Lind, "The Revenge of the Yankees: How Social Gospel Became Social Justice," *Tablet*, November 15, 2020, https://www.tabletmag.com/sections/news/articles/revenge-of-the-yankees.
5. David Samuels, "Q&A: The Marriage Vows of the American Elite: A Conversation with Benjamin Ginsberg," *Tablet*, September 10, 2020, https://www.tabletmag.com/sections/news/articles/benjamin-ginsberg-wasp-jewish-elites.
6. Bari Weiss, "Stop Being Shocked," *Tablet*, October 14, 2020, https://www.tabletmag.com/sections/news/articles/stop-being-shocked.
7. Christian Picciolini, *Romantic Violence: Memoirs of an American Skinhead* (Chicago: Goldmill, 2015).
8. Allum Bokhari and Milo Yiannopoulos, "An Establishment Conservative's Guide to the Alt-Right," *Breitbart*, March 29, 2016, https://www.breitbart.com/tech/2016/03/29/an-establishment-conservatives-guide-to-the-alt-right.
9. Clark S. Judge, "The Rust Belt Is Right to Blame Obama," *Wall Street Journal*, December 19, 2016, A21.
10. Victor Tan Chen, "All Hollowed Out: The Lonely Poverty of America's White Working Class," *Atlantic*, January 16, 2016, https://www.theatlantic.com/business/archive/2016/01/white-working-class-poverty/424341.
11. Chen, "All Hollowed Out."

12. Michael Goldfield, *The Decline of Organized Labor in America* (Chicago: University of Chicago Press, 1989).

13. Jefferson Cowie, *Stayin' Alive* (New York: New Press, 2012).

14. Nate Cohn, "Why Trump Won: Working-Class Whites," *New York Times*, November 9, 2016, https://www.nytimes.com/2016/11/10/upshot/why-trump-won-working-class-whites.html.

Appendix

Parts of this chapter appeared in the following publication and, with permission from the copyright holder, are reproduced with amendments: Benjamin Ginsberg, *The Fatal Embrace: Jews and the State* (Chicago: University of Chicago Press, 1993). © 1993 University of Chicago Press.

1. Esther Benbassa, *The Jews of France* (Princeton, NJ: Princeton University Press, 1999), 8.

2. Salo Baron and Arcadius Kahan, *Economic History of the Jews* (New York: Schocken Books, 1975), 41.

3. Max I. Dimont, *Jews, God and History* (New York: Penguin Books, 1962), 269.

4. Baron and Kahan, *Economic History of the Jews*, 45.

5. Baron and Kahan, *Economic History of the Jews*, 46.

6. Cecil Roth, *A History of the Jews in England*, 3rd ed. (Oxford: Clarendon, 1964), 14.

7. Roth, *Jews in England*, 38.

8. Roth, *Jews in England*, 158.

9. Benbassa, *Jews of France*, 16.

10. Benbassa, *Jews of France*, 25.

11. John A. Crow, *Spain: The Root and the Flower*, 3rd rev. ed. (Berkeley: University of California Press, 1985), 110.

12. Crow, *Spain*, chap. 4.

13. Crow, *Spain*, 112.

14. Edward Peters, *Inquisition* (Berkeley: University of California Press, 1989), chap. 3.

15. Cecil Roth, *The Spanish Inquisition* (New York: Norton, 1964), chap. 1.

16. Henry Kamen, *Inquisition and Society in Spain in the Sixteenth and Seventeenth Centuries* (Bloomington: Indiana University Press, 1985).

17. Peters, *Inquisition*, chap. 3.

18. Roth, *Spanish Inquisition*, chap. 2.

19. Peters, *Inquisition*, 84.

20. Roth, *Spanish Inquisition*, chap. 2.

21. Stanford J. Shaw, *The Jews of the Ottoman Empire and the Turkish Republic* (New York: NYU Press, 1991), 94.

22. Shaw, *Ottoman Empire and Turkish Republic*, 95.

23. Bernard Lewis, *The Jews of Islam* (Princeton, NJ: Princeton University Press, 1984), 134.

24. David Biale, *Power and Powerlessness in Jewish History* (New York: Schocken, 1987), 65.

25. Lewis, *Jews of Islam*, 22–23.

26. Werner Sombart, *The Jews and Modern Capitalism* (Glencoe, IL: Free Press, 1951), 14–15.

27. Jonathan I. Israel, "The Republic of the United Netherlands," in *The History of the Jews in the Netherlands*, ed. J. C. H. Blom, R. G. Fuks-Mansfeld, and I. Schöffer, and trans. Arnold J. Pomerans and Erica Pomerans (Oxford: Littman Library of Jewish Civilization, 2002), 103.

28. Israel, "United Netherlands," 111.

29. Israel, "United Netherlands," 108.

30. R. A. Stradling, *Europe and the Decline of Spain, 1580–1720* (London: Allen & Unwin, 1981), 35.

31. J. H. Elliott, *Imperial Spain, 1469–1716* (New York: St. Martin's Press, 1964), 305.

32. Elliott, *Imperial Spain*, chap. 8.

33. Elliott, *Imperial Spain*, 338.

34. John Lynch, *Spain under the Habsburgs*, vol. 2, 2nd ed. (New York: NYU Press, 1984), 149.

35. Israel, "United Netherlands," 107.

Index

About the Author

BENJAMIN GINSBERG is the David Bernstein Professor of Political Science and Chair of the Center for Advanced Governmental Studies at Johns Hopkins University. He is the author, co-author, or editor of more than thirty books, including *The Fall of the Faculty, Presidential Government, Downsizing Democracy, The Captive Public, Politics By Other Means, The Value of Violence, How the Jews Defeated Hitler, Disconnected Democracies, What Washington Gets Wrong,* and *Warping Time*. His college text, *We the People*, has been the nation's most frequently used American government text for the past three decades. Ginsberg received his PhD from the University of Chicago in 1973 and was professor of government at Cornell until 1992, when he joined the Hopkins faculty.

Independent Institute Studies in Political Economy

Independent Institute Studies in Political Economy

100 SWAN WAY, OAKLAND, CA 94621-1428

For further information:
510-632-1366 • orders@independent.org • http://www.independent.org/publications/books/